I0902418

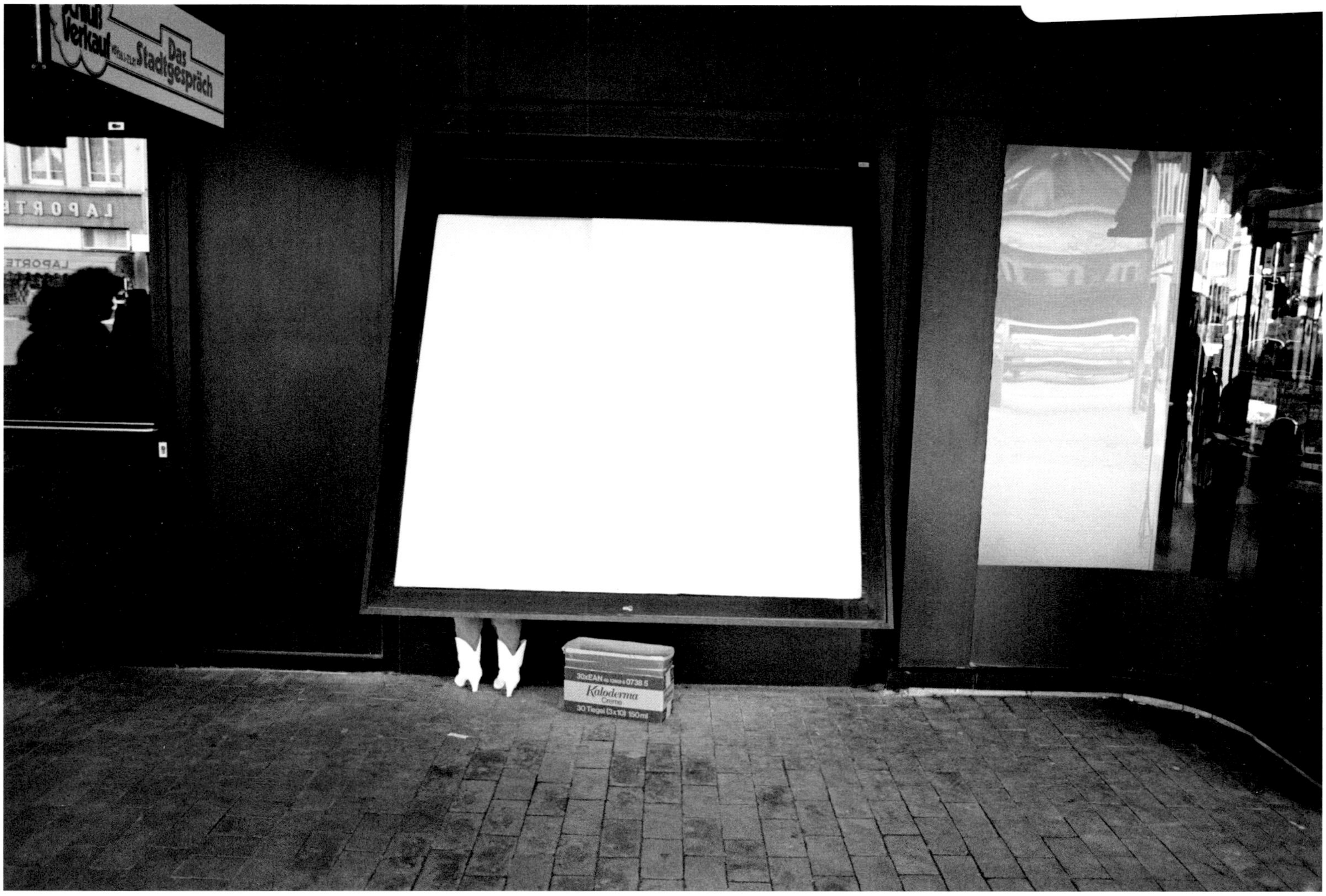

Stuart Cosgrove
David Chandler
Ken Grant
Val Williams

GOST

Paul Reas

1982–2012

Fables of Faubus

Stuart Cosgrove

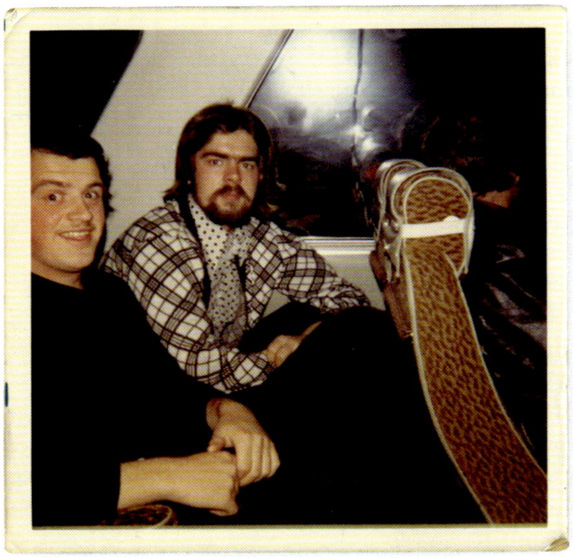

A Northern Soul:
The Photography of Paul Reas

Paul Reas and I had very similar upbringings. He was raised by his mother as one of five boys and grew up on a tough post-war council estate called Buttershaw in Bradford, the spiritual home of the infidelity comedy film *Rita Sue and Bob Too*. But in the years before the movie brought notoriety to Buttershaw, it was one of a swathe of working class communities that became the heartlands of the northern soul scene, the subculture that swept through the industrial north of Britain and bequeathed young people there, with a near obsessive love-affair with the music and social conditions of black America.

When I look back at Paul's earliest photographs in housing schemes of West Yorkshire, I am reminded of the great Harlem photographer Gordon Parks Sr. It may seem strange to dwell on the ghetto-tenements of Harlem to introduce a photographer whose work is ostensibly British but there is a deep connection that needs to be more fully explained. Like Paul's earliest photographs, there is a sense of being embedded there. This is not the distant romanticism of the photographer on a day-trip, or the social explorer who has discovered some obscure tribe, be they in remote rainforests or in a junkie alleyway. Paul is from theses housing schemes and knows their many mysteries. Gordon Parks spent a year of his life living with a local Harlem family, the Fontenelles, and with their co-operation produced photographs which laid bare the poverty of an inner-city ghetto in ways that were both intimate and disturbing. Some of Paul's earlier work has the same intimacy; we want to know more about these people as they stand by their fireplaces, dance romantically in the most unromantic of places and pass their precious time as change scythes through their communities. It is an eloquent and yet anxious portrait of deprivation.

Paul is one of the many remarkable graduates of the Northern soul scene, a learning centre for a generation mainly born far from power and who were often disillusioned with formal education. It was an academy of sorts. There was never formal teaching or even books to take home but the music which was rich in energy and often saturated in the story of civil rights movement. The music became an informal route to knowledge. Paul was precociously young, when at thirteen years old, he first visited the legendary Twisted Wheel, an underground nightclub in a decaying area of Manchester. The Wheel, as it was known, was a tense and amphetamine-fuelled Mecca where mods listened to imported R&B and danced through the night until the morning light or a police raid ended their sojourn. By his own admission, Paul's awkwardness led him to watch the dancers rather than dance himself, but something about the music and its stories of estranged love, civil rights and burning injustice, stuck in his mind like a persistent hook-line, never to be forgotten. It was at The Wheel that he first heard Sam Cooke's 'A Change is Gonna Come,' Curtis Mayfield and The Impression's 'People Get Ready' and James Carr's 'Freedom Train.'

Paul was a studious soul fan. 'I listened deeply to this incredible music,' he once told me. 'It struck me early on that the music, coming as it did from mainly small independent labels, was an expression of the social circumstances of the recording artists. Yes, many of them were telling the staple boy-meets-girl stories, but others were ambiguous and dark. There was something I related to in these particular records. They talk of racial issues, but they also talk of class. These tracks became expressions of situations and circumstances which I knew and felt.'

It was through the music that Paul felt compelled to read about civil rights and the racially divisive attempts to desegregate Little Rock High School in the state capital of Arkansas. It was in those young and impressionable years that he first came across the strange name of Orval Faubus, the Governor of Arkansas in 1957, who used his local powers to impede desegregation, by instructing the National Guard to block the way of nine black students entering the city's all-white Central High School. The infamy of Orval Faubus spread like a malign virus through the civil rights movement, and along with 'Bull' Connor, the pathologically racist mayor of Birmingham, Alabama, he came to be seen as a dark force holding back social change. The story of Little Rock was a moment of tense realisation. For the local Arkansas soul singer Johnnie Taylor it was a time he witnessed naked institutional racism close-up. Al Bell Jr. was a teenager, a local DJ who spun R&B records at protest meetings and went on to become an executive at Stax Records in Memphis. And for President Bill Clinton, born and raised in Little Rock, it was the event that forced him to face up to the failures of the segregated South. But most vividly, the Little Rock confrontations inspired the late great Charlie Mingus to record the song 'Fables of Faubus,' a caustic title intended to bring racial segregation to vinyl. Such were the racial sensitivities of the time that Columbia Records refused to allow Mingus to include the lyrics 'Oh Lord Don't Let Them Shoot Us,' and so the original song was released only as an instrumental.

For the next ten years of his life, long before he had discovered jazz and Charlie Mingus, Paul was working as a bricklayer and was a regular at northern soul clubs including VaVas in Bolton,

Paul Reas (L) with Bob Chappell travelling to the Highland Room at Blackpool Mecca. 1973. Photo courtesy of Bob Chappell.

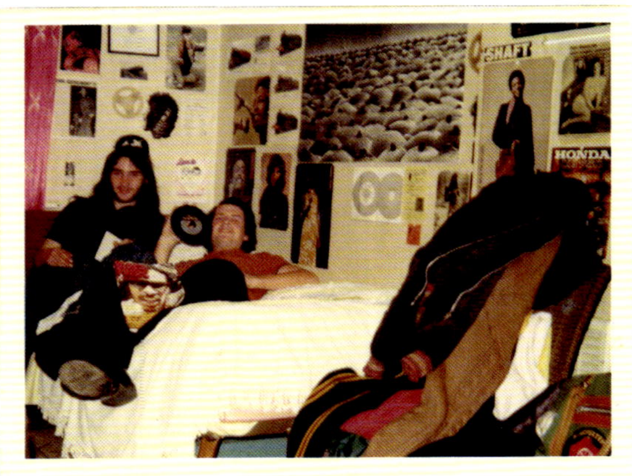

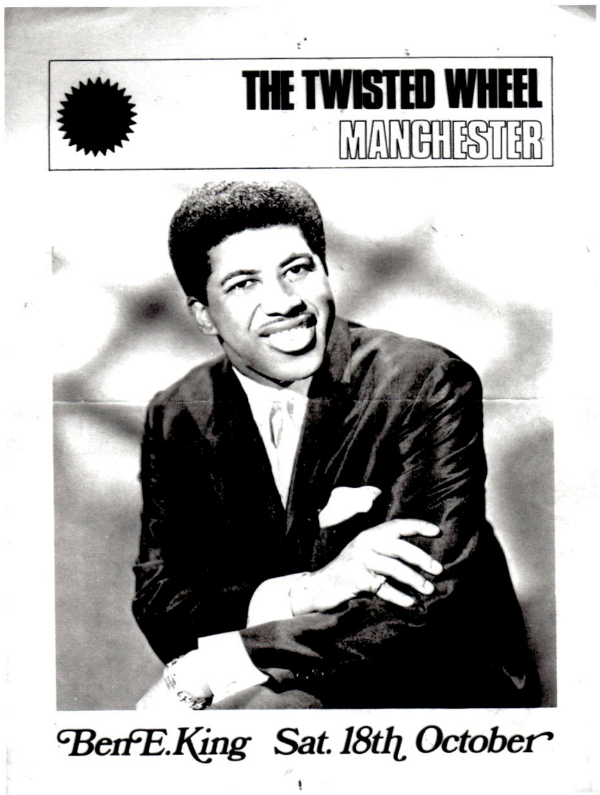

Andy Simpson and Paul Reas, Bradford, 1972. Photo courtesy of Andy Simpson.
Twisted Wheel Flyer. Courtesy of John Massen.

with its paranoid mirrored-walls; the famous Wigan casino all-nighters in a once grand northern ballroom; and one of the most revered clubs on the scene, The Highland Room at Blackpool Mecca. Despite what he has ruefully described as 'the chemical assistance,' he was a 'shy and awkward lad who never had the confidence to dance' in a club scene that attracted some of the most forthright and self-confident people in the soul underground.

Paul's days on the northern soul scene may well be one of the great missed opportunities of British social photography. One of the UK's best photographers inside a scene that is notoriously difficult to penetrate at a time when the British working class and their institutions were witnessing profound change—the miners' strike, the three-day week, power blackouts and deindustrialisation, subjects his later photographs reflect. It was a scene that lacked a commanding photographic presence, the clubs were pitch dark, there was a reluctance to allow outsiders to film, and most photographs were cheap snapshots of friends on buses, outside clubs and only periodically dancing.

Paul came to the northern scene before his passion for photography was fully unleashed and so much has gone unseen. The more I look at his photographs, the more I have become fascinated with that lost journey. Something about our shared upbringing has forced me to look back to Paul as a young man. These impressions are entirely made up, but they have an imagined truth. I see him near the front of the stage at the Twisted Wheel crouched down beneath Ben E. King's sweating brow, looking up at him, hoping that a shaft of stage light will illuminate his emotionally pleading face, a boy trying to catch a glimpse of a legend. I see him on a crowded single-decked bus leaving the decaying outskirts of Bradford as music blares from old cassette recorders, and mouthy boys and shameless girls fool around in the aisle. Saxie Russell's 'Psychedelic Soul' is screeching to escape from the crowded bus. Paul is sitting watching them with the quiet intensity of the photographer cradling his sports bag as if it holds precious treasures—a tissue wrapped round a handful of amphetamines and a Polaroid, whose images would never last the decade.

By the mid-1980s as northern soul went though one of its many schisms, Paul had become one of the most significant photographers to emerge from the new wave of British colour documentary. He is part of a pioneering generation of photographers that included Paul Graham, Martin Parr and Anna Fox, photographers who revealed and critiqued British class and culture. His abandonment of black and white was not an abandonment of interest in the time-honoured veneer of social photography, it was a recognition that the working class had not atrophied with history, but were living new lives, after industry, and being exposed to new challenges and different methods of exploitation.

My third impression of Paul relates most directly to his colour photography and the volume of work contained in 'I Can Help' and 'Flogging A Dead Horse.' Here is working-class Britain fractured into consumerism, the suburban stores, the industrial theme parks, and the garish invitation to spend money which remains preciously hard to come by. In this image, Paul is walking into Blackpool Mecca. Downstairs, in this chain-store nightclub, the cavernous bottom floor is populated by palm trees and Hawaiian kitsch, and upstairs via the indoor escalators, is the legendary Highland Room, the ultimate Mecca of rare soul. The walls are improbably surrounded by claymores, tartan drapes and battle decor that would shame Braveheart, a nod to the armies of working class Scots who flooded to Blackpool every summer. This is what passed as mass entertainment; cheap, plastic and ephemeral but hidden away among the fantasies is something very real, the beating heart of northern soul, wholly working-class and hidden away from the coercive mainstream. This is where Paul's photography truly flourishes—in the afterlife of industry.

Then there was northern soul—the unique subculture that thrived despite mainstream mass entertainment, hidden away in places that society could never quite understand it, dancing to music from the American ghettos they could never buy, and taking amphetamines that baffled the pharmaceutical industry. Paul's photography has that sense of the other; it is aware of post-industrialism, looks askance at consumerism but is never fully immersed within it. There is always a detachment, a nod that things could be better, a feeling that if kitsch nightclubs must exist at least they could have the common decency to abandon the Top Twenty and play underground records from the ghettos of our imagination.

Paul is a very special photographer because he has found a way of giving life to a society that is otherwise so casually ignored. One of the famous closing songs at Wigan Casino all-nighter was by the unknown soul singer Tobi Legend entitled 'Time Will Pass You By.' It was a song about time and mortality, but like Paul's photography it speaks to the story of change and the flux of the people impacted by their times. It is a story of quiet socialism and is known and loved by everyone in the northern soul scene: 'Life is just a precious minute baby/Open up your eyes and see it baby/Give yourself a better chance/Because time will pass you right on by.'

As the youngest of a family of five boys, and as someone whose early working life was spent on building sites, I was used to the company of men. I realise now that all my early college projects at Newport College of Art and Design, were made in predominantly male-dominated environments. These were spaces where I not only felt comfortable, but I could also relate to the circumstances of those whose lives I was trying to represent. These working environments of coal and steel were typical of the heavy industries of South Wales at this time in the early 1980s.

I recall, as a student, being shown the work of August Sander for the first time. I was so struck, not only by the scale of his endeavour, but also by the grace, beauty and dignity he bestowed upon his subjects. My portraits were a poor attempt at trying to get close to some of the majesty of Sander.

Desmond's Mine was a small, independently owned drift mine by Pantygasseg, near Pontypool in the South Wales Valleys. It was one of only a handful of mines in Britain which still used pit ponies, and it did so right up until 1999, making Desmond's the last mine in Britain to do so. I photographed in the mine over a period of months in 1982, whilst still a student on the Documentary Photography course at Newport. The camaraderie and banter amongst the men was reminiscent of my time working on building sites and I felt instantly at ease in their company. With hindsight, one can see clearly why I would have been attracted to Desmond's as a subject. At this time, so much of documentary photography in Britain was concerned with the preservation of ways of life which were under threat of change, or photographers were drawn to the quaint and whimsical. This was a tendency I would deliberately resist in later projects.

1982

Industry

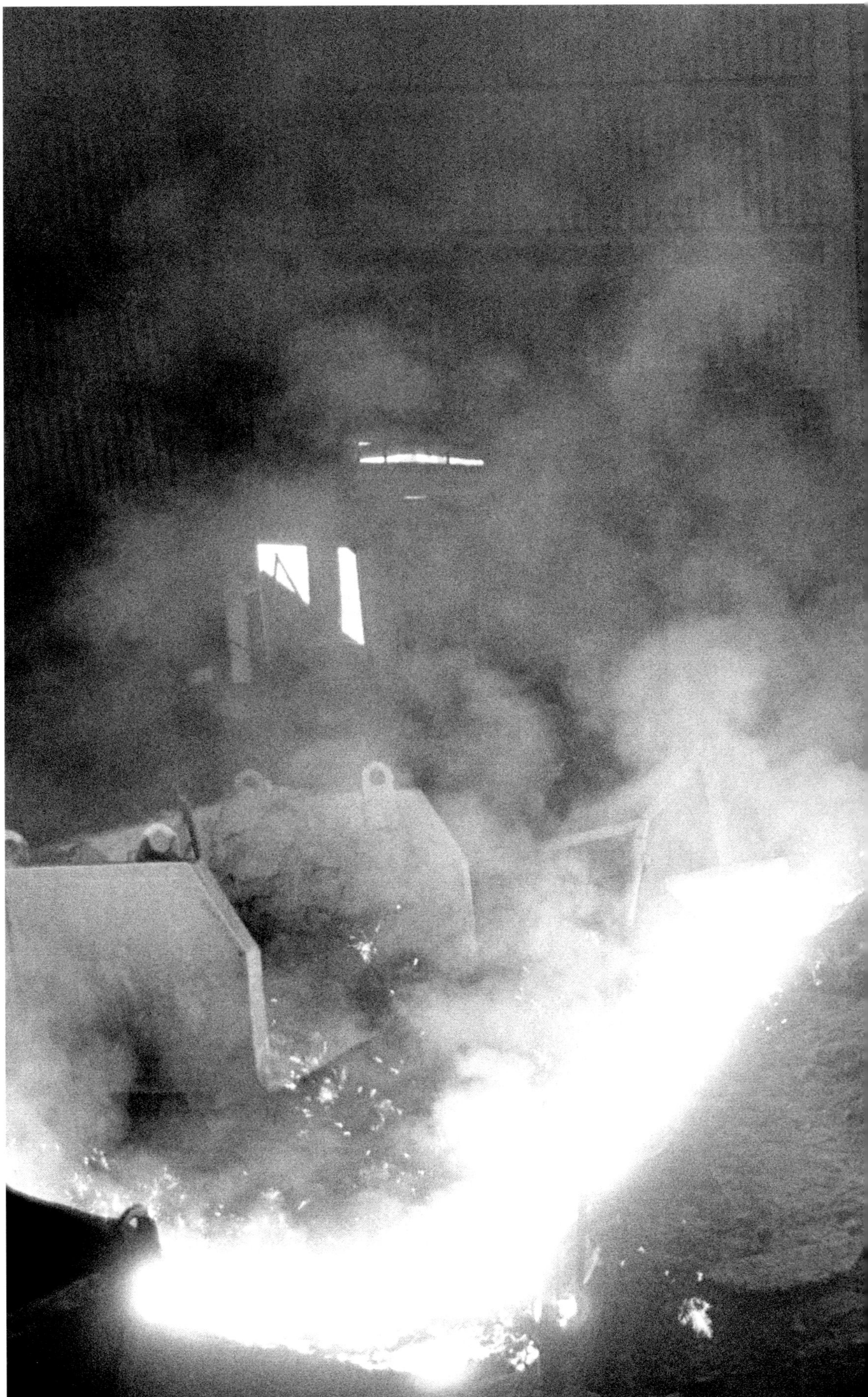

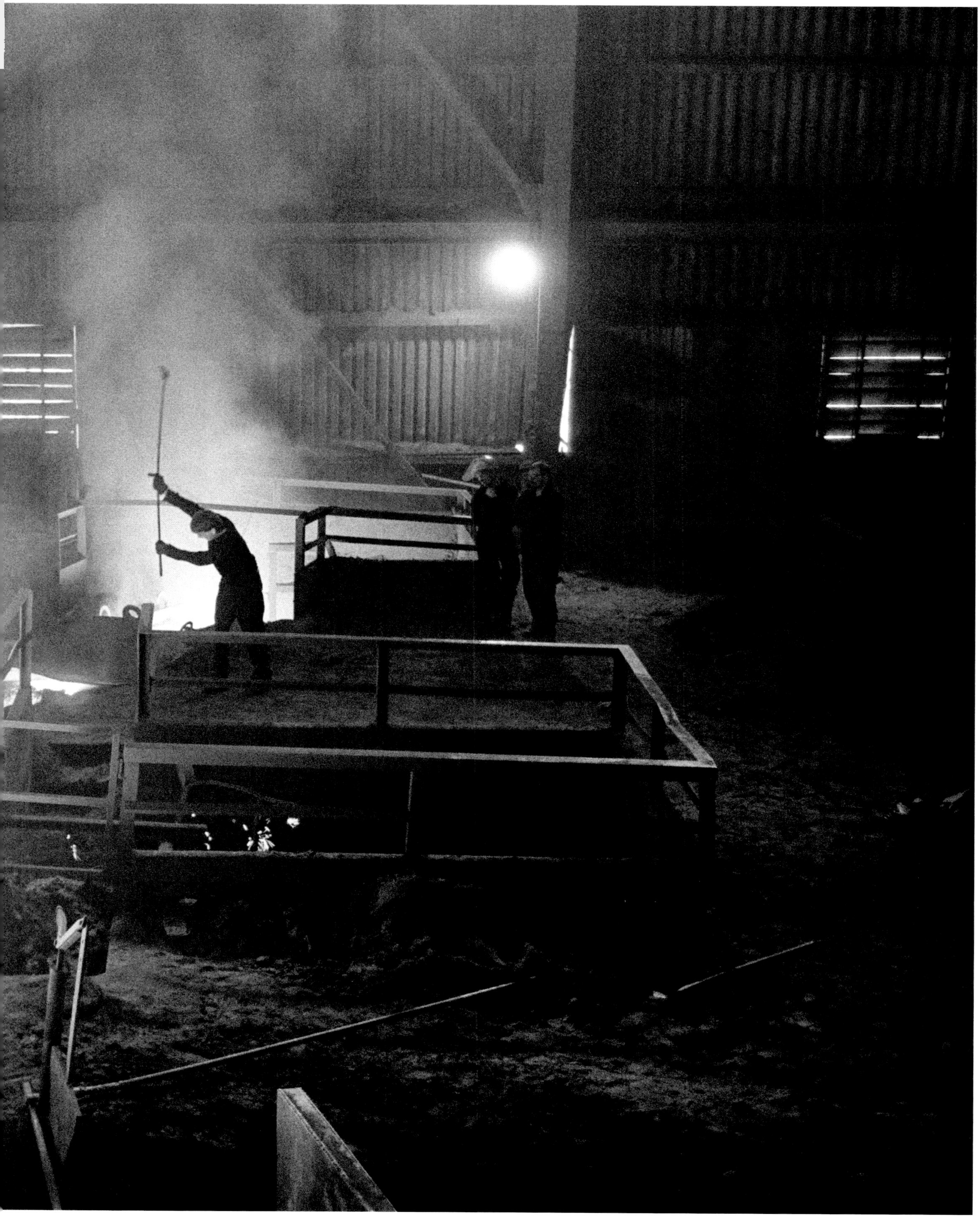

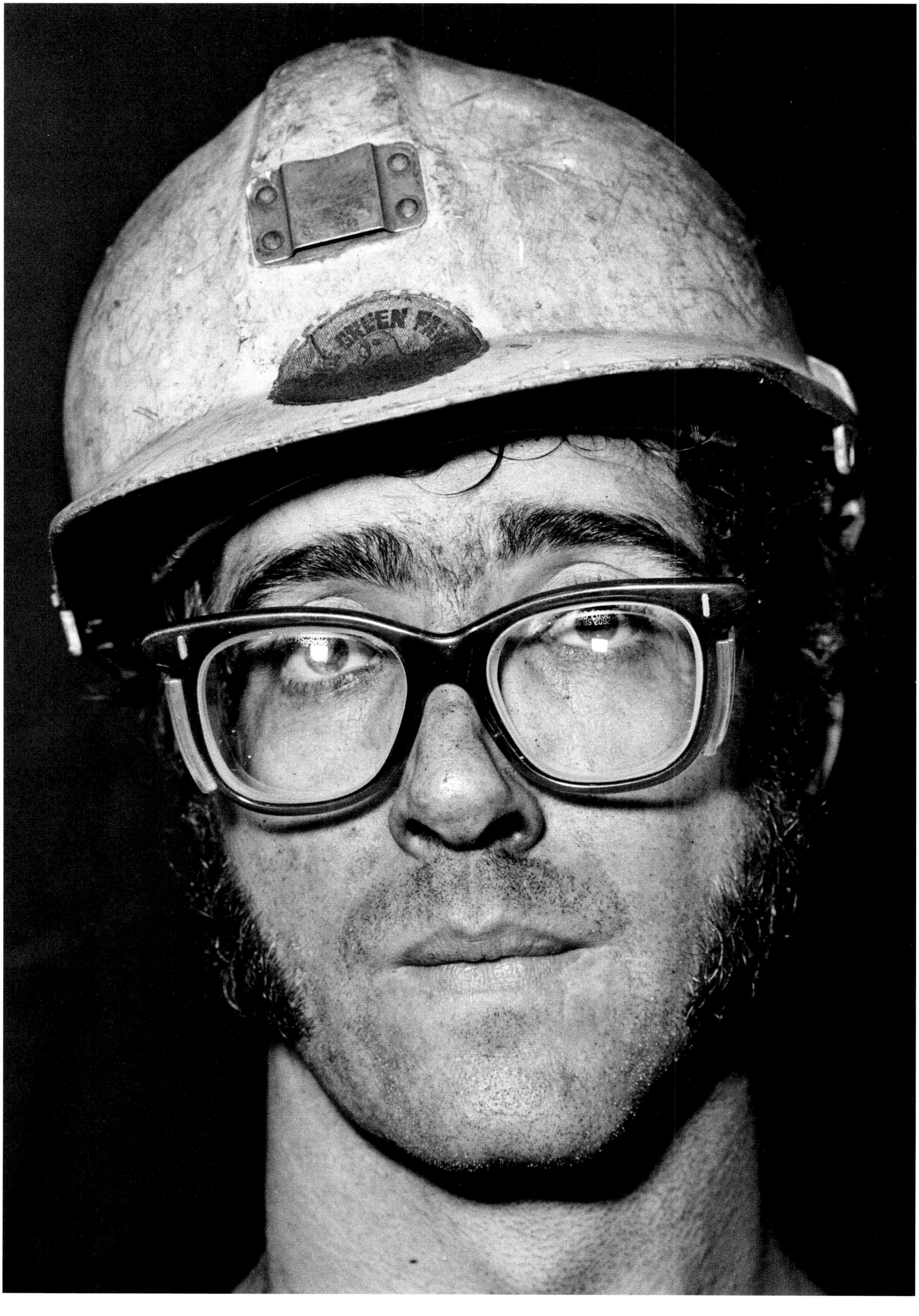

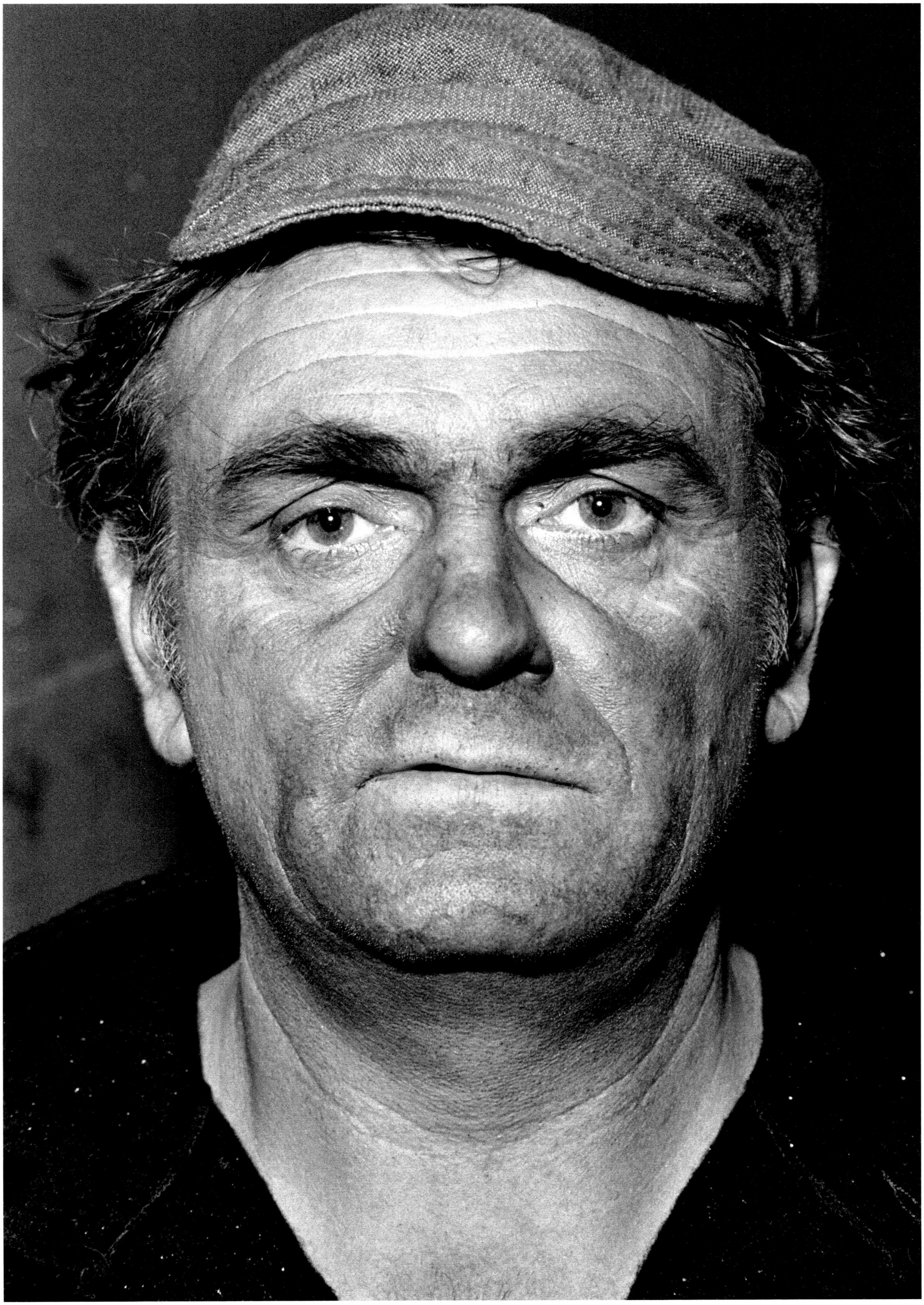

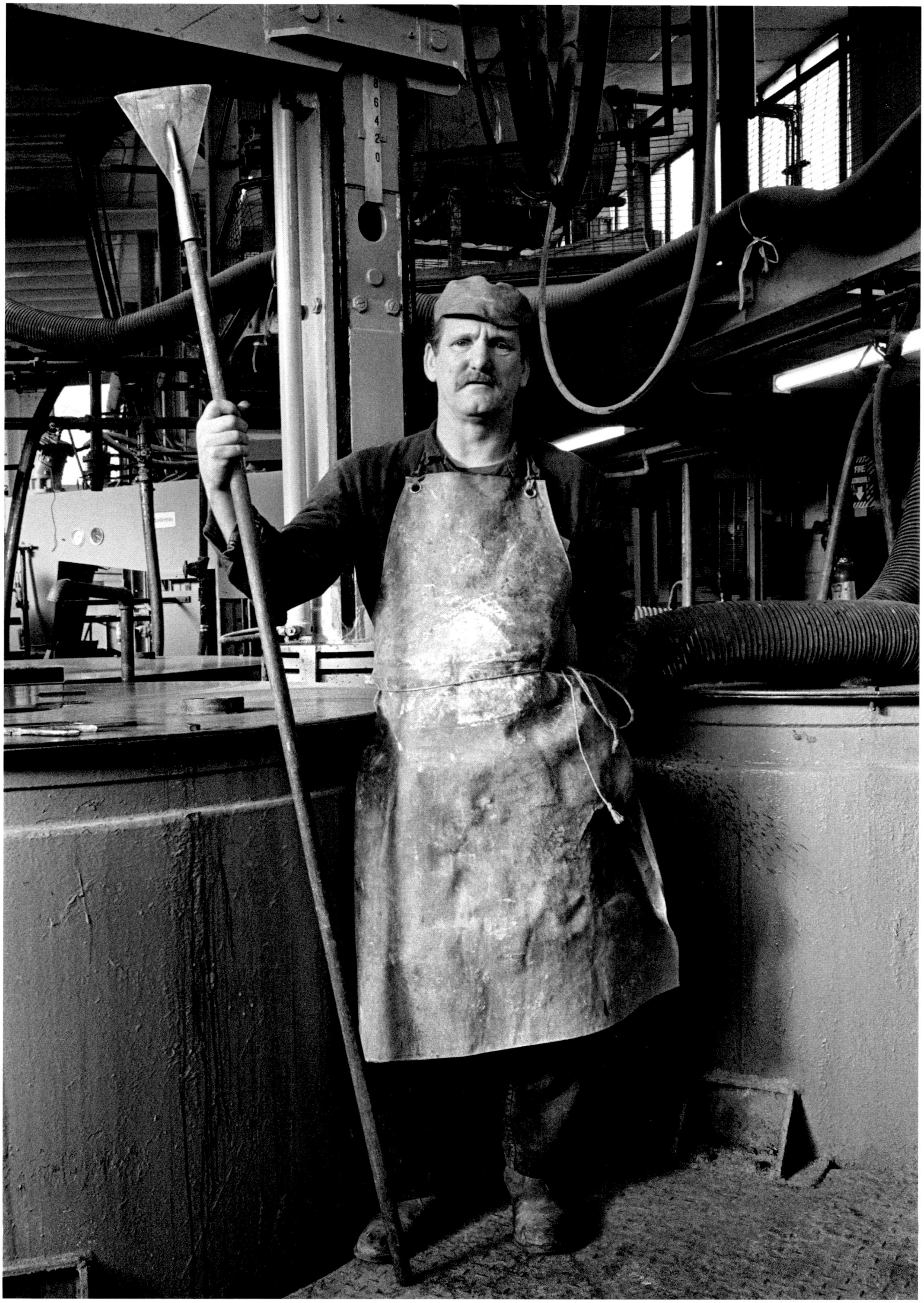

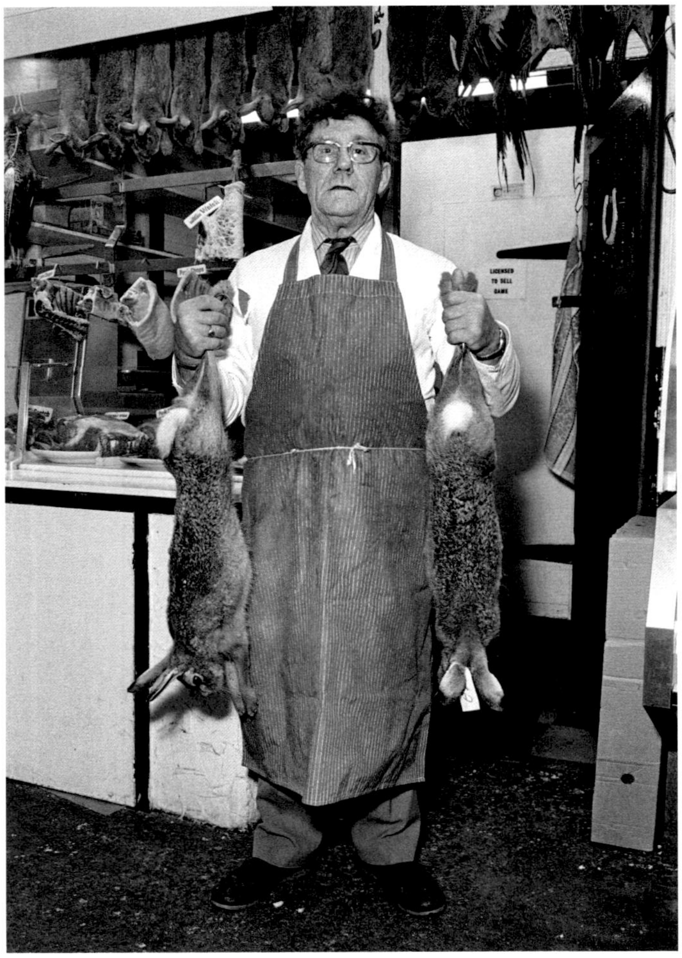
LICENSED
TO SELL
GAME

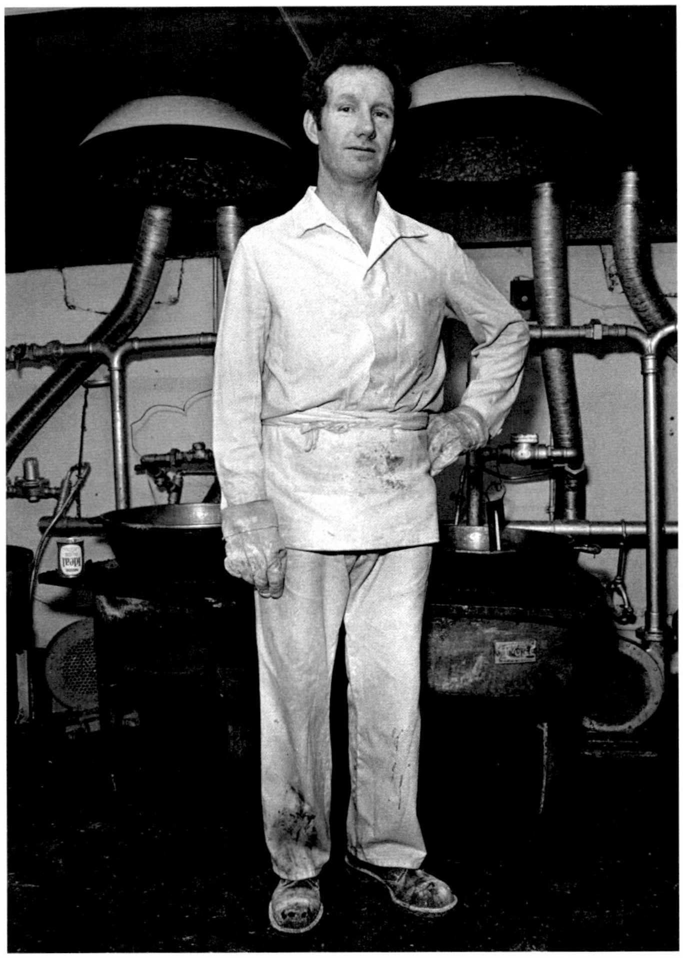

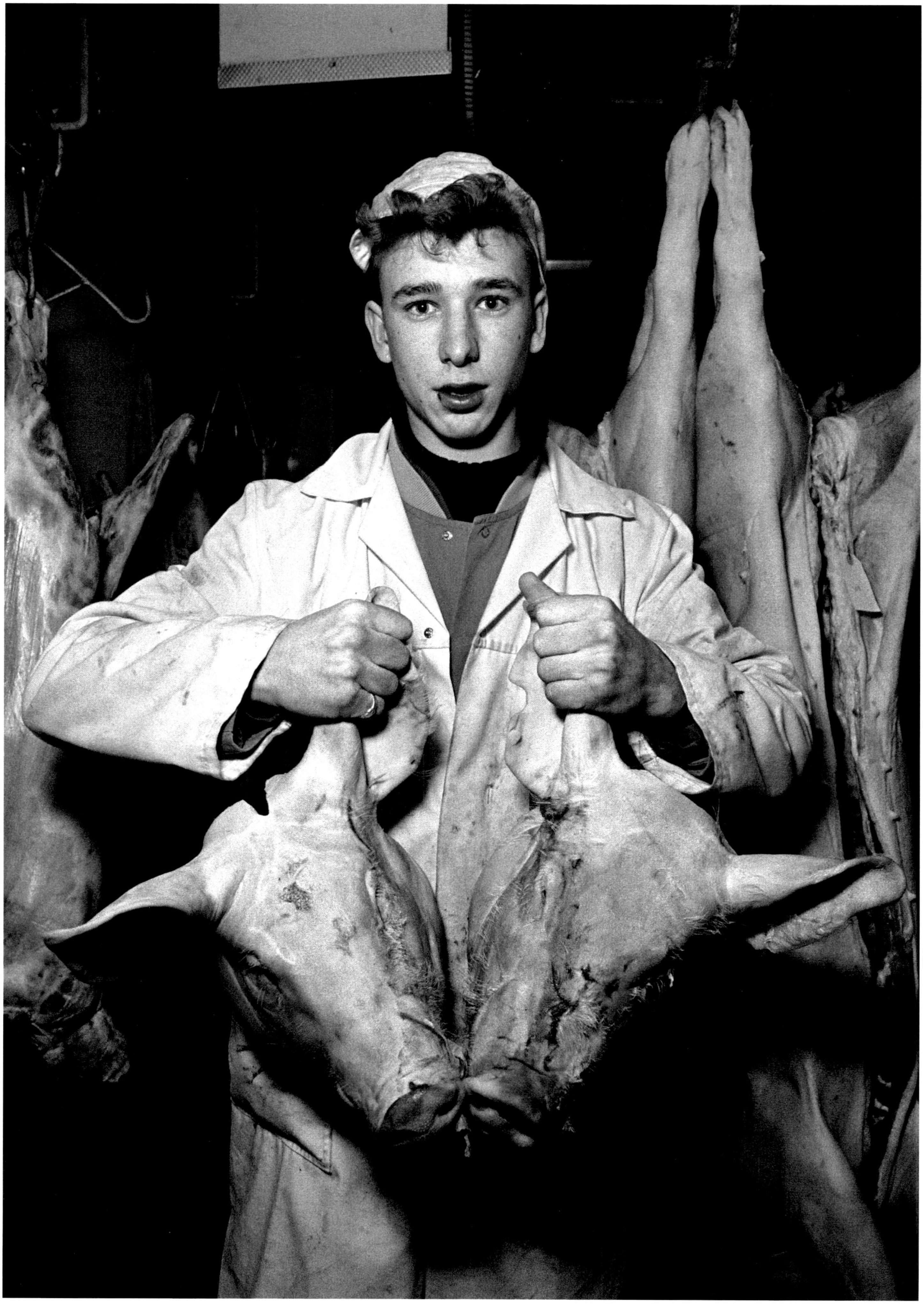

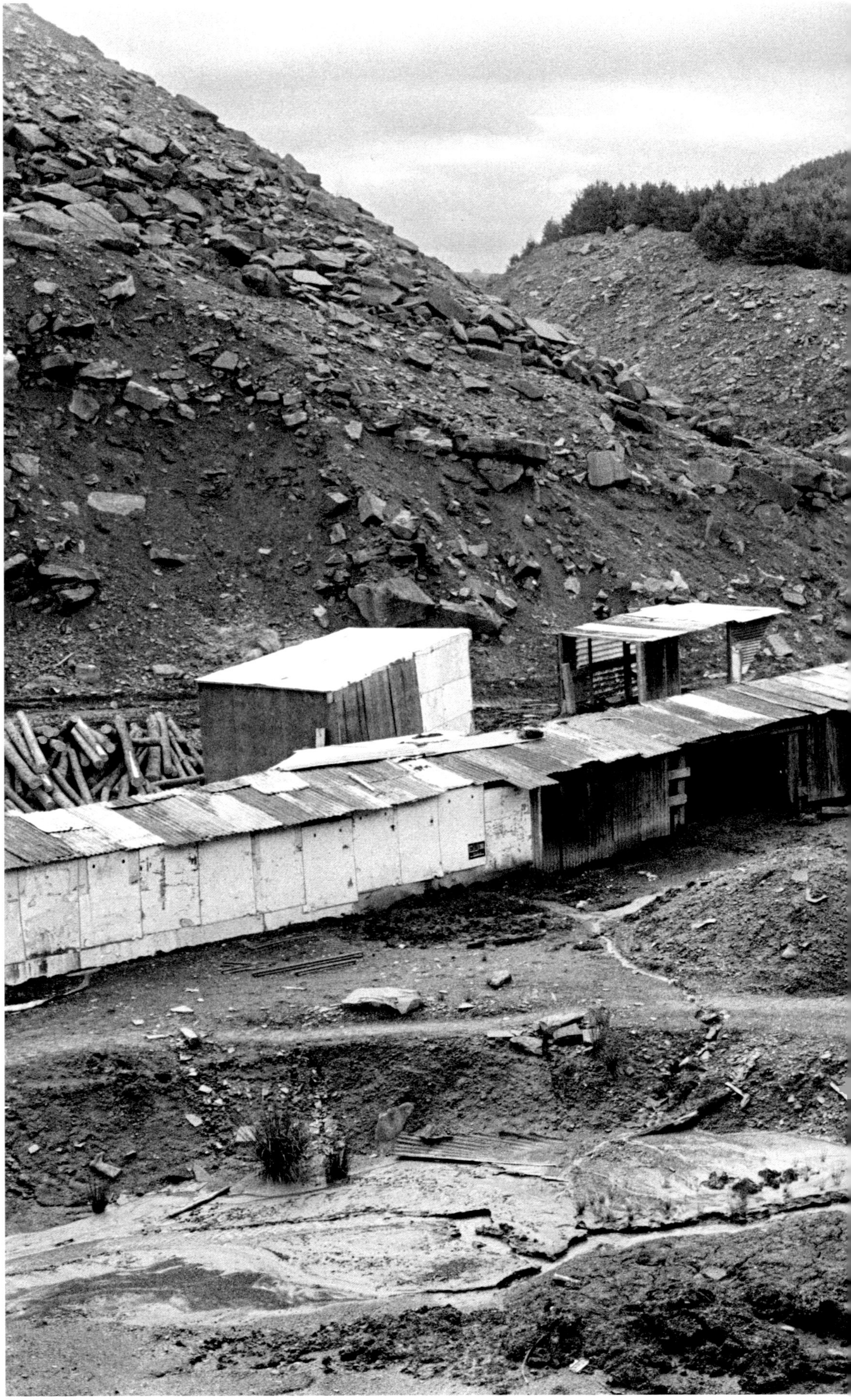

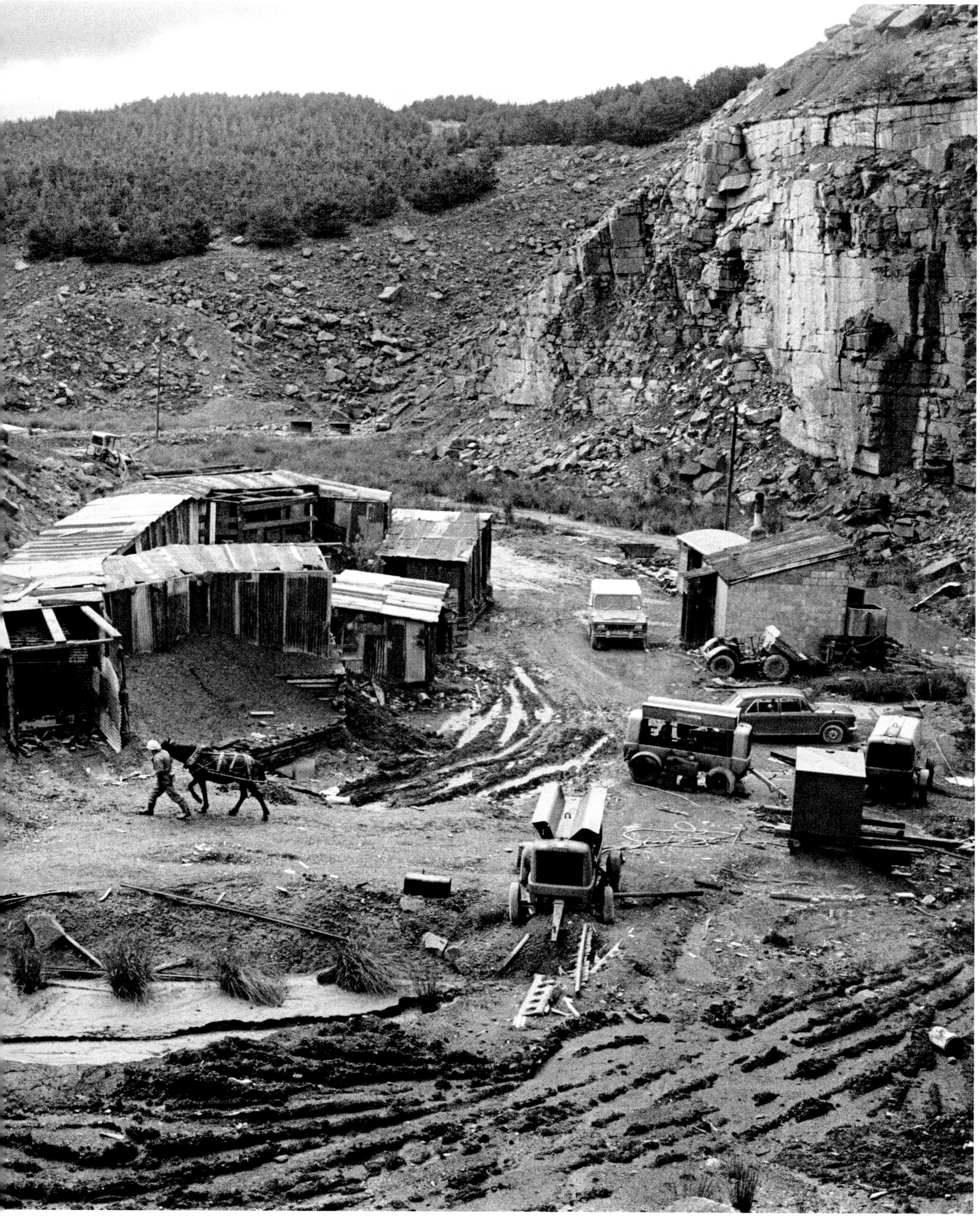

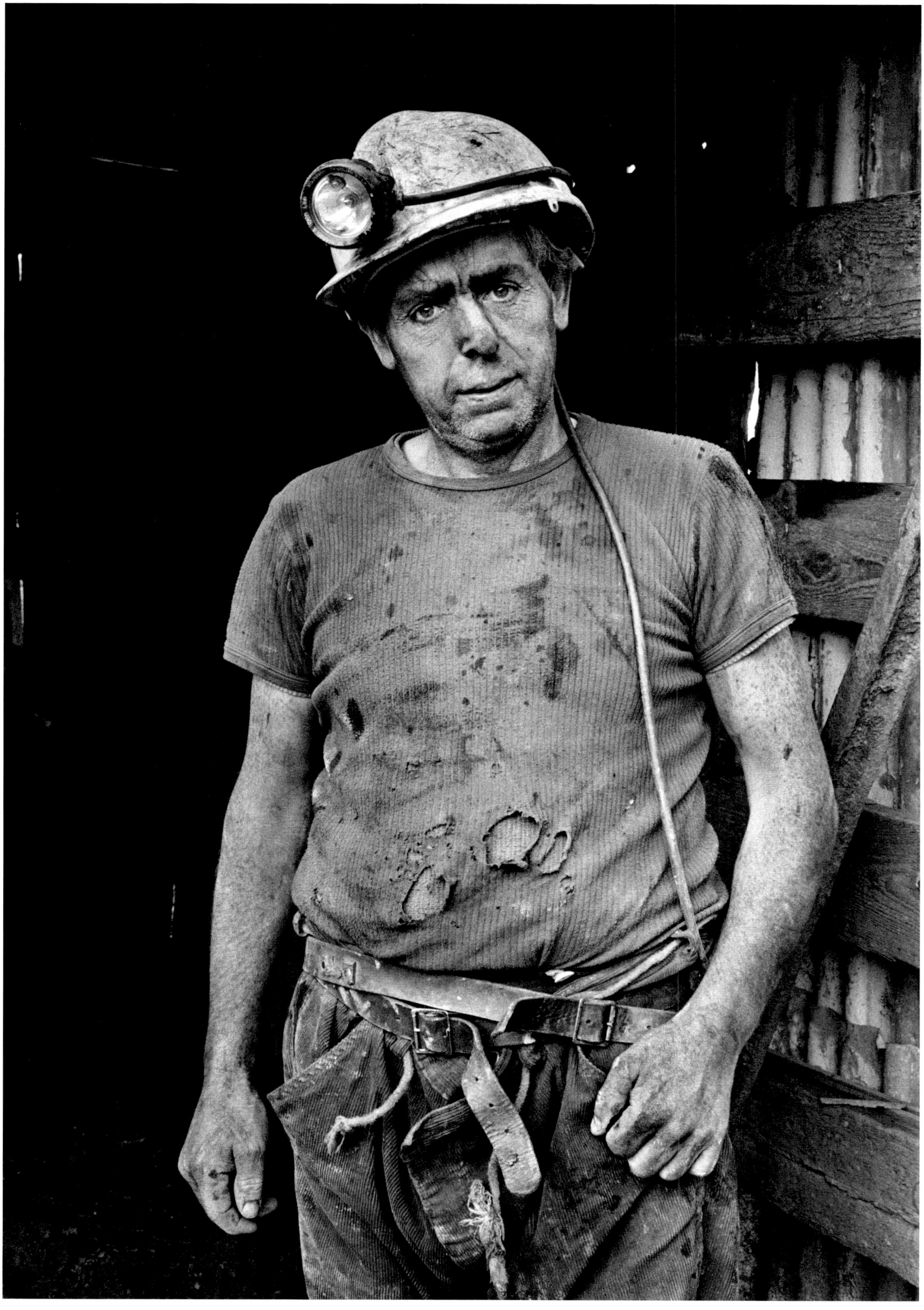

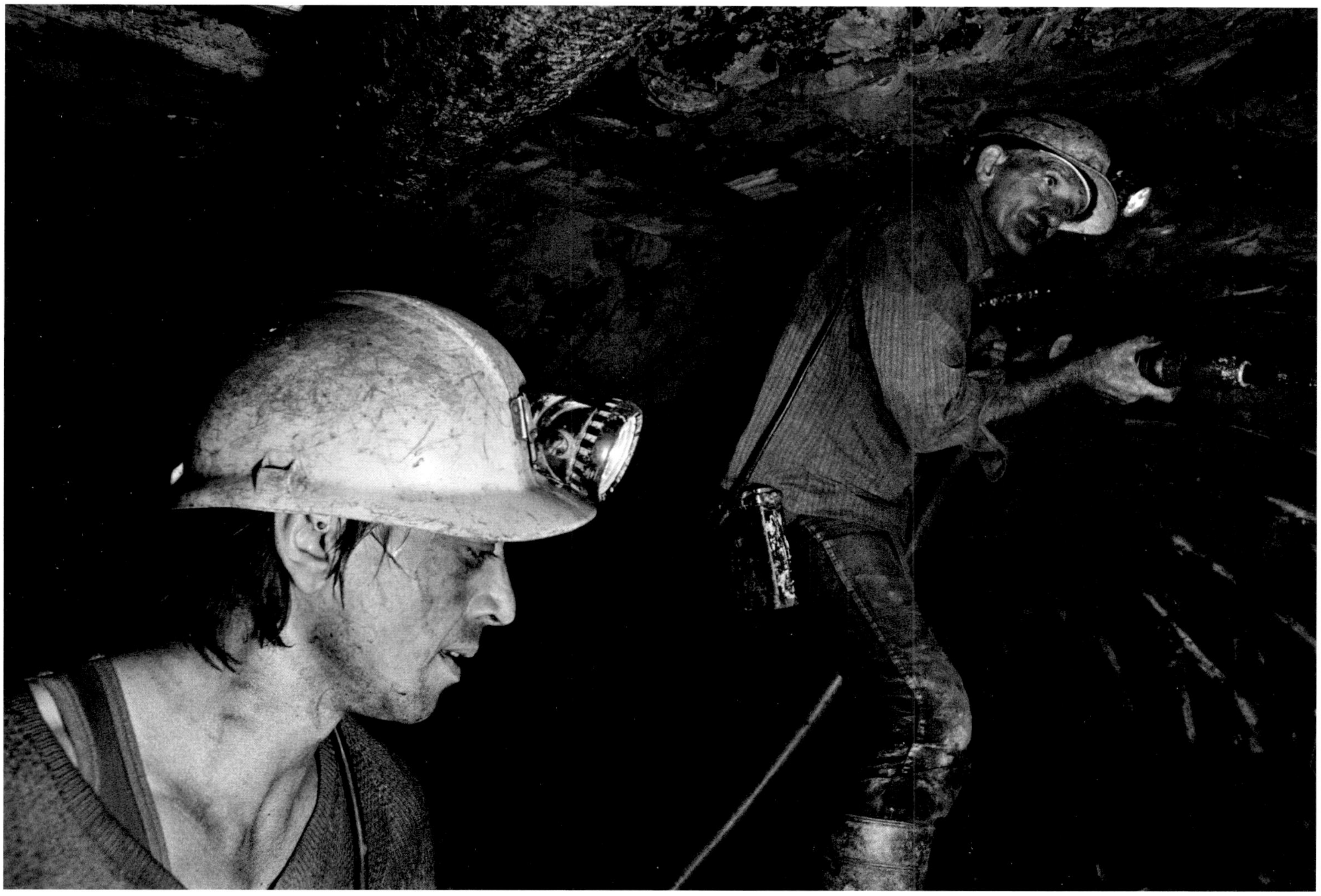

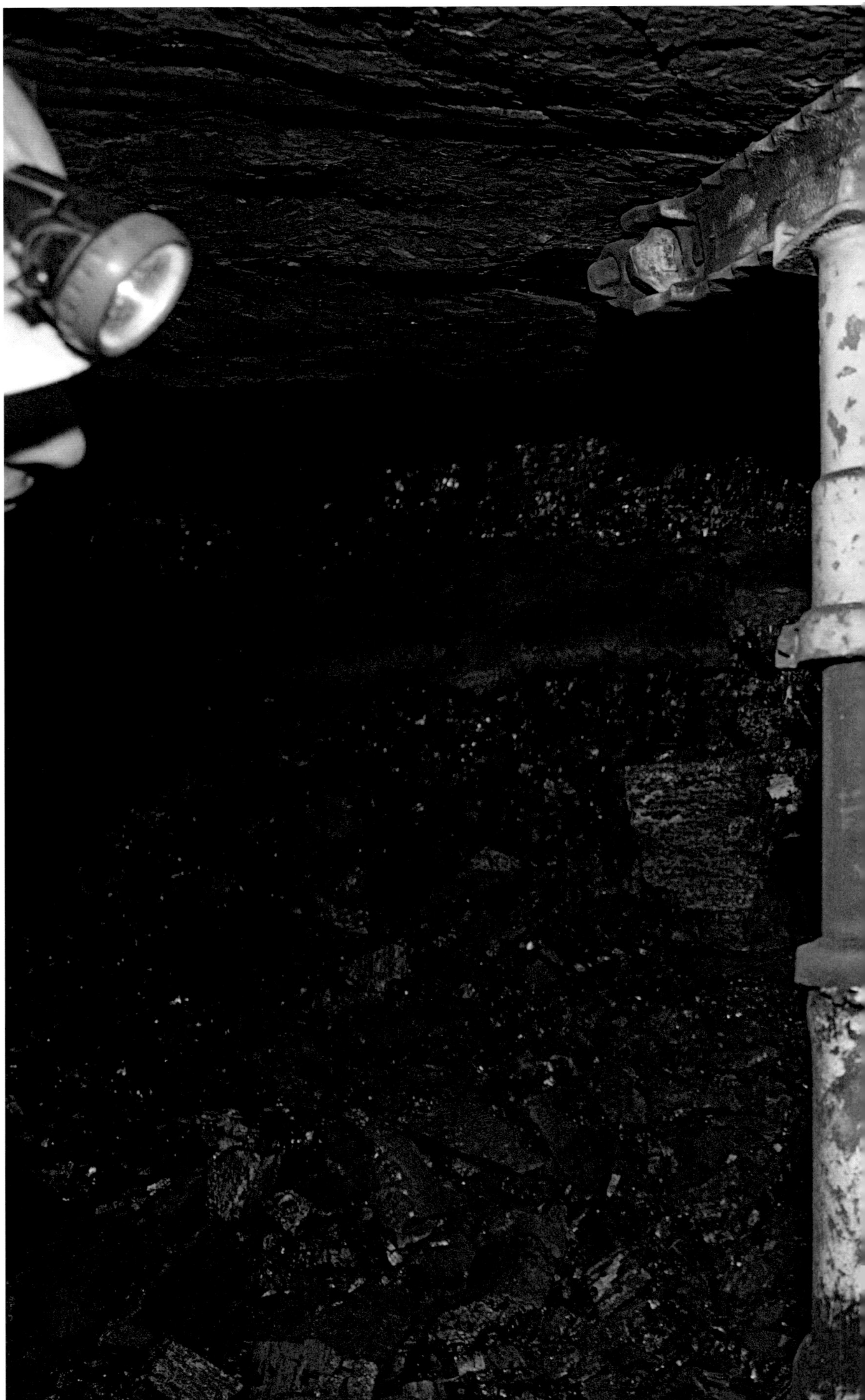

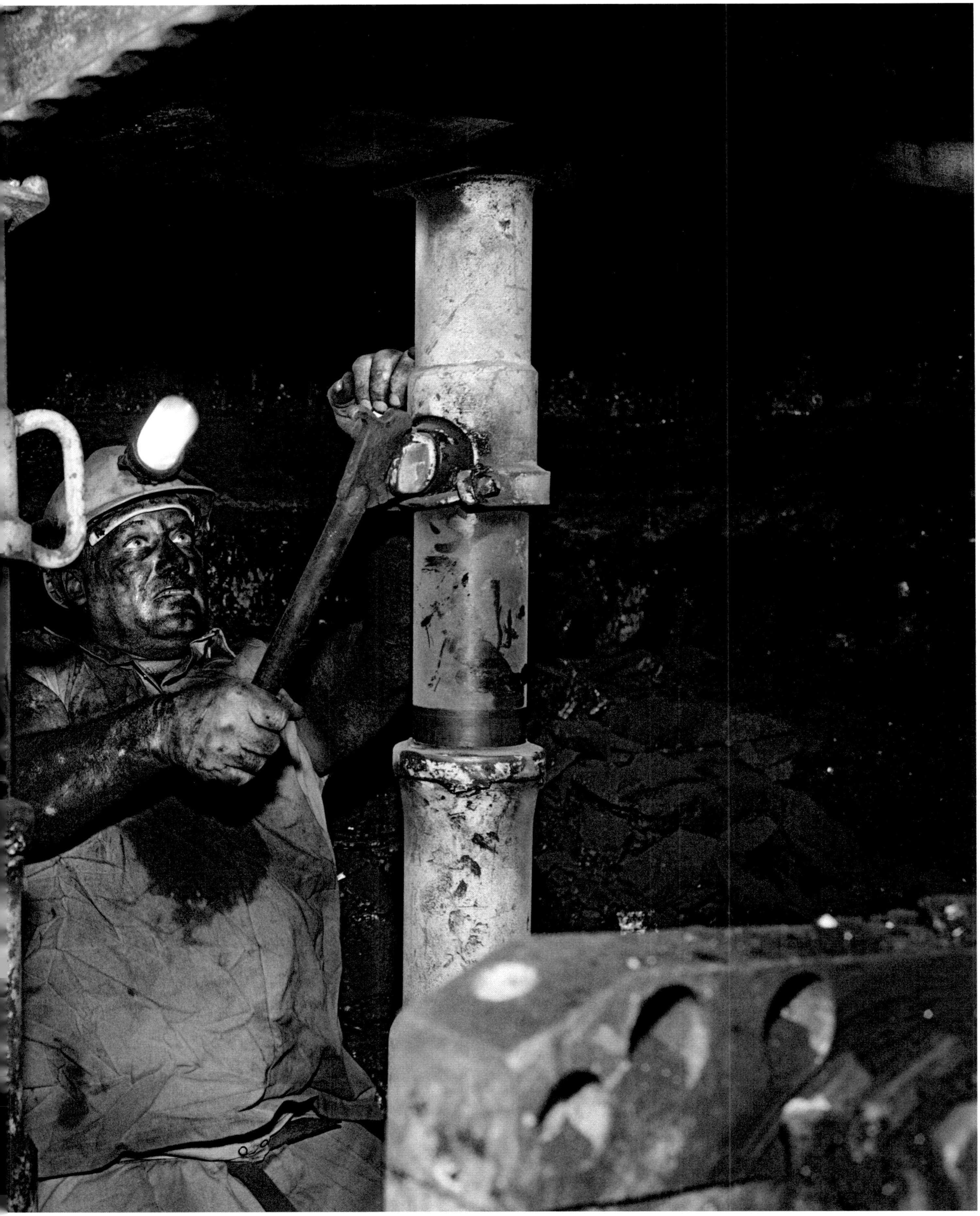

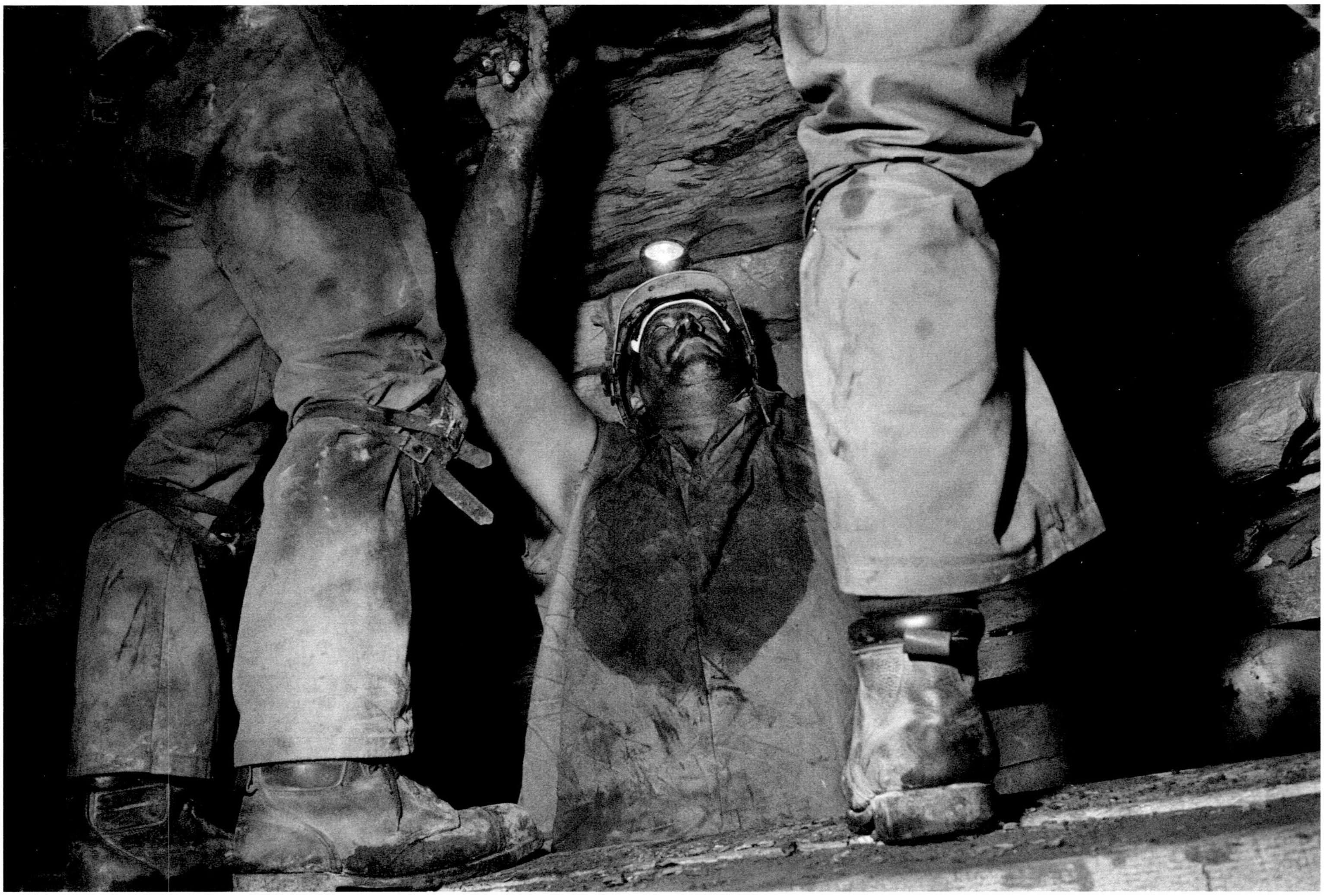

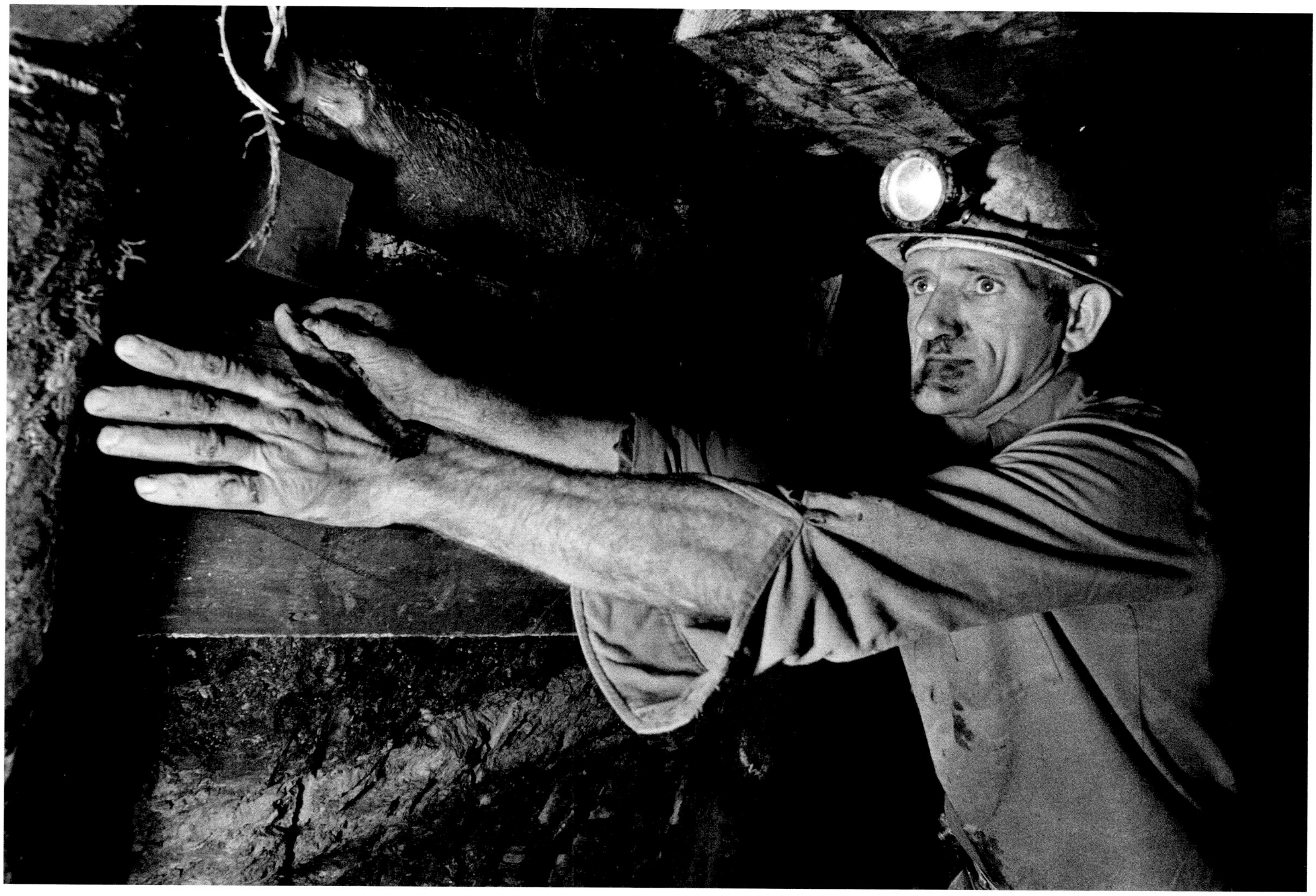

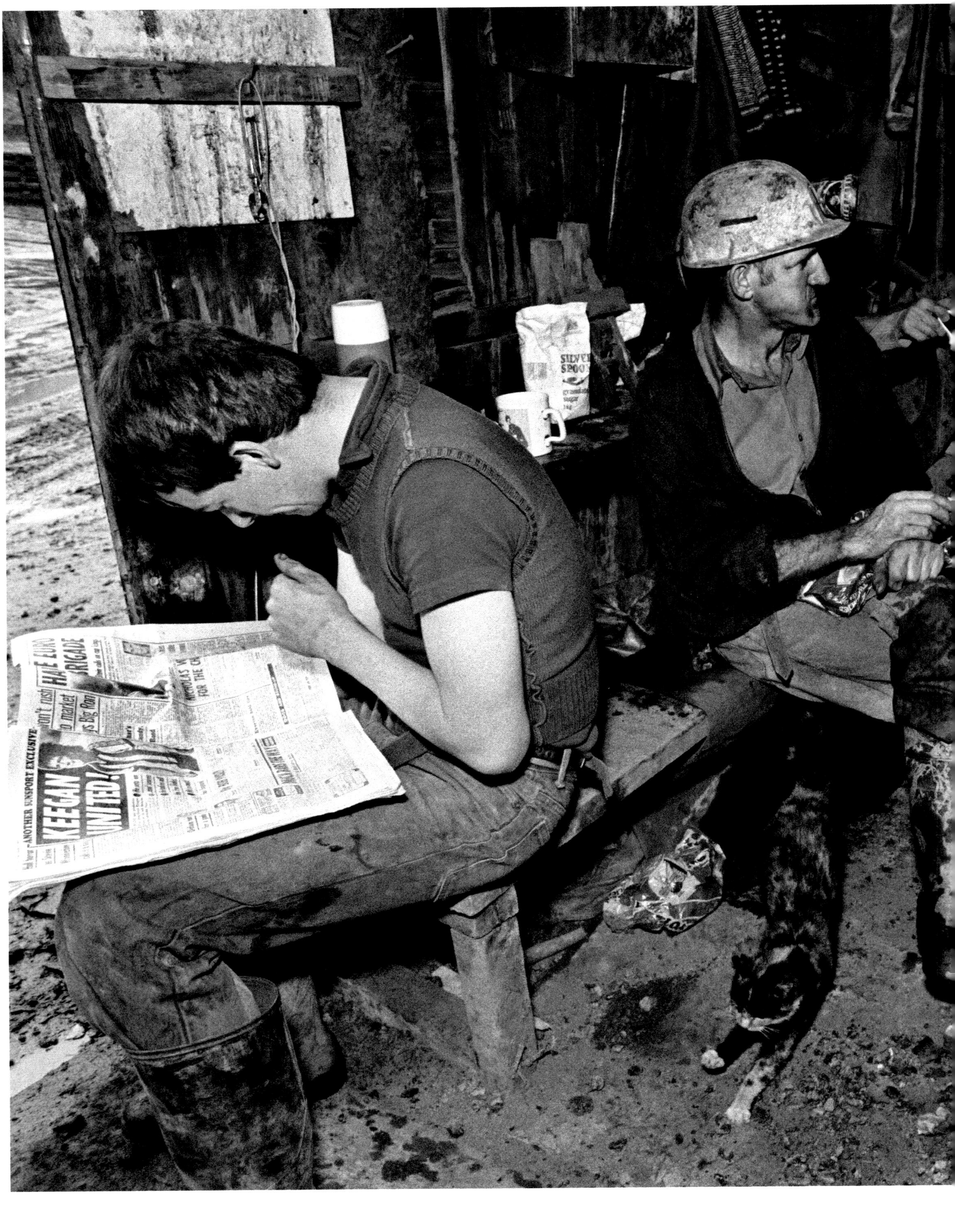
ANOTHER SUNSPORT EXCLUSIVE
KEEGAN UNITED!

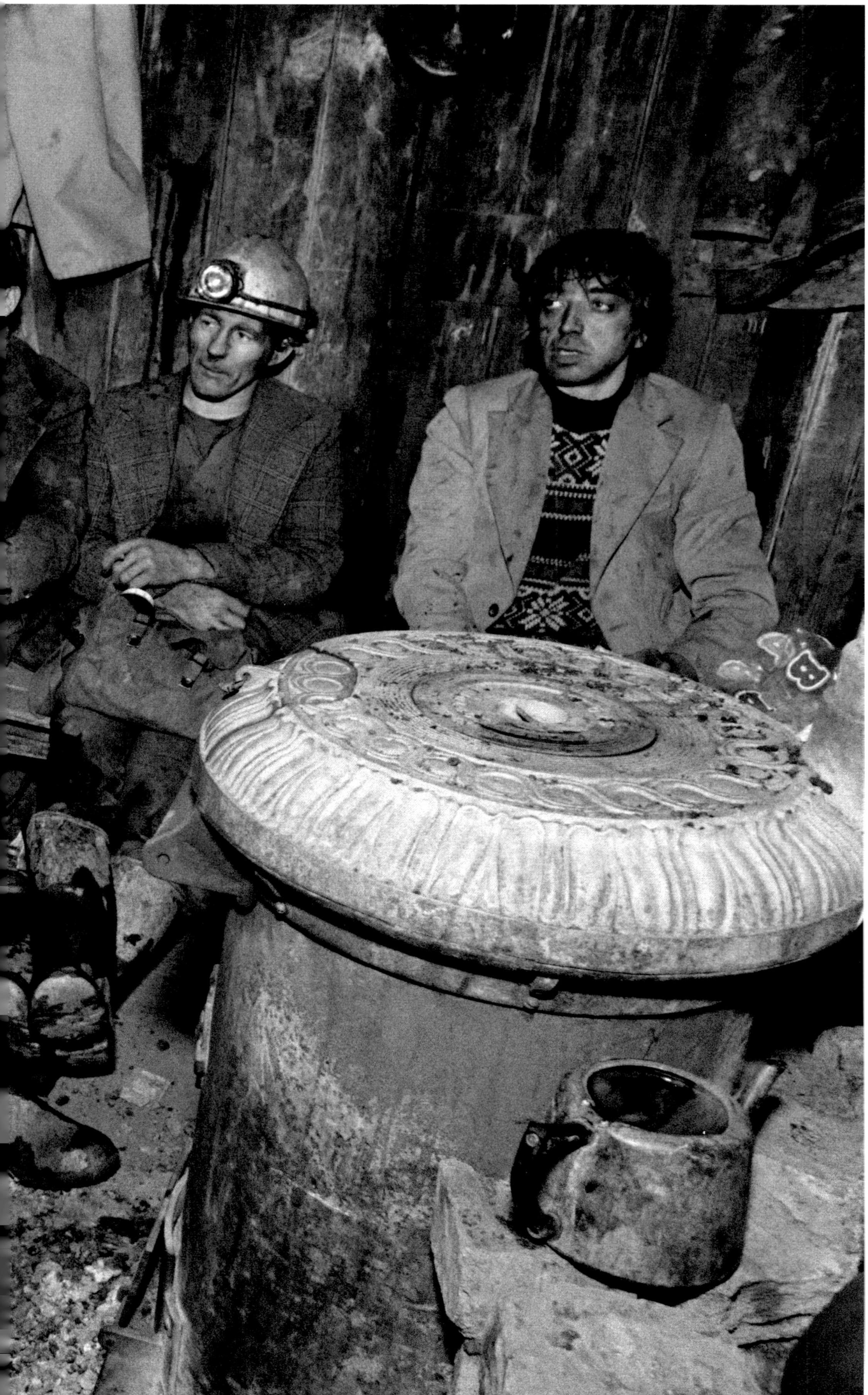

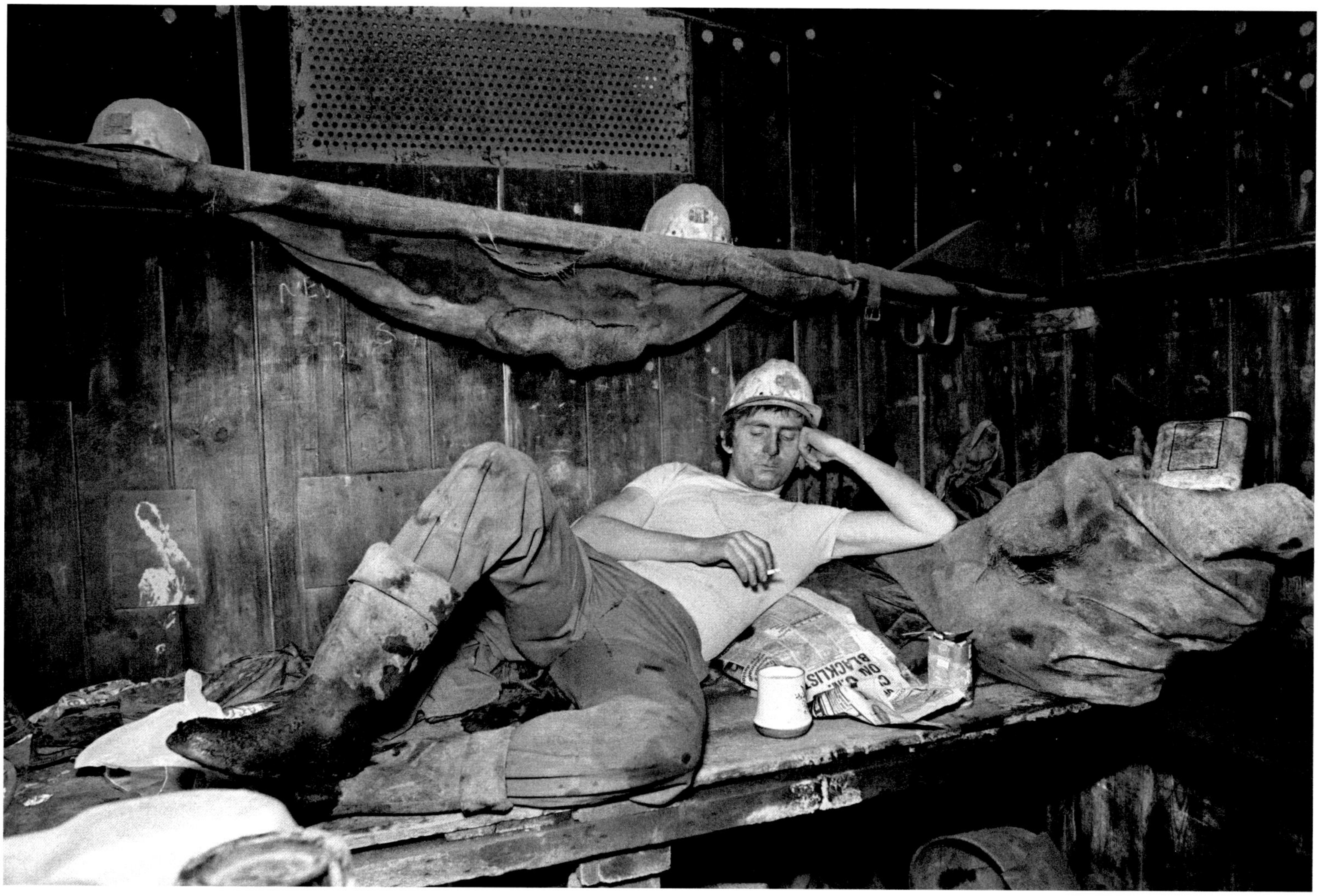

David Chandler

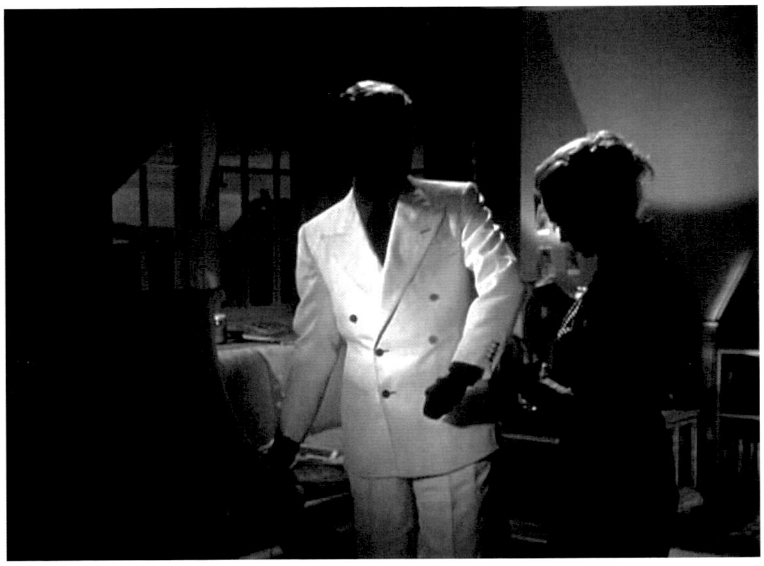

Whispers (Getting Louder): Paul Reas, The Dance Class, Penrhys Estate, 1984

In Alexander Mackendrick's 1951 Ealing Studios film *The Man in The White Suit*, a young Alec Guinness plays a Cambridge-educated scientist/inventor who gains access to the research departments of several northern textile mills in order to pursue what has become his personal quest—the development of an everlasting fabric. Guinness's Sidney Stratton is a man out of place, a socially naïve middle-class obsessive, who floats through the rigid class structures of a post-war England terrified of change. In this world, at the centre of one of Mackendrick's typically ambiguous moral fables, Stratton is both hero and villain. In one sense, he is the parody of a disinterested scientist in the new nuclear age, an idealist completely oblivious to the social ramifications of his work. But he is also a restless and energetic creative, a disruptive force who, as he insinuates his 'buccaneer experiment into the conformity of the research lab,' signals radical change on the horizon, and whose ultimate failure in the film has been seen as a 'pessimistic allegory of the artist.'

But the most powerful symbol of this radical spirit is the white suit itself, made from the 'indestructible' fabric that Stratton eventually produces, and which he wears throughout the second half of the film—or, as one character remarks, it is the suit that wears him. Luminous against the darkening terraced streets, cobbled alleyways and stark factory skylines of a generic northern urban landscape, the white suit stretches the sense of realism on which, from its opening documentary footage of working mills, the film is grounded. It is a glowing spectre from the world of dreams, alive in a place stoically resistant to its implications. And its ultimate (and literal) unravelling—a reflection, it has been said, of Mackendrick's 'cosmic scepticism,' especially in relation to science and scientists—does nothing to dampen or diminish the uncanny mood and liberating sense of possibility that the suit comes to embody.

I first saw *The Man in the White Suit* on TV sometime in the mid-sixties. It was one of the many British films of the 1940s and 50s that seemed to be shown constantly at the time, so ensuring that the recent past along with its values and sense of national identity lived very tangibly in the present, almost as a source of instruction and comparison at a time when so many of our social co-ordinates were being rearranged. It was partly from these films that my generation learned about the older culture we came from; they became important markers against which we could gauge the extent of our own expanding moral universe. White suits were common in these films. I'd come to associate them with hot climates, exotic locations and a certain class of Englishman abroad, caught up in the machinations of a waning empire—the film version of Graham Greene's *Our Man in Havana* (1959), again starring Alec Guinness, was a good example. Or, perhaps even more than this, I understood white suits as the ultimate sign of a mysterious, sophisticated foreigner: typically, Paul Henreid's cool Victor Lazlo, the real hero of *Casablanca* (1942). But, *The Man in the White Suit* was different. Uniquely and incongruously, it placed that image of exoticism and sophistication at the heart of a worn-out post-war landscape of Englishness, among its stock characters, its predictable conversations and its moribund attitudes and prejudices, all of which felt very familiar to me, a recognisable part of my childhood and my family's history.

Looking back to that time I have a distinct visual memory of the film, partly because the glowing white suit seemed to exaggerate the essential black and whiteness of our TV set in a room awash with 1960s colour, where competing patterns decorated every surface. But, before I was old enough to fully understand it, I also remember the film for the disturbing, subversive power of the suit and the vague sense that, as a beacon in the gloom, it was beckoning from another more exciting reality. The fact that Sydney Stratton is victimised for his invention by mill bosses and workers alike, and hounded by them through those dark streets in the film's nightmarish final sequence, only seemed to confirm the suit as a kind of rebel emblem.

For me, in one fundamental sense, the white suit in Mackendrick's film was about a kind of bravado, its luminosity a surreal incarnation of daring to be different, of being unafraid to stand out. From where I came from, and as a relatively timid youth, that message seemed awkward and confusing, but also incredibly transgressive. Underlying Sydney Stratton's reckless experimentation was not simply the threat of cultural renewal but a bold reinvention of the self. Don't worry about drawing attention to yourself, the film seemed to say, just relax and let the suit wear you!

Almost twenty years later, these memories were rekindled during a visit to the exhibition *Image and Exploration*, shown at The Photographers' Gallery, London, in the summer of 1985. The exhibition was a survey of British photography at the time and very much reflected a moment of transition, when the photographic image had become a point of confluence for many different artistic interests and traditions. I remember that diversity of styles and approaches being slightly chaotic and difficult

Film still from *The Man in the White Suit*, 1951

to navigate, but one photograph, with its strange echoing of the uncanny white suit, stood out for me in crystallising the show's quizzical mood and its eclectic sphere of reference. As if in recognition of this status, Paul Reas's *The Dance Class, Penrhys Estate* (1984), was used as the frontispiece of the exhibition catalogue and the picture's distinctively bizarre sense of everyday mystery remains undiminished by the passing years. As this rambling introduction suggests, I have always associated Reas's photograph with the film of *The Man in the White Suit*, and the connection has only become more meaningful for me over time. In both cases, the white suit's appearance is completely out of kilter with its surroundings, and in both it represents a turning point, a catalyst for change where one set of rules, one way of seeing and thinking, gives way to another. These are the personal preoccupations and lived histories that we all bring to our reading of images. But like all the best photographs, *The Dance Class* draws you back again and again because it refuses to be fully explicable or resolve itself around one coherent subject. It speaks to me now, as it has always done, as a quietly weird, unassuming masterpiece.

As a picture, *The Dance Class* is formed around a powerful intersection between its sweeping movement left and the strong sunlight angled across the image to the right. Leading the leftward motion by walking their way out of the photograph are a middle-aged couple straight out of British photography's lexicon of post-war ordinary. They are instantly familiar to me: in appearance and bearing they're a reminder of everyone's parents I met in the 1970s and early 80s; in fact, they could be my own parents, only a slightly smaller version. That they are a 'petit' couple is partly understood by the man's jacket, which looks too large for him, too long in length and in the sleeves; or perhaps it betrays a lingering affinity with drape jackets of the fifties favoured by Teddy Boys, a style this man may have flirted with in his late teens and twenties. But their size gives this couple a certain compactness, they are neat and tidy, upright, self-consciously respectable; and you can see they're trying their best. They belong to a generation of grateful survivors, those who have come through war and austerity and who, living their lives as a form of protection or containment, are very happy with keeping things simple. In this picture, they also have the look of Butlin's ballroom veterans, moving in an elegant dance stride, stepping lightly with a well-practiced poise, the man supporting but not exactly leading the woman, just gently holding her hand. It's a formal gesture and yet with this particular couple it suggests to me a similarly gentle domestic arrangement, the private equality and understanding that, certainly in my own experience, was common among working class men and women by the 1980s, and which, although likely to be played down in the more bullish public domain of the time, is able to express itself freely here in the measured body language of a community hall dance class.

In fact, so intent is this couple on their artful gliding, so lost in the moment, that they seem oblivious to the strange sun-bleached figure of a man, much taller, who looms so closely behind them, whose step exactly mirrors theirs, and who, with a raised hand, seems to be about to speak. Caught at that moment, and glowing in the sunlight, he appears as an apparition knocking on the door of their insular world, a ghostly refugee from some other reality politely asking to be let in.

In a commonplace setting where things should make sense, where we might expect everything to be comfortingly predictable, nothing here quite adds up. Not least that blackboard the dancing couple are about to pass, its chalked words a litany of apparent nonsense that we suspect has something to do with Bingo, but which—beginning with the end—floats into this otherwise innocuous space as the dispirited background noise of economic decline. Similarly, the glowing white man is a figure of disjunction; he stands out, literally, as a negative silhouette, a kind of anti-matter in this documentary realm, one that announces both an awakening and an act of photographic transformation. Once again, the white suit, this radiant body so wildly re-imagined by the camera, is a sign of new dimensions opening up while others slide out of the frame.

Despite the strong sun flooding into the space, Paul Reas's photograph was taken on a bitterly cold day, during the morning of Wednesday the 8th of February 1984 in the Penrhys community centre in South Wales. A heavy fall of snow had covered the streets outside and whitened the landscape of the Rhondda Fawr and Rhondda Fach valleys that the village overlooked from its hilltop site, some 1100ft above sea level. Reas had been coming to photograph here every day for the past six weeks, driving the 39 miles in his bright red Citroen 2CV from Newport where he was in his second and final year of the Documentary Photography course at Newport College. He had come to Penrhys partly because it reminded him of the place he grew up in, Buttershaw in Bradford, which had a similarly elevated position, as well as far-reaching social problems, rooted in high levels of unemployment and poor housing. In both places, Reas noted, the sense of physical elevation, the feeling of space and the views out over the surrounding landscape, was countered by the negative charge of a collective despondency spiralling downward, a condition common to 'sink estates' as they came to be called by the media around this time.

Drawn by the felt connections to his own experience, and by the ingrained sense of social inequality and injustice that in Penrhys seemed both highly specific and representative, Reas's aim was to make the place and the lives of its people visible in a series of 35mm documentary photographs, to build what he has described as a 'classic form of humanist reportage' in the manner of the photographers he admired at the time, such as Don McCullin, or those socially engaged contemporaries in Britain who were part of the Exit Group, such as Paul Trevor and Chris Steele Perkins.

Having made his photographs in and around the Penrhys community centre that cold February morning, Reas headed back to Newport to assess the results. When he arrived, the college was unusually quiet and, having printed his contact sheet, Reas was surprised to find two tutors, Martin Parr and Daniel Meadows, available to offer him some feedback. The contact sheet of *The Dance Class* they looked at is a vivid and absorbing record of Reas's physical and mental process as he worked around his subject, responding to the dancers' parade of movements and gestures while recognising the visual impact of the morning sun as it drenches the room in light. Daniel Meadows, as Reas remembers, was 'passionately in favour' of frame 30A, a picture that draws a deft comparison between the grace of the dancing middle-aged couple, entwined and in full flow, and the sweeping downward arc—the ribbon bow—of the curtains behind them, tied together to allow the sunlight to illuminate the otherwise dark and grey room. The image succeeds because it draws an uncluttered and elegant moment from what was a much more chaotic scene, and in so doing, it tells one notable story of time and place through a clear, simple, yet deeply poetic, association of elements. It suggests a photographic imagination schooled in the realist traditions of British post-war documentary, and we can safely assume that Meadows's own already considerable investment in those traditions drew him to the sensitivity and skill in this strand of Reas's work. Martin Parr, on the other hand, evidently saw another form potential unfolding in the final frame sequence where Reas begins to concentrate on the play of sunlight in relation to the single figure of a man in a white suit. Parr's choice from this sequence was frame 39A, the photograph eventually selected, which, more than any other of Reas's efforts that day, steps beyond the former realist tradition to conjure an ambiguous, illusory drama from the everyday narrative unfolding in the room.

Significantly, Parr's primary interest was the quality of the photograph and not its fidelity to the subject. During the tutorial Reas remembers him saying, 'You can only experience this moment by looking at the photograph, because real life doesn't look like this.' Crucially for Parr, Reas had added a new visual dimension to the scene; the white-suited figure existed purely as an invention of the camera and as an expression of the photographer's own restive response to his subject. Reas remembers that Parr backed up his observations by quoting Garry Winogrand's now well-known dictum, 'I photograph to see what the world looks like photographed,' always provocative for a documentarist, and deployed as a kind of general license to abdicate responsibility for anything but the photographer's creative preoccupations as a picture-maker.

This was very much Parr's own position. Having come under the formative influence of Tony Ray Jones in the 1970s, Parr's evolving photographic sensibilities had always favoured personal creative expression over hard documentary evidence. But in February 1984, as a picture-maker, humourist and melancholy poet of British eccentricity and whimsy, his priorities were being tested by the social and political challenges emerging since the election of Margaret Thatcher's conservative government in 1979. In many ways, the photographs he was making in New Brighton on Merseyside at the time, the pictures that became *The Last Resort*, were an attempt to resolve those new challenges with his commitment to a rapidly developing colour aesthetic. The result was a new kind of mordant, anti-picture-postcard satire on leisure and consumerism in contemporary Britain, one that, too callously for some, cast its local working-class subjects, many of them young families and elderly people, in chaotic, litter-strewn situations they would hardly have recognised. In this sense, *The Last Resort* was fundamentally a photographic invention, a hybrid form, conceived by Parr's acute eye for the incongruous and produced in saturated colour heightened by his use of fill-in flash in the already searing sunlight.

Back in Newport, Parr's preference for frame 39A and his reasoning, had an immediate and far-reaching impact on Reas, as he has said: 'Prior to this moment I aspired to the humanistic social documentary cannon of people like Eugene Smith... picture-makers who were using the photograph primarily as evidence in an attempt to right the world's wrongs...(but) this one single critique of

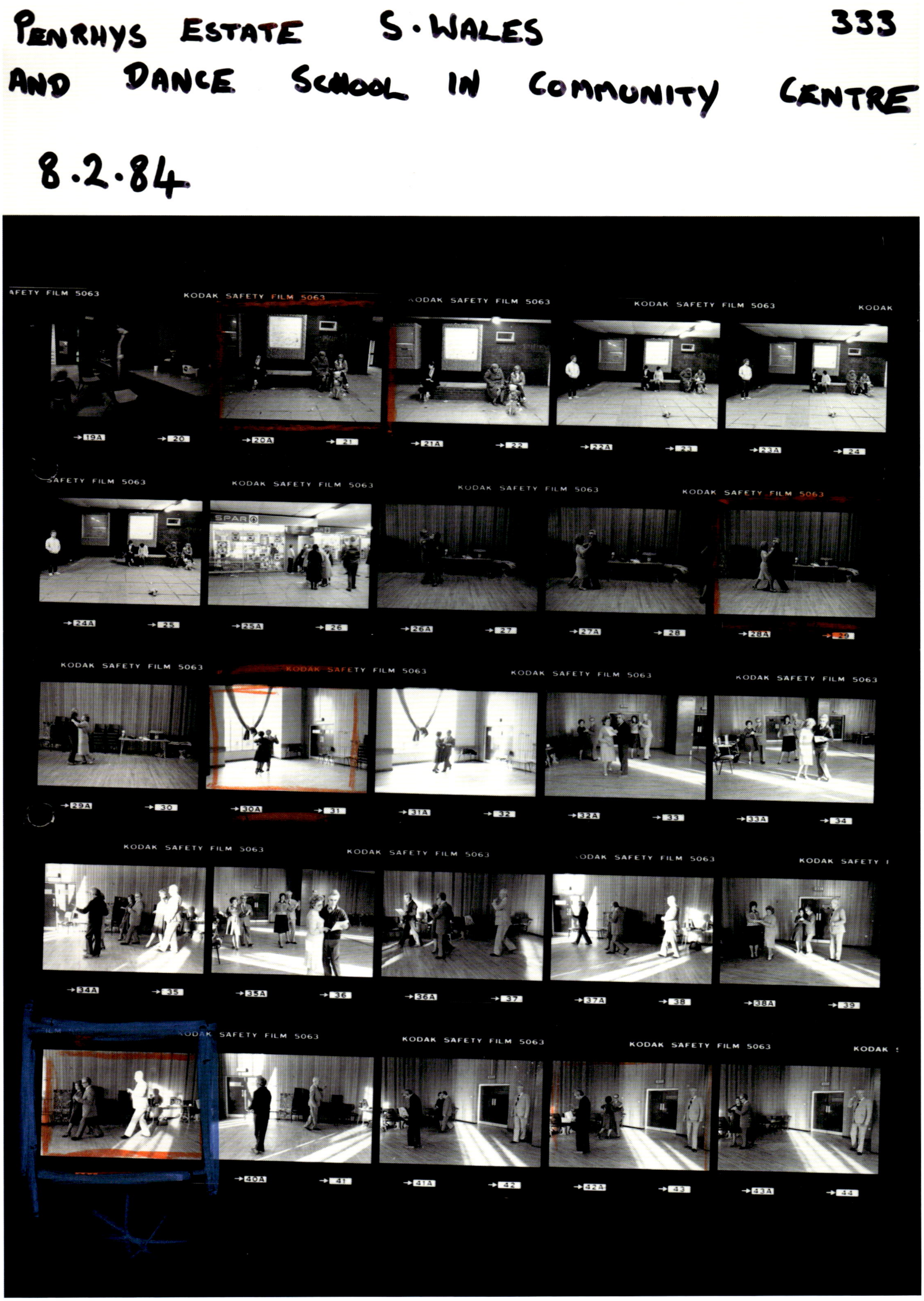
PENRHYS ESTATE S. WALES 333
AND DANCE SCHOOL IN COMMUNITY CENTRE
8.2.84
KODAK SAFETY FILM 5063

my work completely altered the way I thought about photography and started to determine the kind of work I looked at and aspired to create myself.'

Following Parr's suggestions that work would have included the photographs of Ray Jones and, perhaps more importantly, key examples of the new American photography: notably Lee Friedlander, the exciting, almost illicitly single-minded example of Winogrand, and then, later, the colour work of William Eggleston, Joel Meyerowitz, Joel Sternfeld and Stephen Shore, among others. What happened over the next five years or so, as Reas gradually developed his own hybrid form of acerbic, satirical, subjective social commentary in seminal works such as 'I Can Help' and 'Flogging a Dead Horse', is now part of the history of recent British photography and is well chronicled in this book. It would be wrong to say that, for Reas, the story began in the community centre in Penrhys, but it's tempting to see that otherwise uneventful morning, with all its modest and gracious endeavour, as a symbolic moment.

Because of the cold weather the streets of Penrhys were almost deserted when Reas arrived to photograph that day, so he made his way to the community centre where he knew local residents tended to congregate. In the desolate spaces outside the centre, part of a cavernous concrete shopping precinct, Reas photographed a few people hanging around: sitting, waiting, killing time or queuing by the Spar. The images have the same sense of torpor common to many of his Penrhys estate photographs, an energy-drained stillness that registers as a kind of grey weight in the air. But stepping into the hall where the dance class had already begun, he found a new kind of alertness. In contrast to the cold inertia outside, here was movement, not fast and furious but something more measured, like a formal presentation that Reas might watch and study, tuning in to a different tempo and trying his hand at something more demanding. Growing up in Buttershaw, Reas had become a devotee of northern soul music, but during those sweaty, high-octane nights at the Twisted Wheel in Manchester or The Torch in Tunstall, Staffordshire, he had always been an observer, a shy watcher on the side-lines rather than a dancer. So, long before he became a photographer, he was a keen student of human energy and movement, and it is interesting to imagine how some trace of that experience may have informed his response to the swaying middle-aged dancers in Penrhys. Into this framework of implicit memory, we might also place Reas's interest in the man in the white suit, who, his partner having left the lesson, dances alone and so awkwardly through the final eight frames of the contact sheet. And following this thought a little further, we might just feel a faint click in the photographer's unconscious as he prepares to expose frame 39A, when the white-suited man finally steps up to the rhythm, when the game suddenly changes and when, for one split second, he finds his own place in the spotlight.

My memories of *The Man in the White Suit* were further informed by a chapter on the film in Philip Kemp's book *Lethal Innocence: The Cinema of Alexander MacKendrick* (Menthuen, 1991). The essay also drew on comprehensive notes written for me by Paul Reas, some of which I've quoted from, and on conversations between us over several years. My thanks to Paul for his generosity and patience during this time.

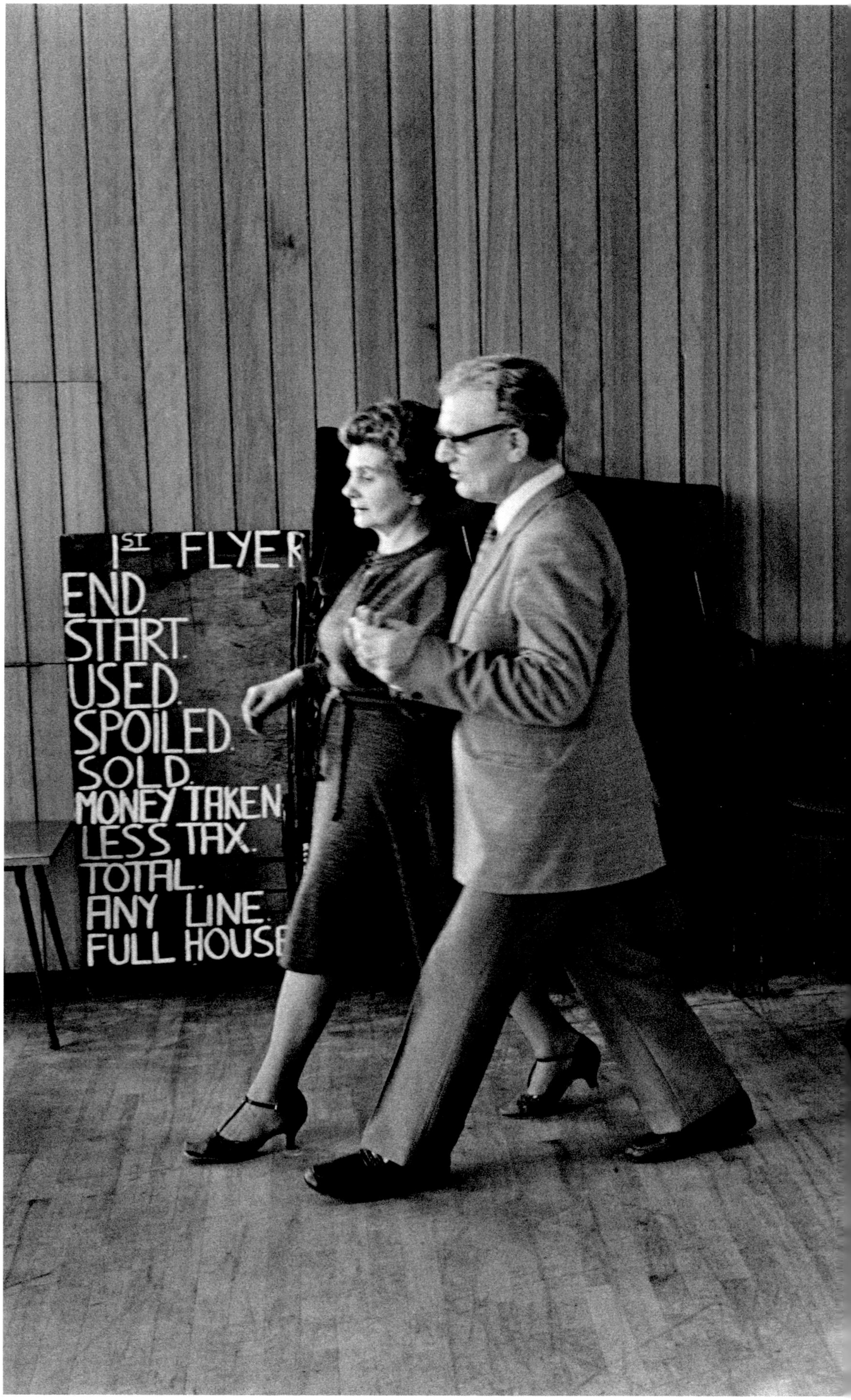
1ST FLYER
END.
START.
USED.
SPOILED.
SOLD.
MONEY TAKEN
LESS TAX.
TOTAL.
ANY LINE.
FULL HOUSE

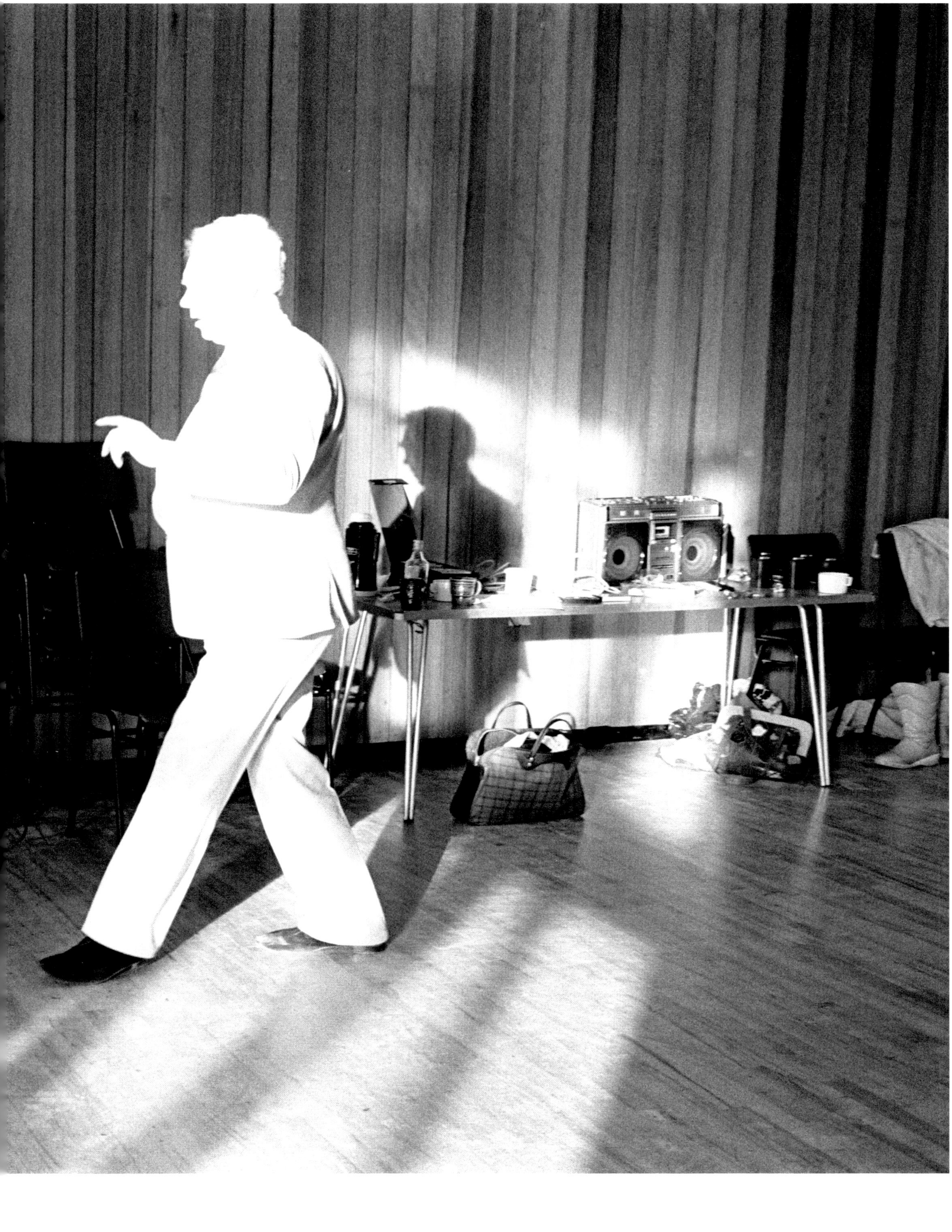

The Penrhys estate sits 335 metres above the Rhondda Valley in South Wales. This hilltop site of a former monastery became the location for 951 homes in 1968. Built originally to house coal miners from the Nottingham coalfield, who were to be relocated to work in a proposed new colliery in the Rhondda Valley, the homes were left empty when South Wales mining began to decline, and the National Coal Board withdrew its order for the houses. Rhondda Borough Council's response was to use the Penrhys estate as a 'dumping ground' for 'problem' families.

My initial interest in the estate stemmed from the similarity it shared with the estate I had grown up on in Bradford, West Yorkshire. The Buttershaw estate in Bradford was built in 1947, on land which had been extensively mined, and at an altitude of nearly 270 metres above sea level it was one of the highest points in Bradford. My mother was one of the first residents to inhabit the estate and it was here, at number two Brafferton Arbor, that she raised her family of five boys. Our family was typical of many ordinary, hardworking families on the estate who were doing their best in difficult circumstances. Like Penrhys, Buttershaw also had a bad reputation locally, as it was also used by Bradford Council as a place to house 'difficult' families. Buttershaw, and in particular Brafferton Arbor, gained notoriety in 1987 when they were featured as the setting for most of the scenes in the film *Rita, Sue and Bob Too*, which was based on plays by local resident Andrea Dunbar, who also lived on that same street.

I knew that Penrhys's reputation, like that of Buttershaw, was ill-founded and that the residents were not the victims of an environment of their own creation; they were by and large decent families who were trapped by circumstances beyond their control.

Since I knew that the Penrhys estate had been the subject of much negative media attention, it therefore felt unwise to suddenly arrive on the streets with a camera unannounced. I decided, as a form of introduction to the community, that I would establish 'The Free Studio' in the estate's undercover shopping precinct. The inspiration for this had come from works such as Irving Penn's 'Worlds in a Small Room' (1974), but most importantly from my then tutor Daniel Meadows and his projects 'The Shop on Greame Street' (1972) and 'The Free Photographic Omnibus' (1973–74). Like Meadows, I would use 'The Free Studio' as a point of contact, a place for conversations, an opportunity to explain who I was and what I was trying to do in the hope that they might trust me. Like Meadows's 'Free Photographic Omnibus' portraits, I saw 'The Free Studio' as a precursor, an entrée to the more 'serious' business, as I saw it then, of the photo reportage.

1984

Penrhys Estate

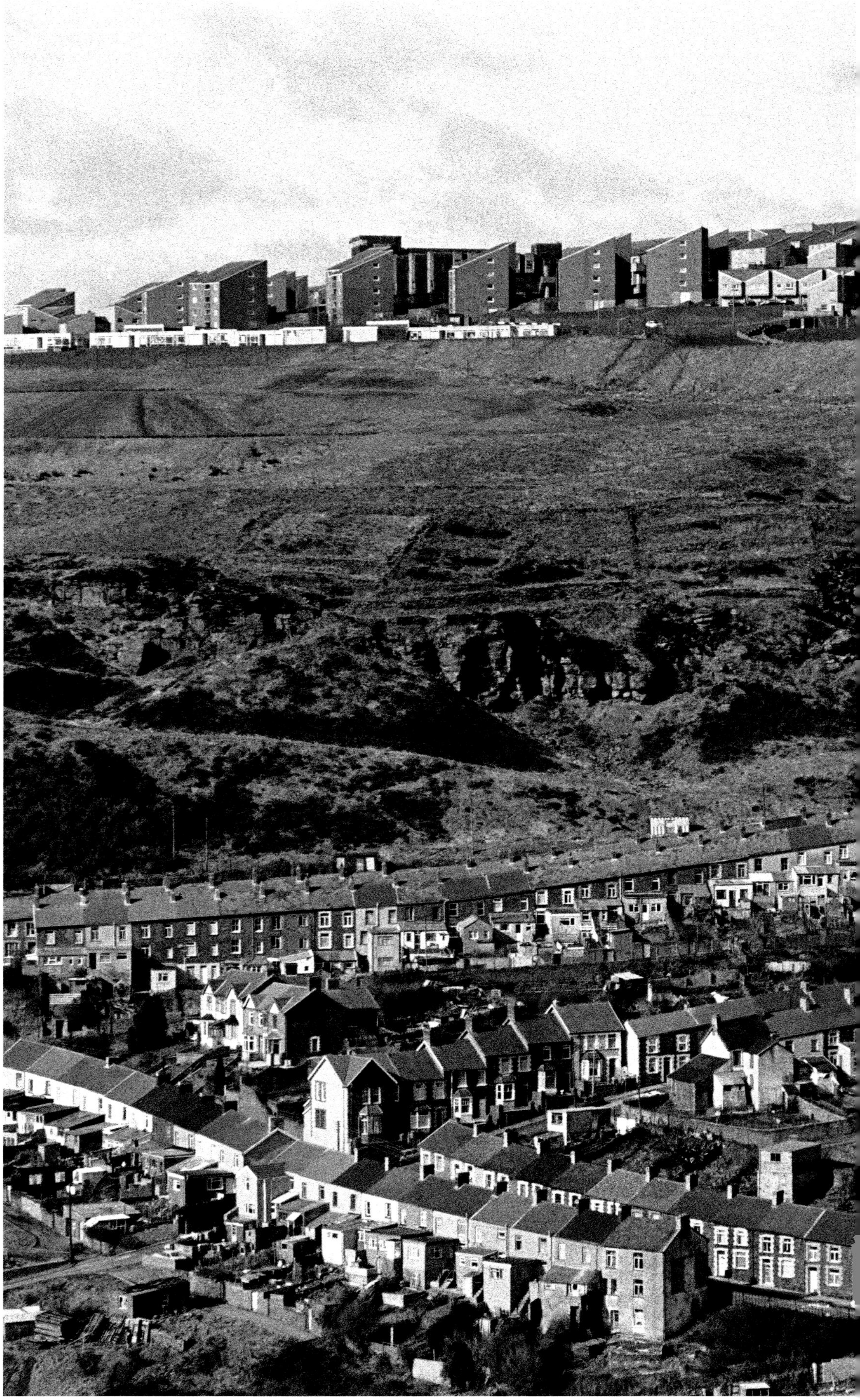

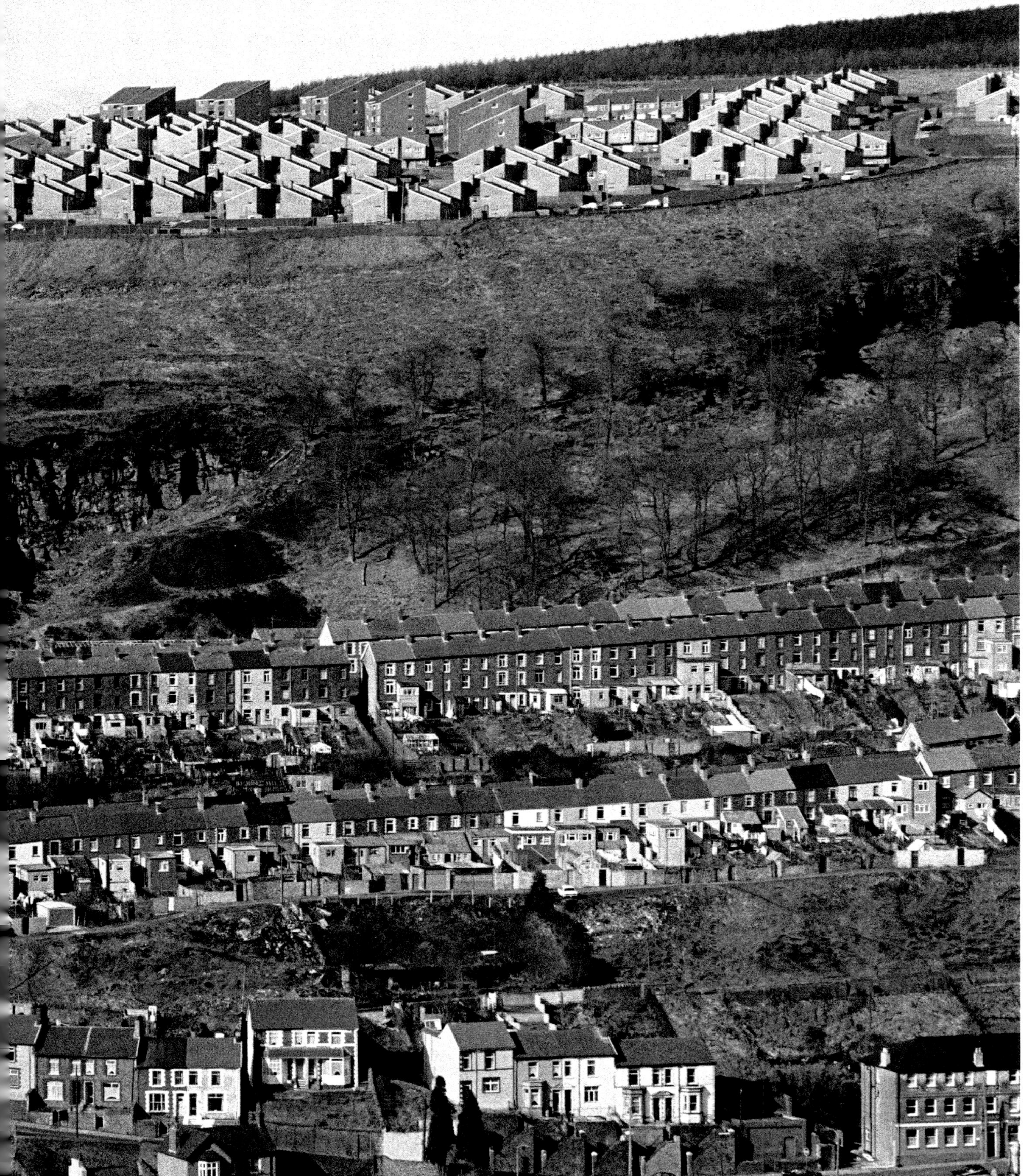

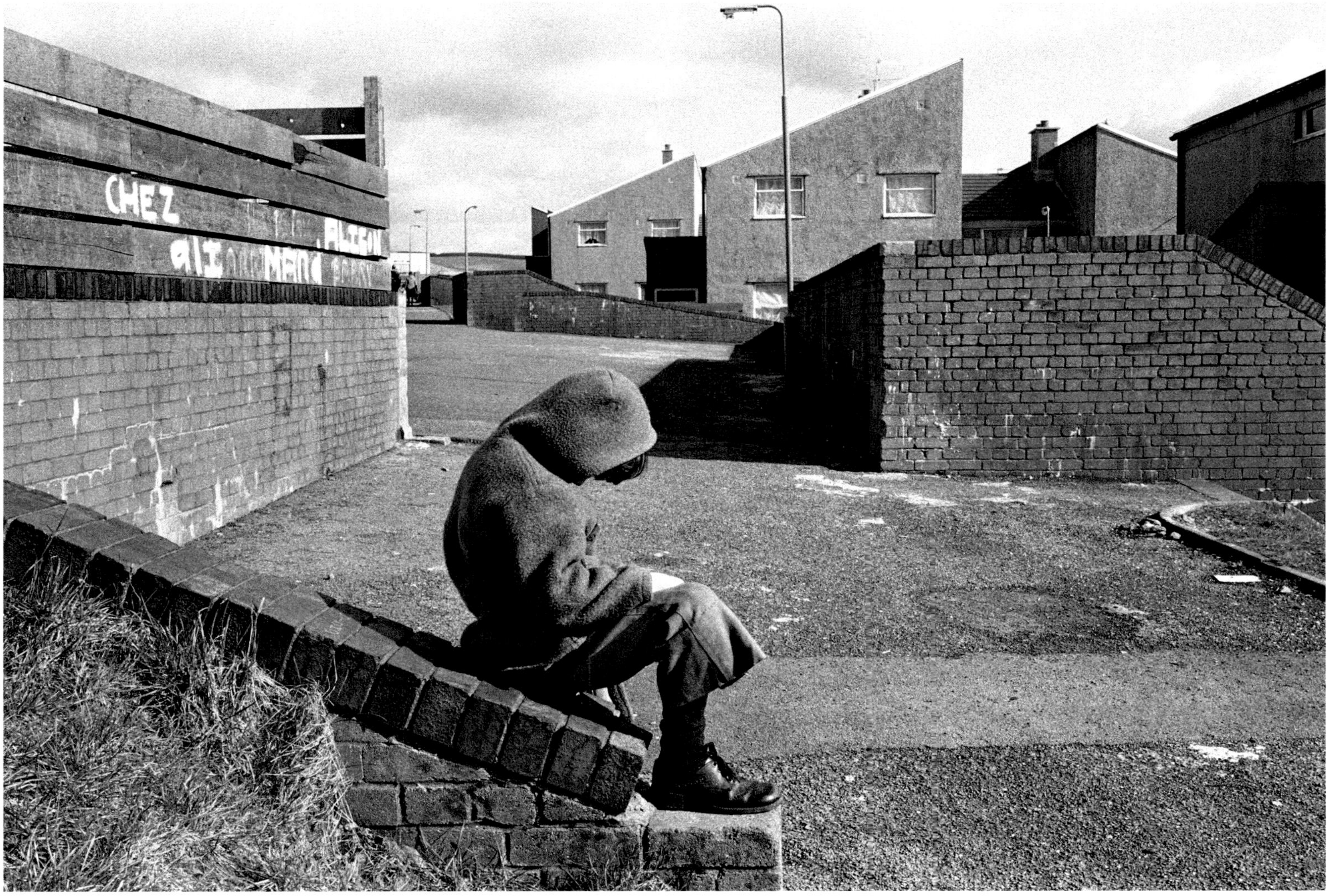
CHEZ

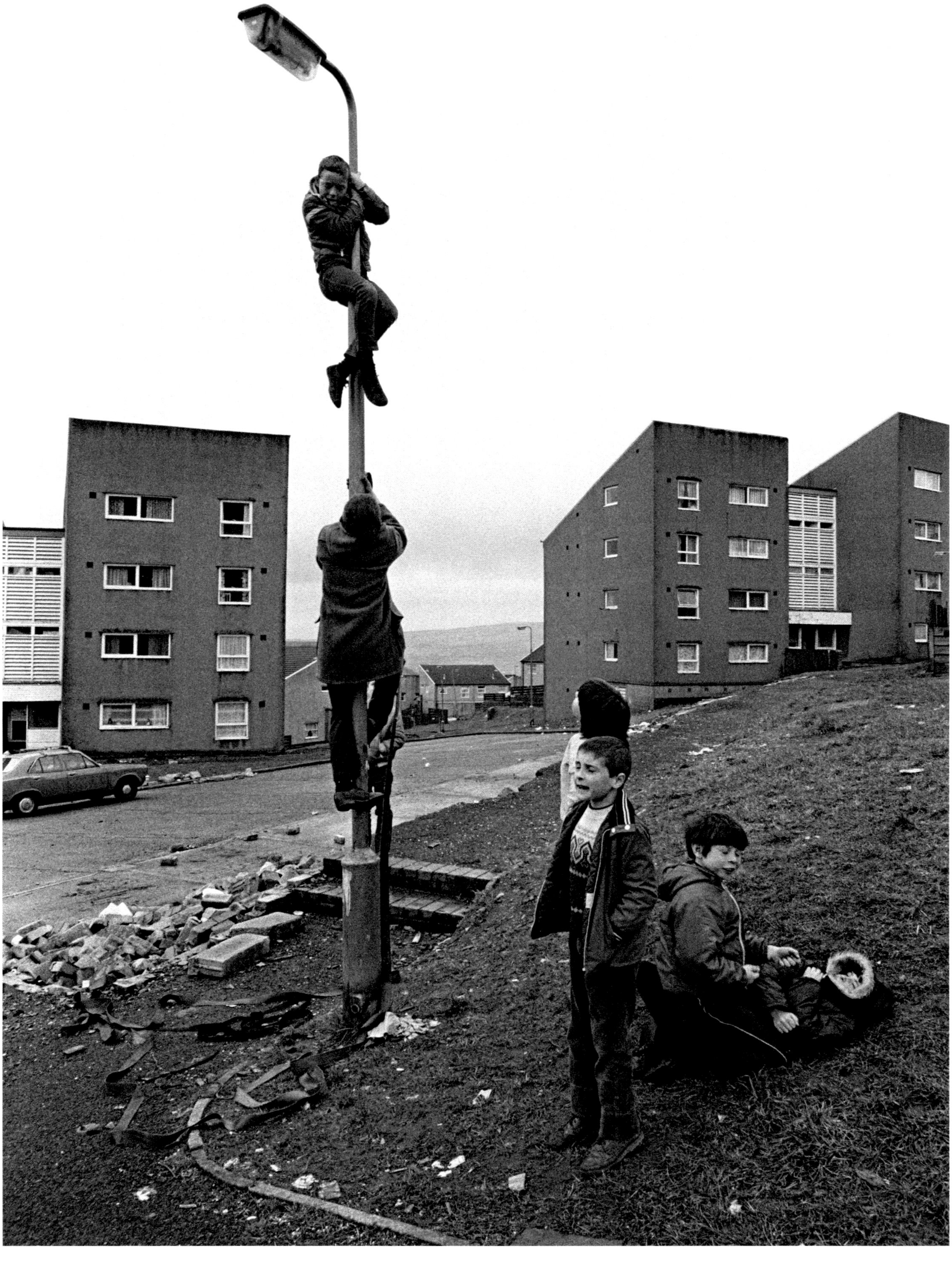

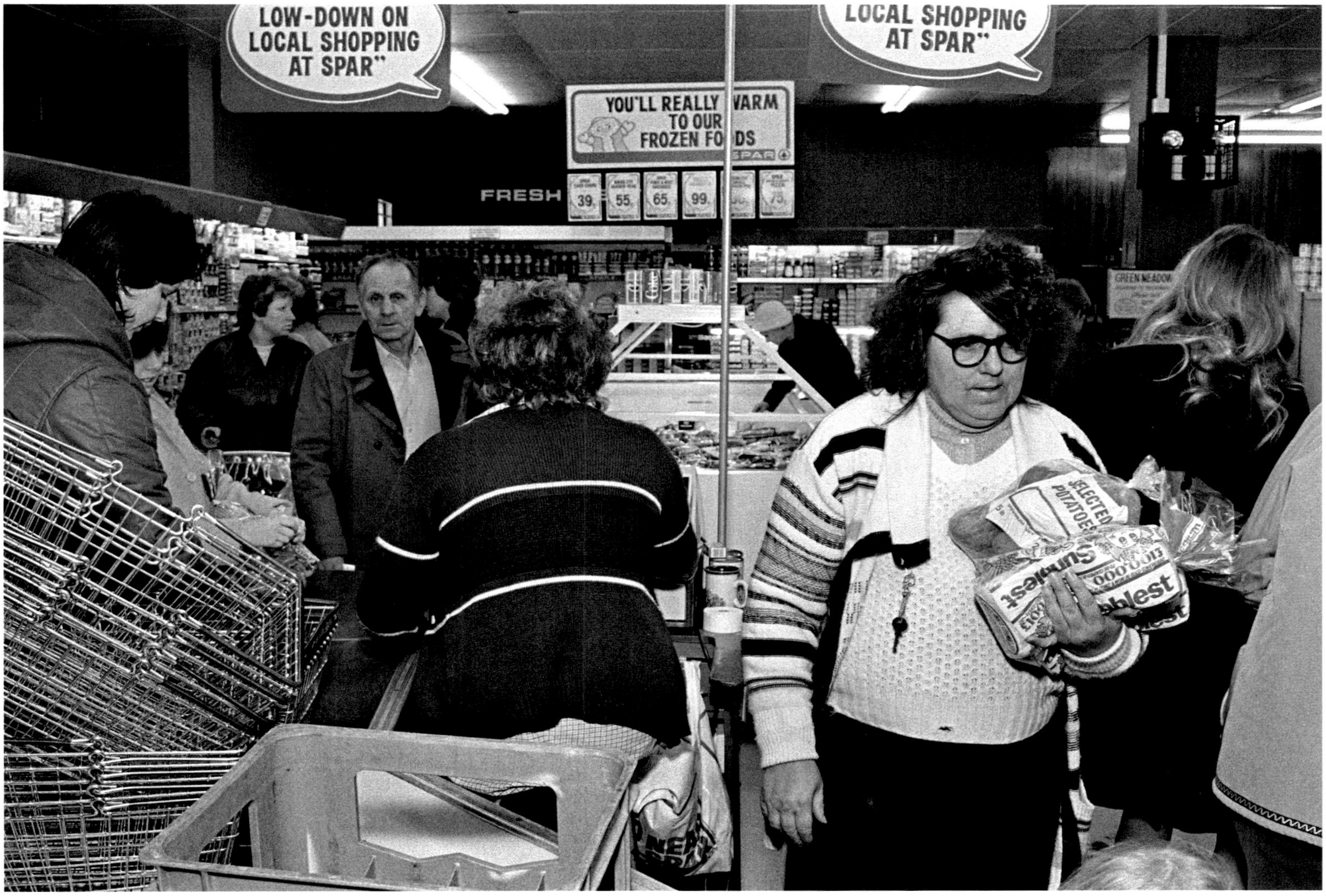
LOW-DOWN ON
LOCAL SHOPPING
AT SPAR"
LOCAL SHOPPING
AT SPAR"
YOU'LL REALLY WARM
TO OUR
FROZEN FOODS
SPAR
FRESH
SELECTED
POTATOES

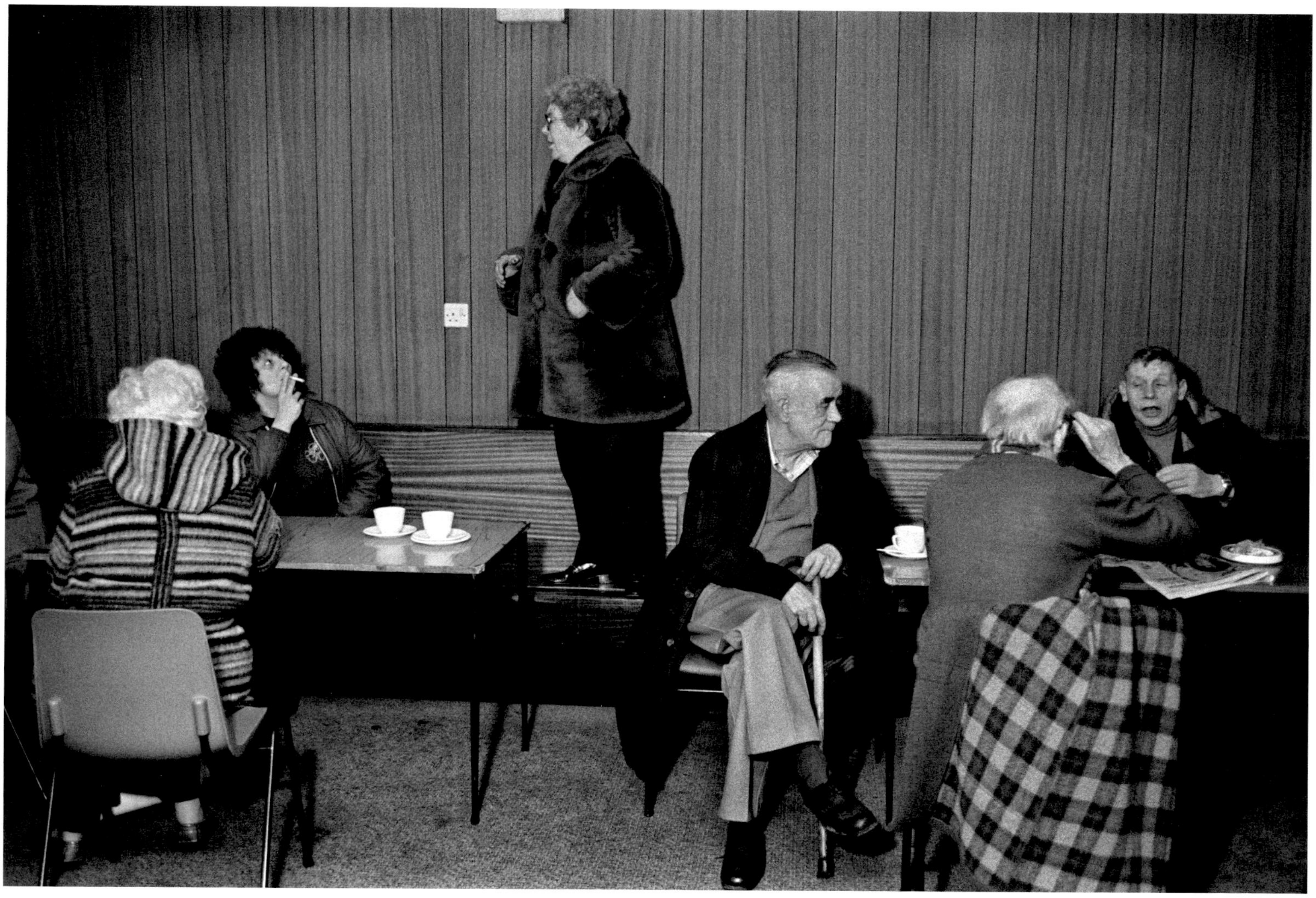

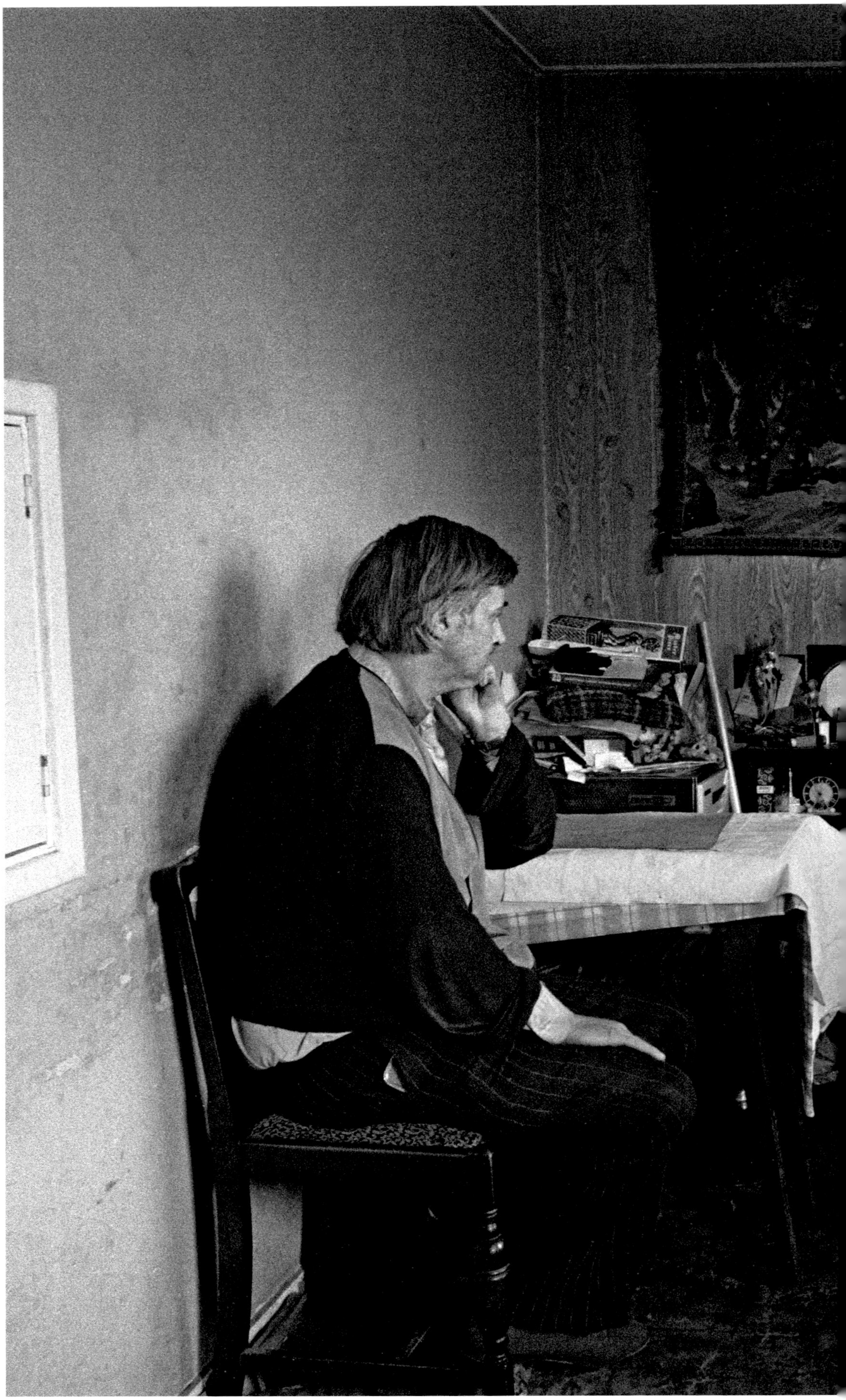

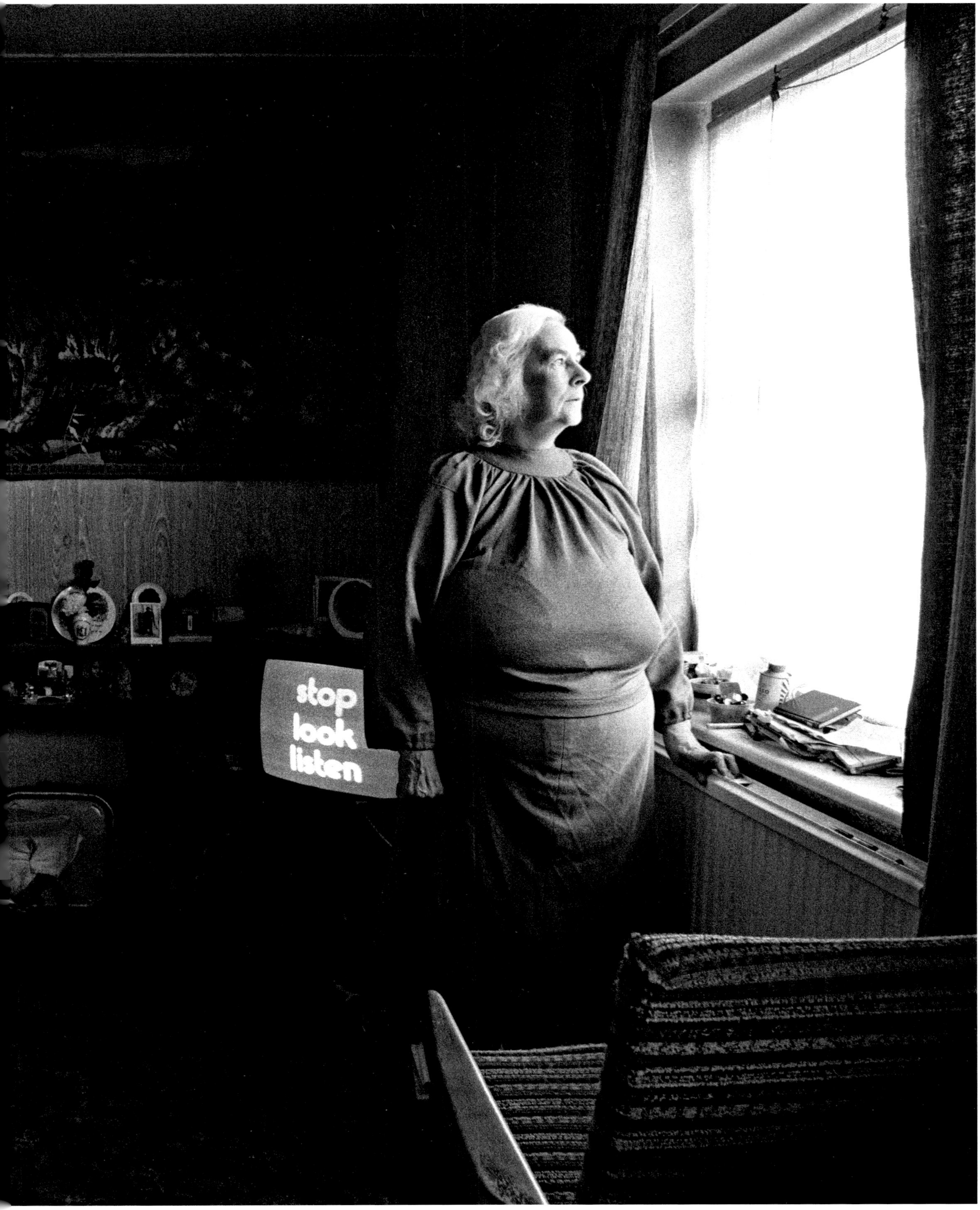
stop
look
listen

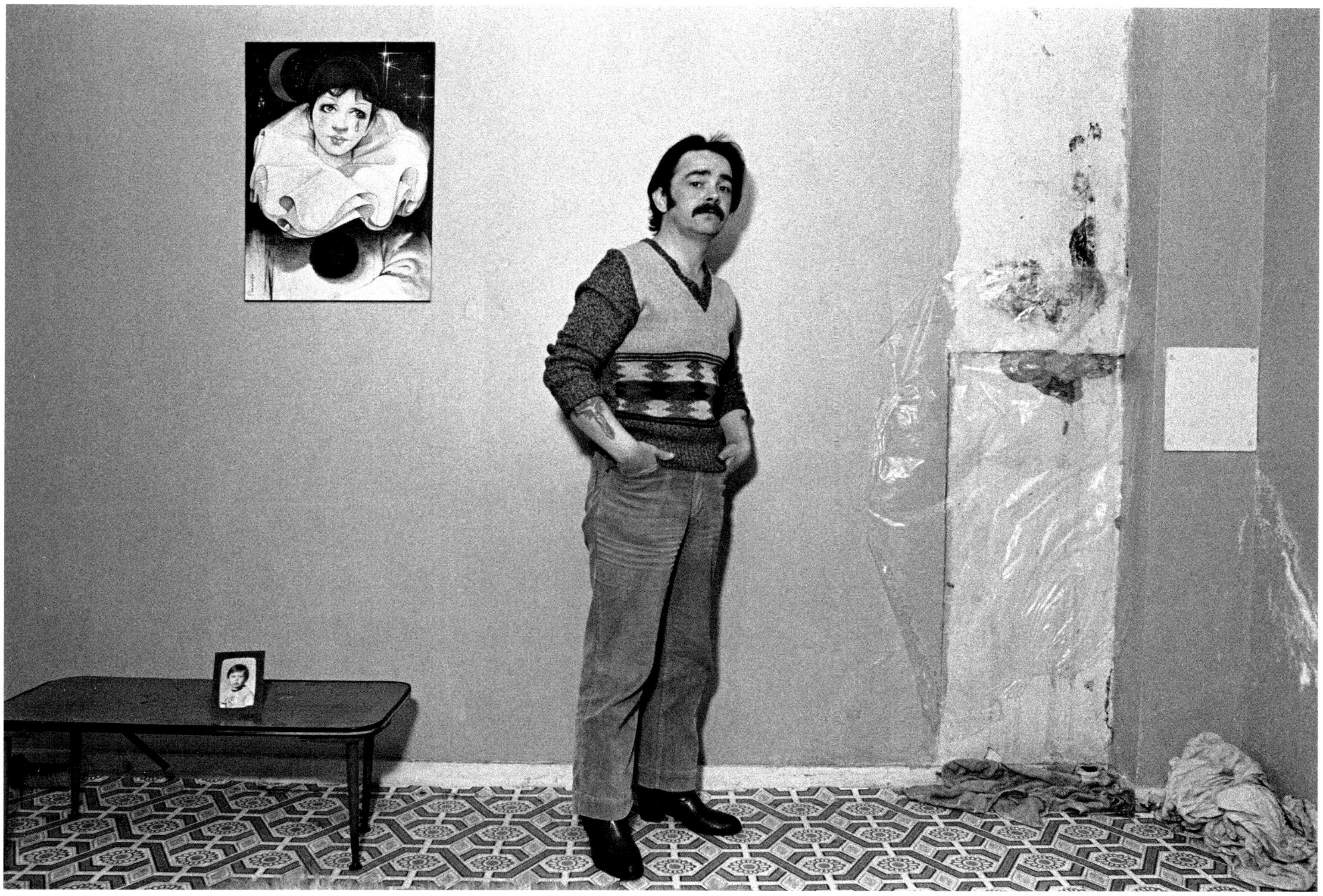

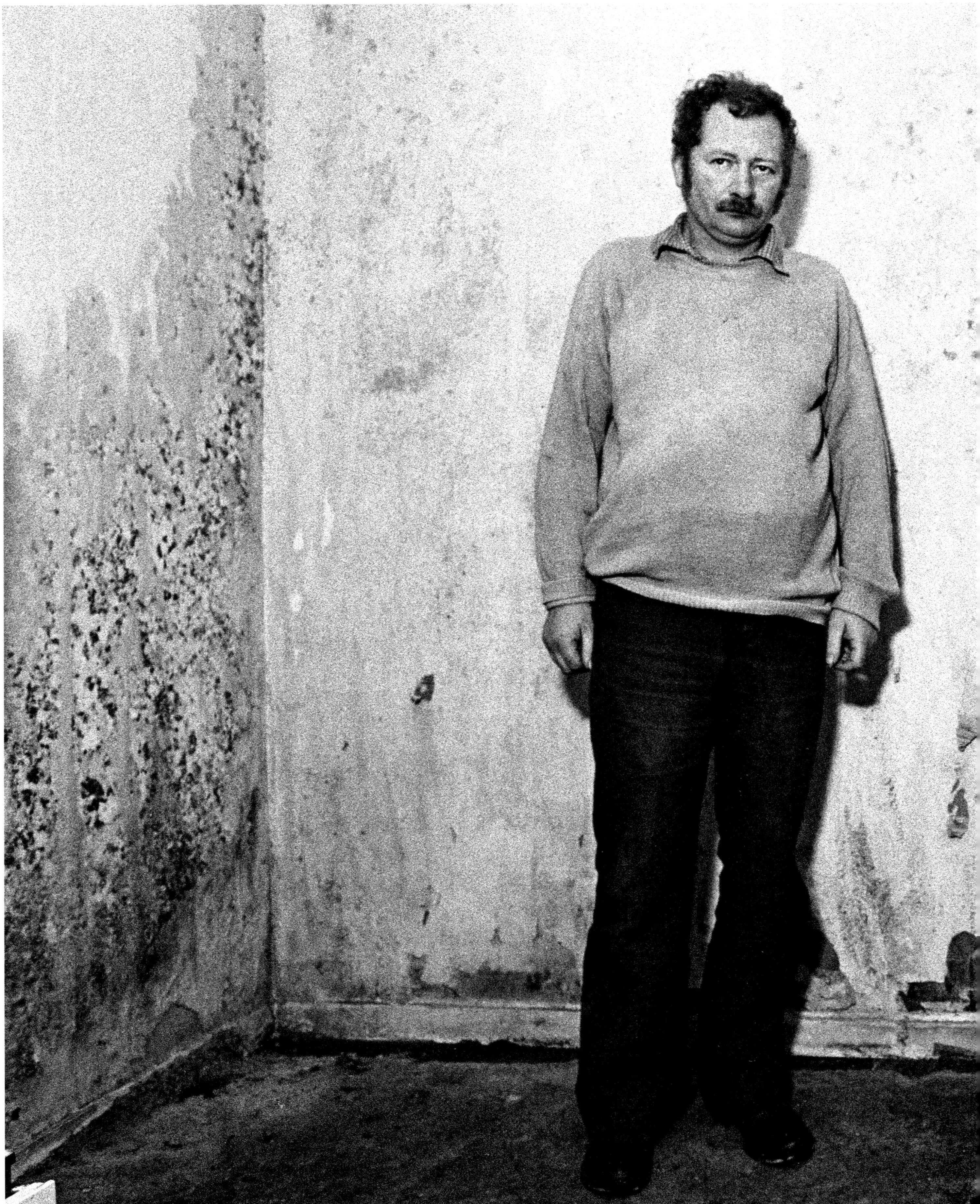

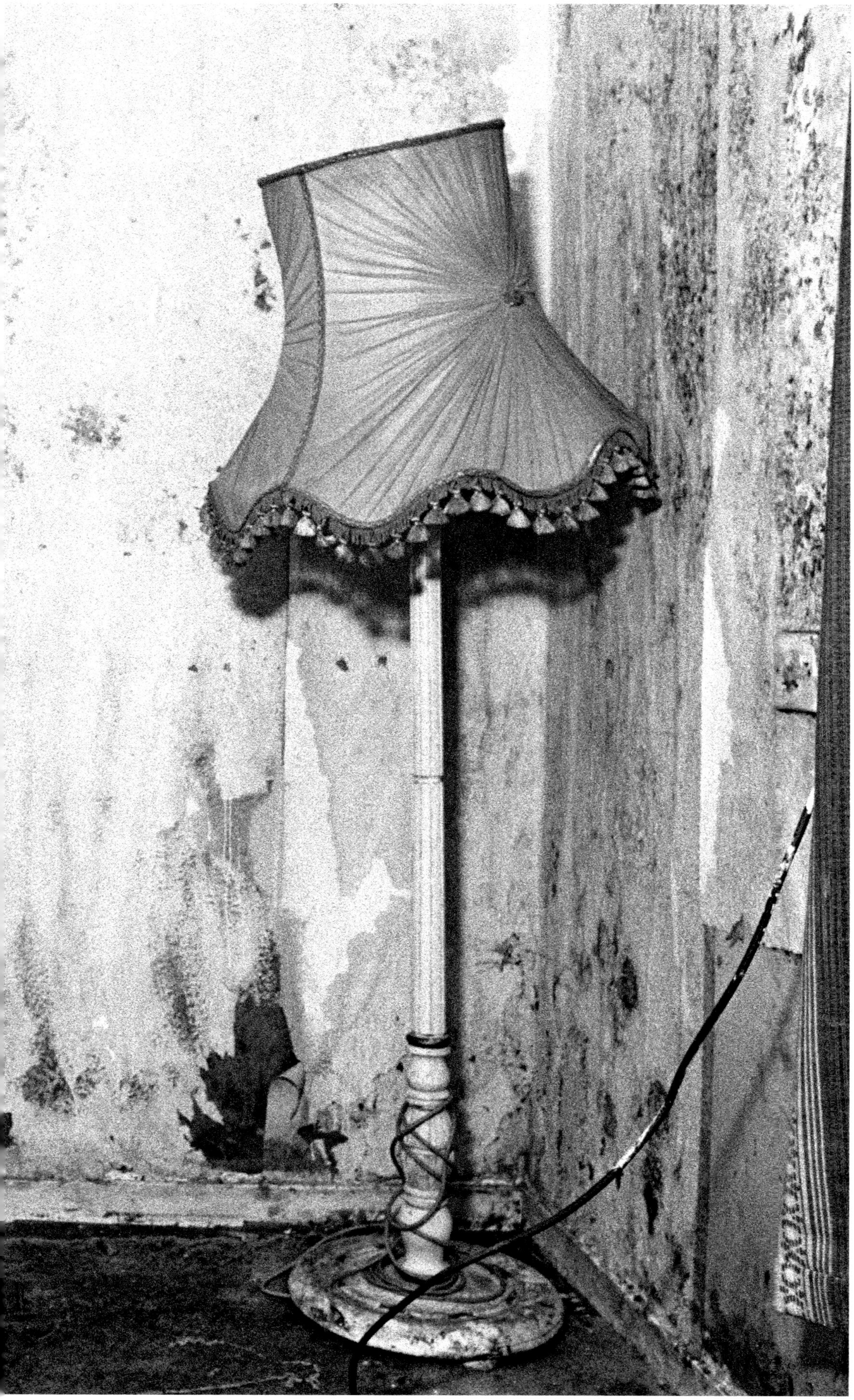

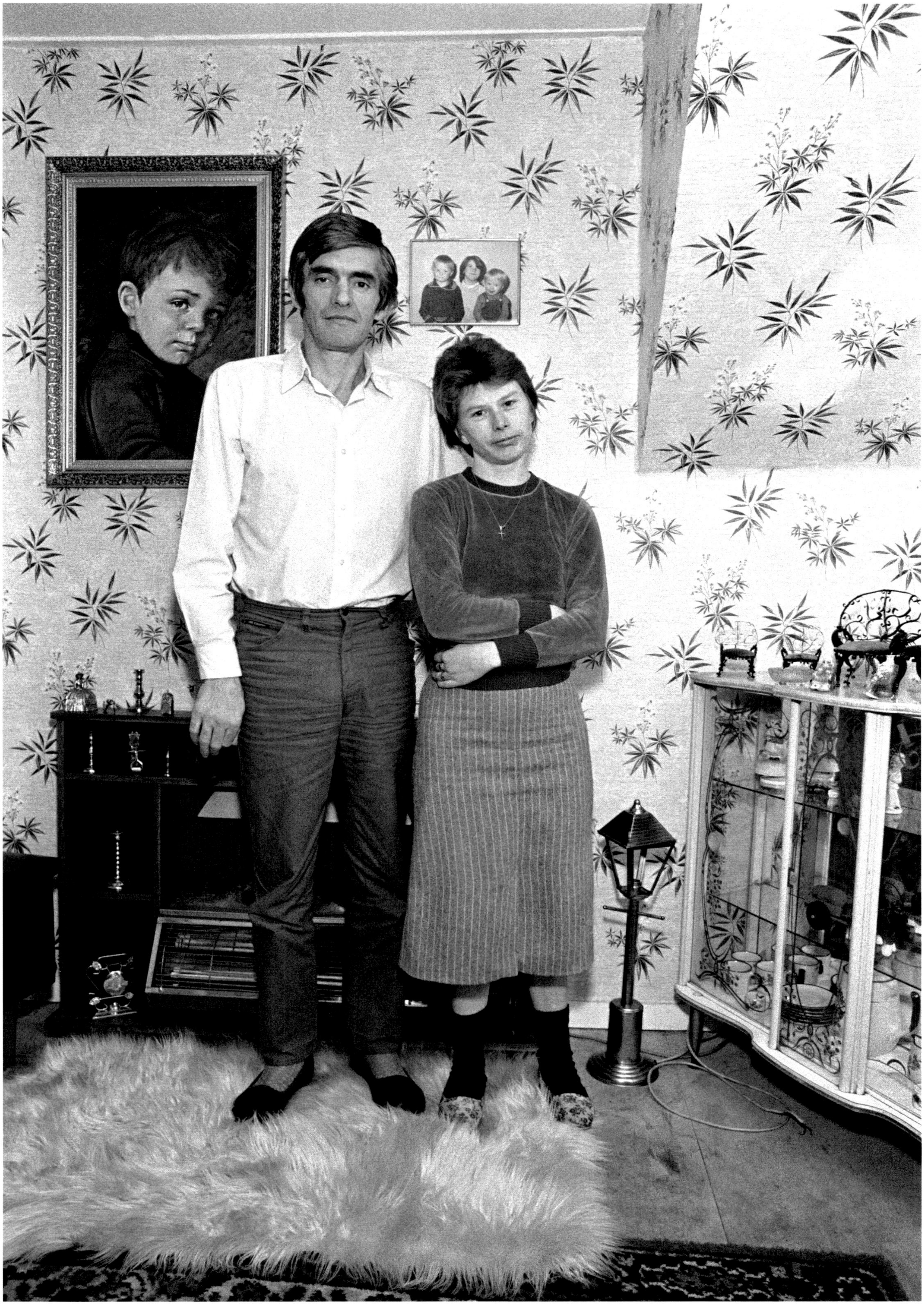

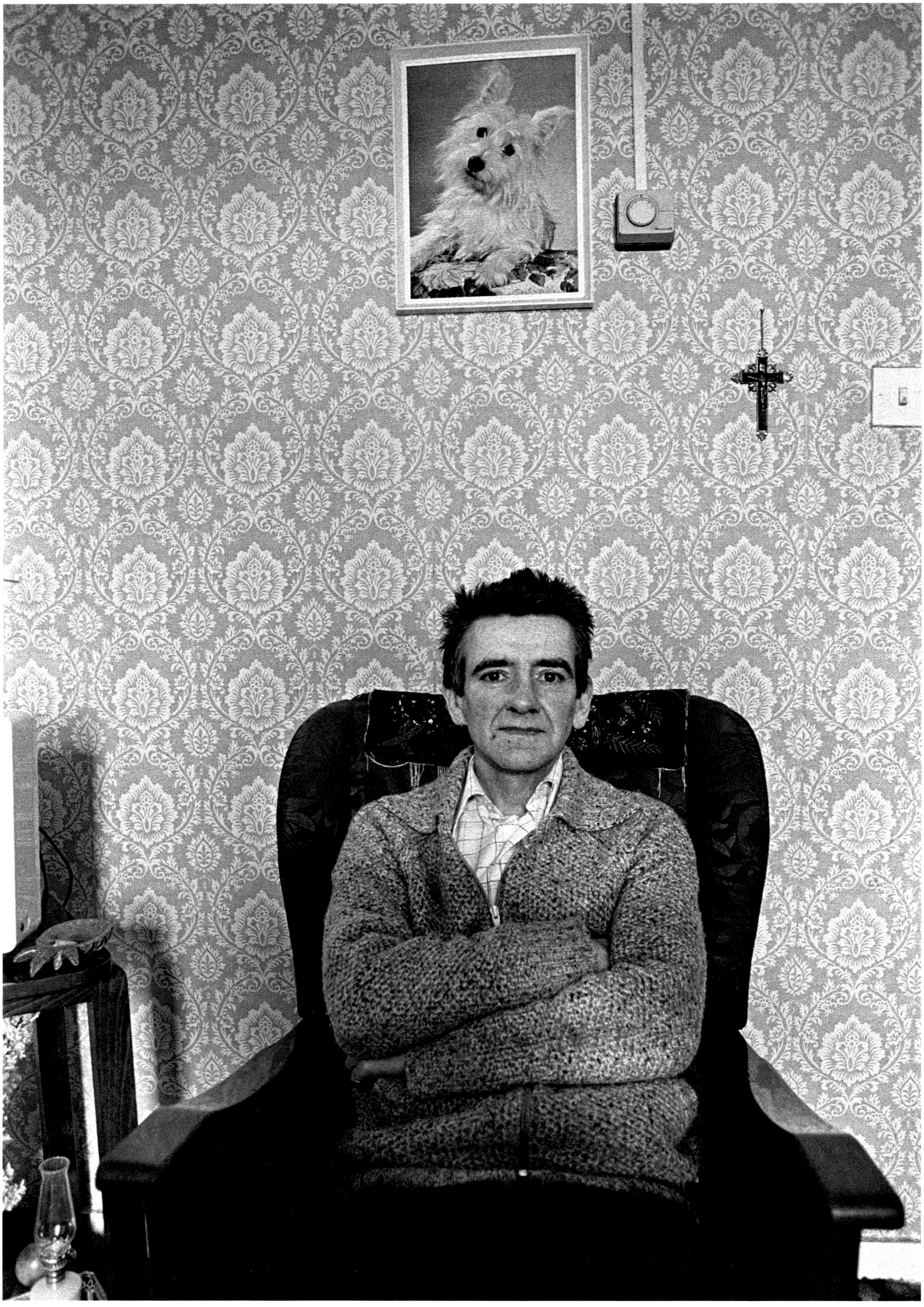

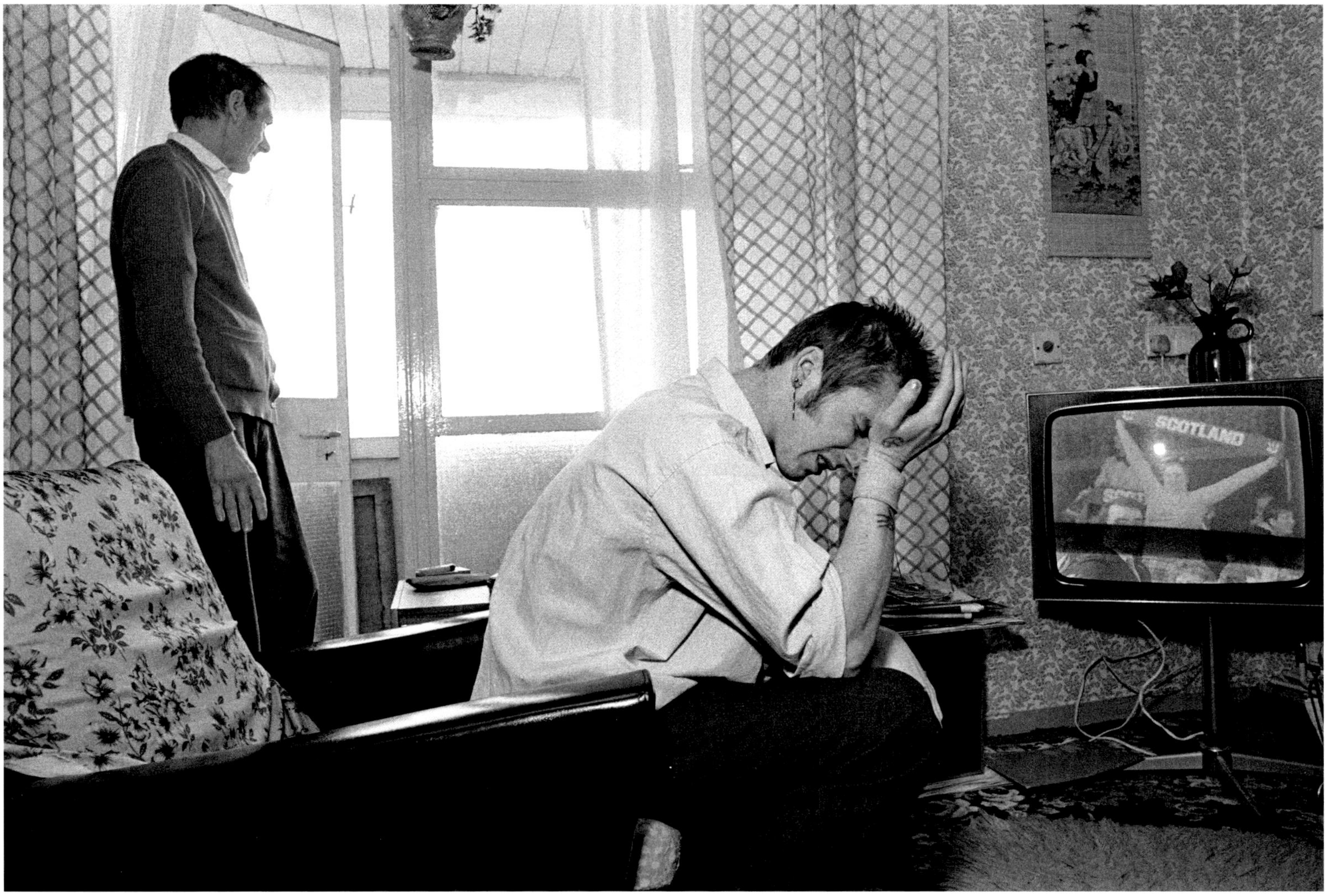
SCOTLAND

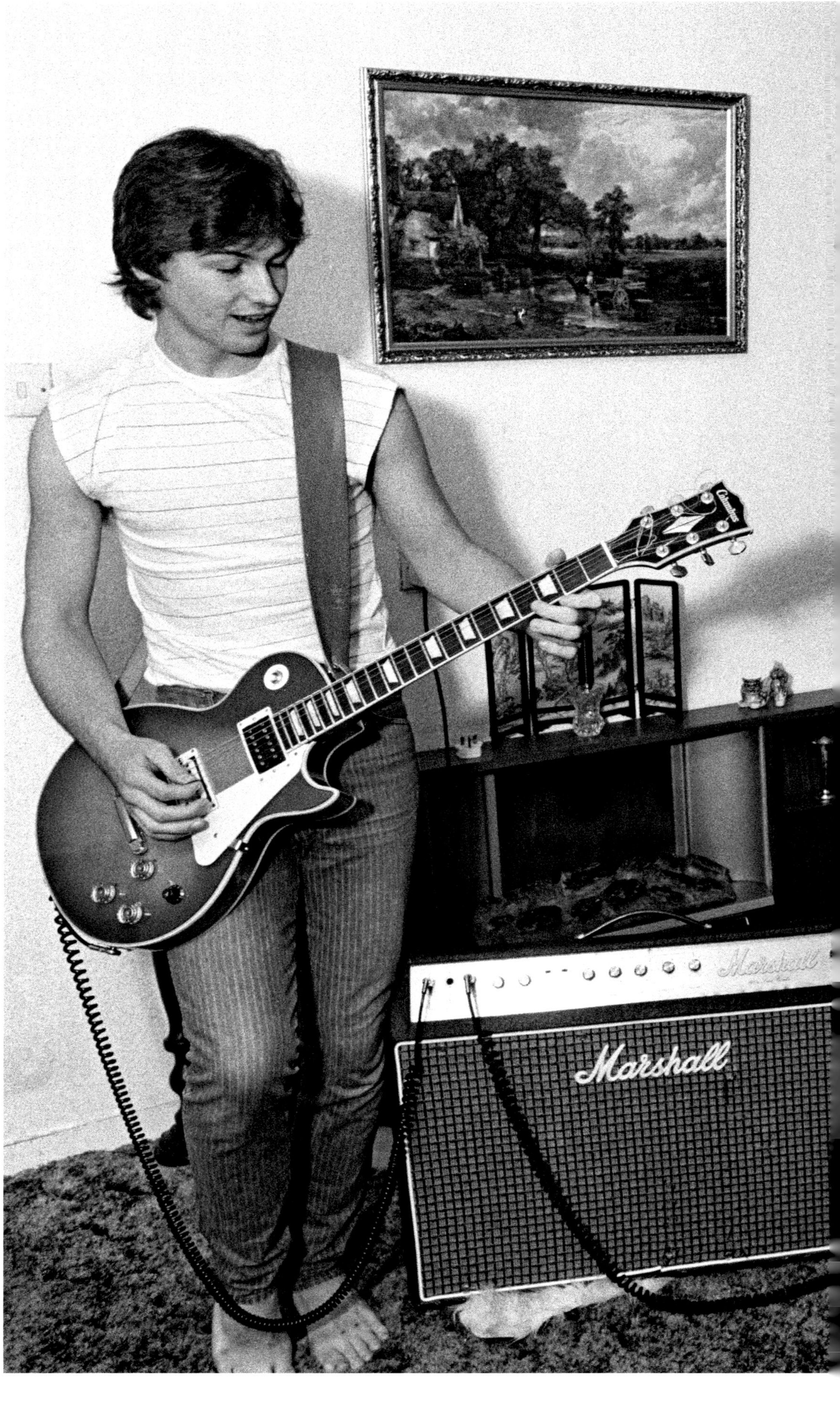
Marshall

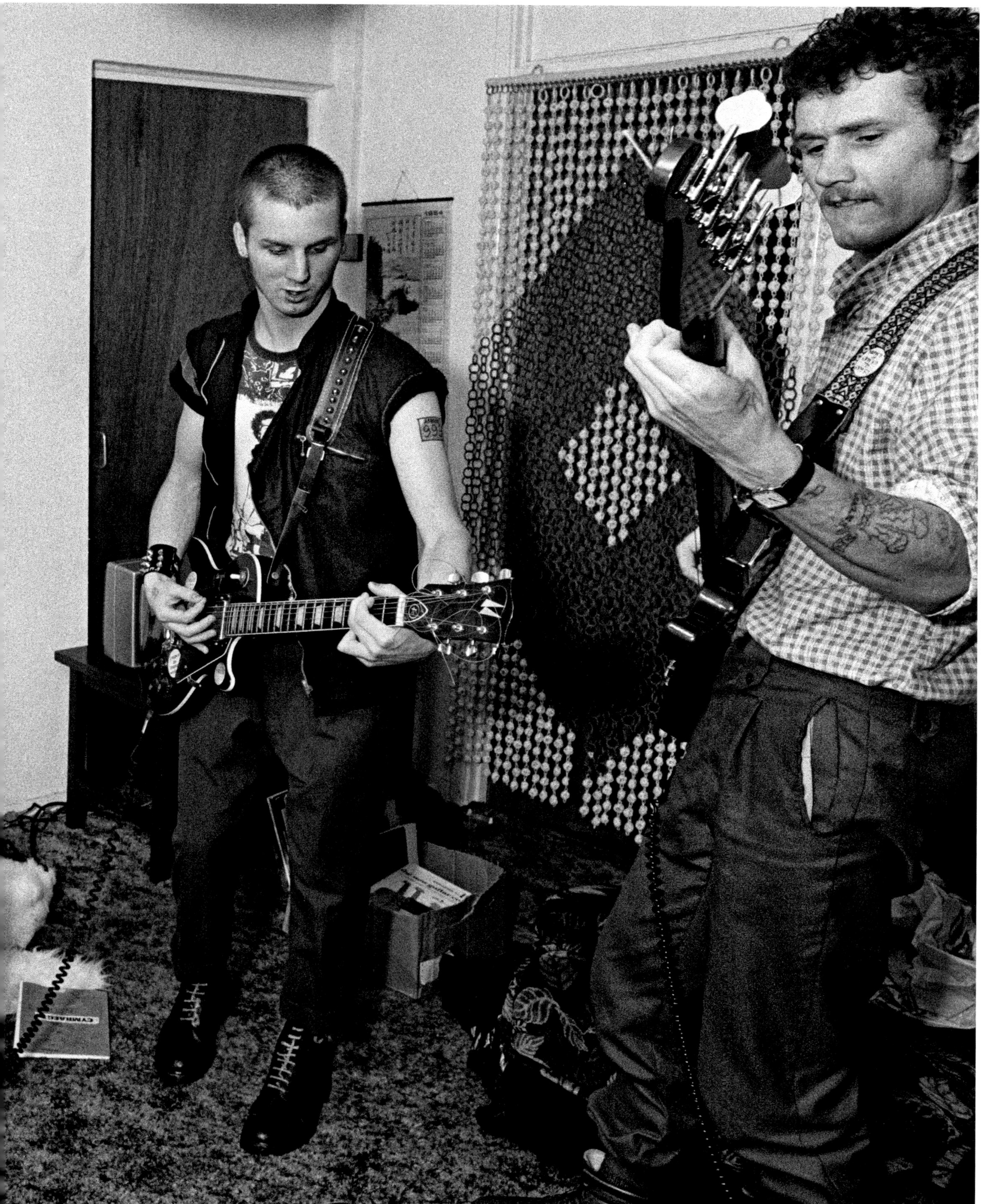
CYMBALS

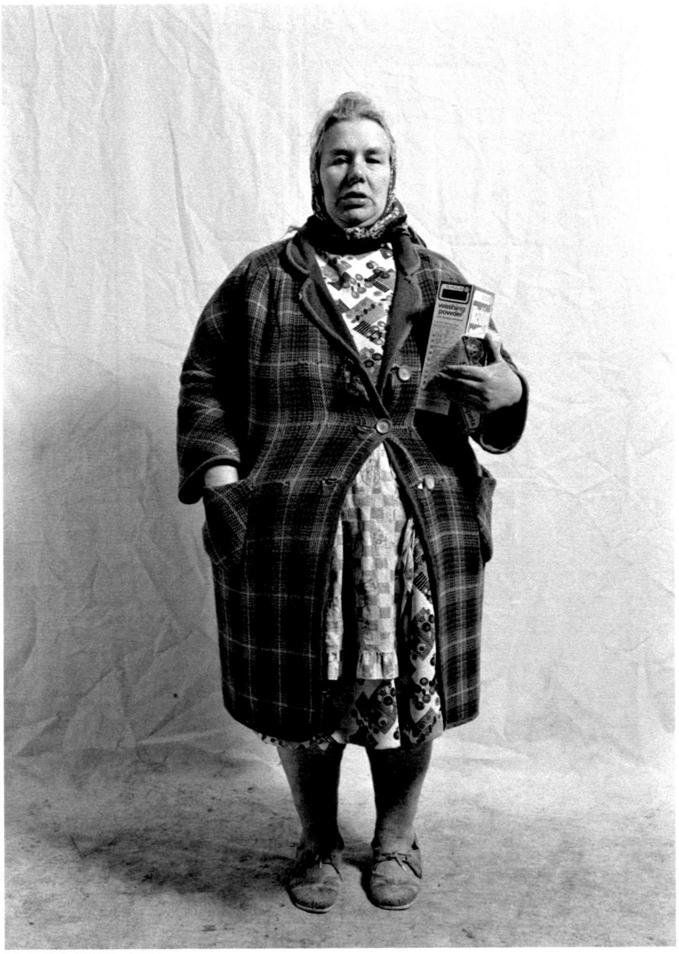

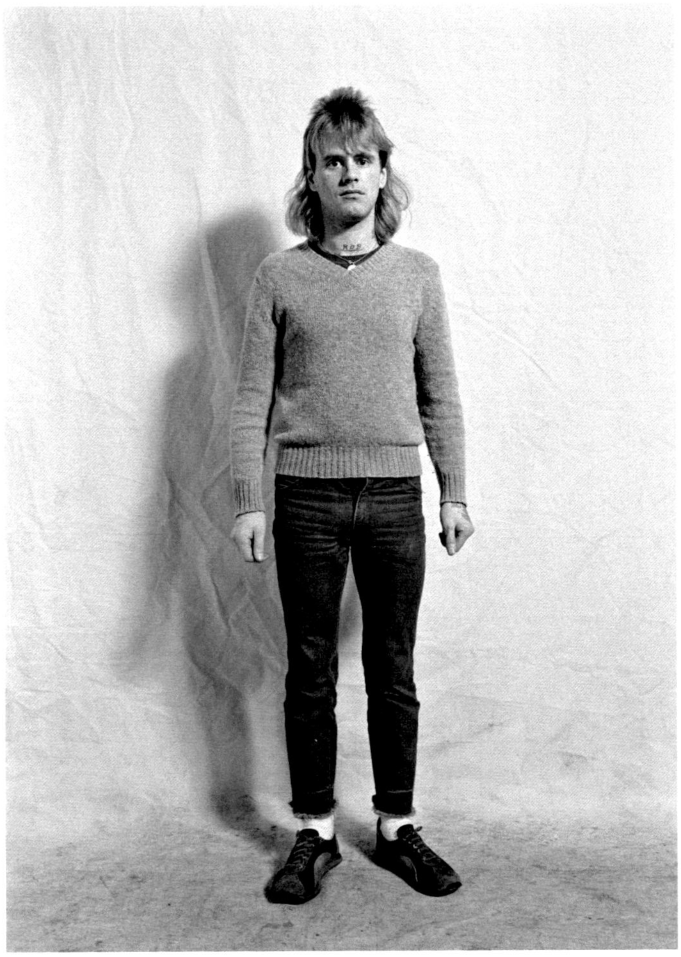

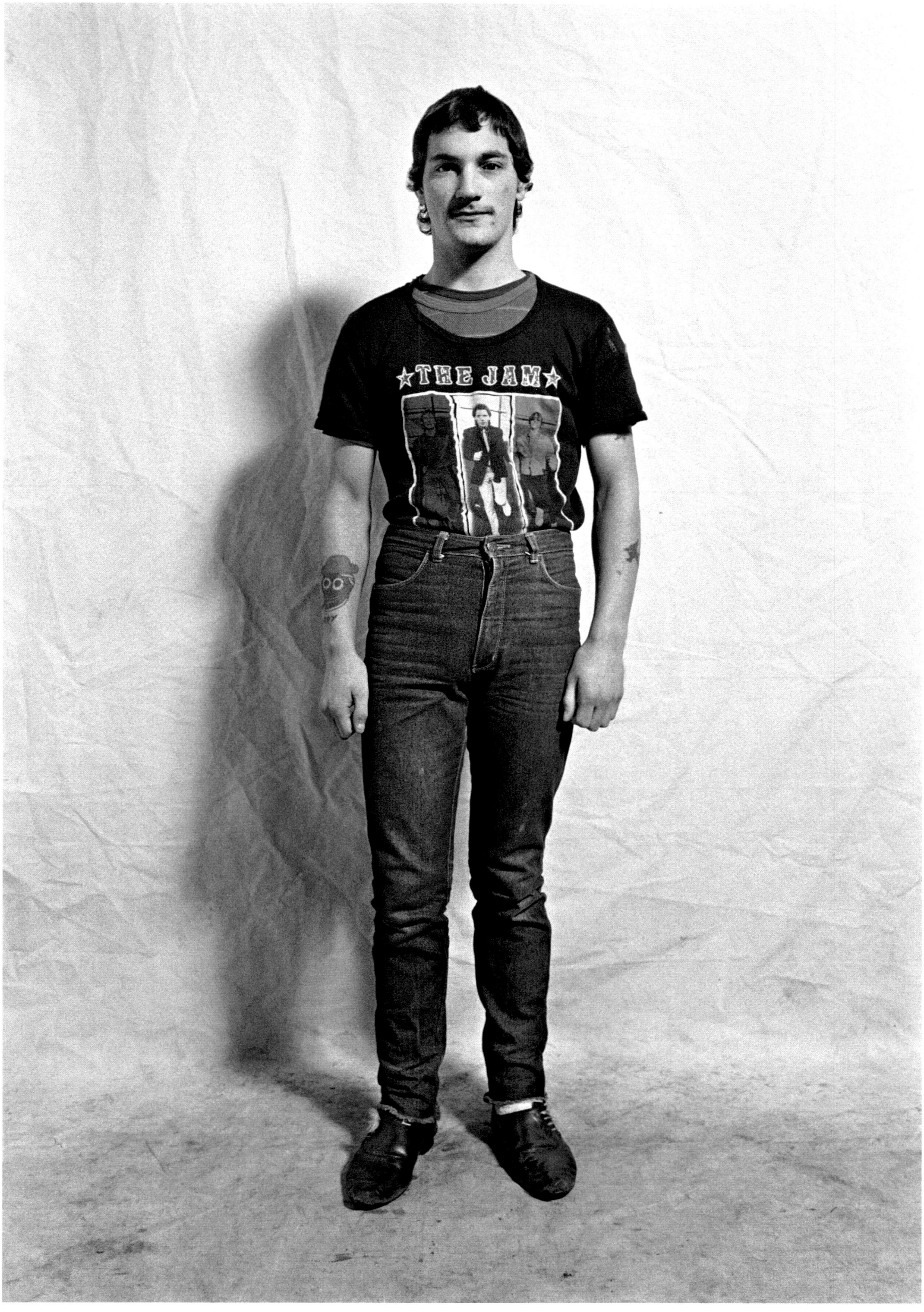
THE JAM

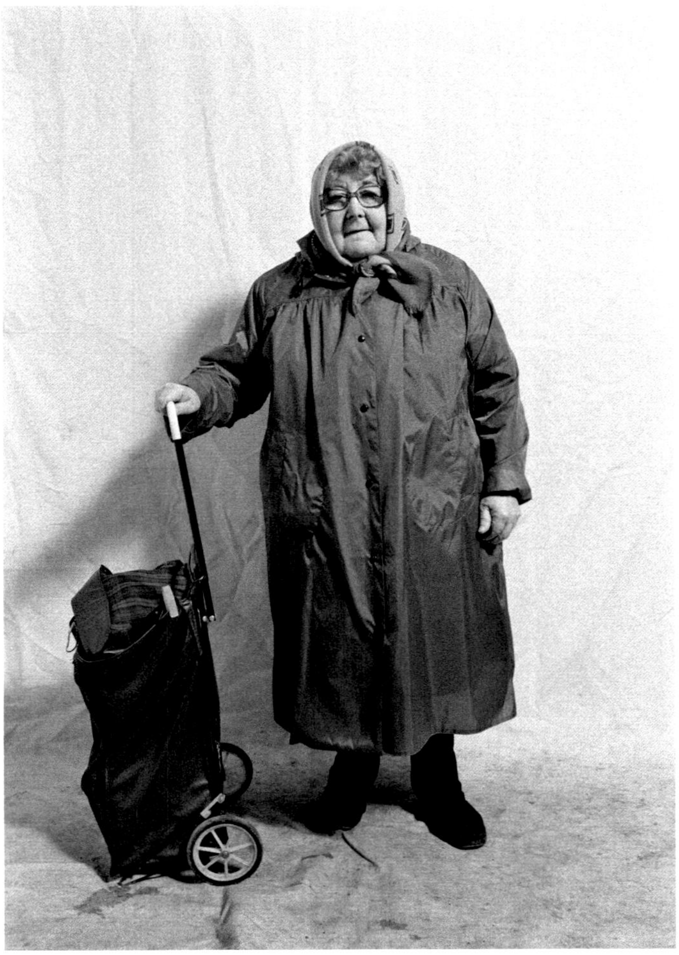

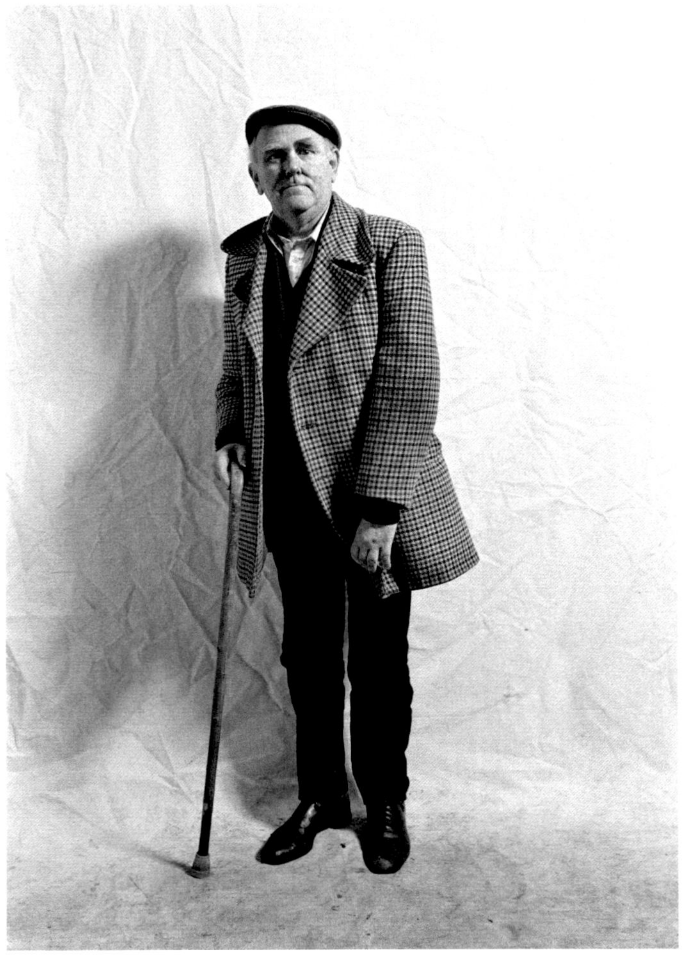

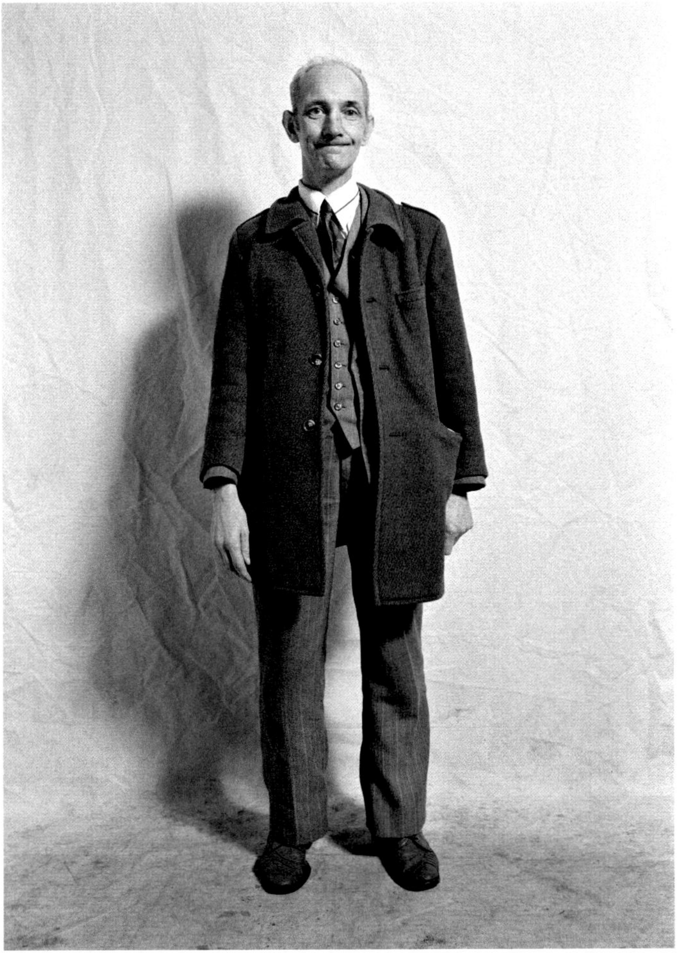

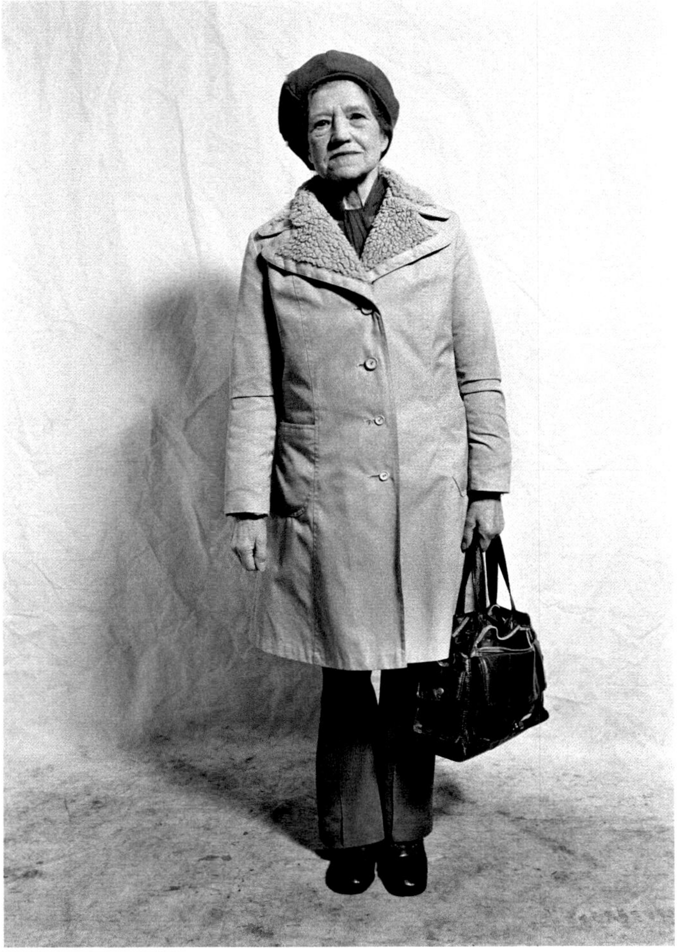

Ken Grant

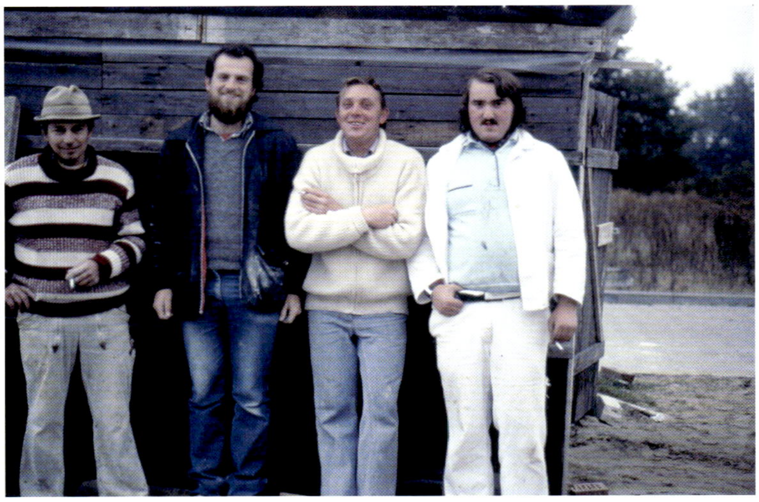

Dreams are what
you wake up from.

The men who sit at the bar in the pub I've taken to visiting finish work early on a Friday. By six in the evening, their brick and paint crusted jeans are woven around stools in the warmth of a bar that will numb the winter cold of the half-built site they've worked on all week at the edge of this northern town. It seems such an easy roll into the night—with work put to rest and money, drink and home stories mulled over in turn. Whilst I work through my own thoughts, I sometimes imagine few such complications will ever foil them—as strong as they seem in their bruising banter and as numbed as they become from the steady rounds that taper into shorts, whilst the TV screens above them bring news updates of war, lies and something that means something to someone somewhere else. It's Friday. It's over.

When Primo Levi's novel *The Wrench* was first published in 1978, he surprised readers by moving away from the dreadful themes of conflict and inhumanity, for which he had become so widely known, to consider Faussonne, a rigger who earned a living on construction sites. The narrator, Levi, a mere storyteller, measured Faussonne's talked up exploits and tales of life being lived so loudly, so fully, against his own worth. Levi was a witness, someone who watches, listens and transcribes but who may never feel the internal tensions of labour or understand enough of the concerns that those on the inside might hold. When I first read it, I was conscious that the same anxieties recur through the brief histories of documentary photography—veering, as they do, between experience and belonging and the compassionate distance of observation and detachment. From James Agee's guilt and self-doubt as he takes the shelter of dustbowl families who have little, to the troubled offloading of Chauncey Hare, half a century later, whilst photographing *Interior America*, the uncertainties are well established. Hare's book might yet become the key turning point for a kind of photography that prevails even now, recognising, as it did, that photography of work needs to go far beyond simply showing what we do and instead, it needs to try—and no matter at what cost—to describe something he for one could no longer ignore...*what work does to us.*

As uncomfortable and incomplete as it may be, photography has kept a close watch on work and working lives in ways that reach back to its earliest uses. From the evolution of 19th century London, with Henry Mayhew's 'deserving and undeserving poor' to its current siren screaming flow, photography augmented journalists in their discovery of the poor quarters of the growing capital; from the plotting and construction of the post-war housing reservations of Kirkby to Paul Reas's Buttershaw and beyond, photography has always attended and recorded—it's even policed. It was commissioned to celebrate the cutting of the first earth and the benign events that distracted from soulless routines—and, as dreams soured and the promise of new worlds disappeared as fast as those companies seeking cheaper land and higher profits did, it would return to evidence, as it so often does, the disasters of a very domestic attrition, with tarnished ideas, homes that implode and the fraying remnants of what writers still call—though it's a stretch to remember when they were—'communities.' *Dreams*... to borrow from the short story writer Raymond Carver, *are what you wake up from...*

It's perhaps easy to understand—even excuse—the limited histories that photography has inspired, accounts that see a Ship's launch celebration whilst the working processes are rarely shown. Photography, and those who live from it, it seems, would be prone to note the exceptions and the exotic and all too rarely the exertions of a working day. When the *Worker's Illustrated News* adopted its new name, in Germany in 1924, the forerunner of so many picture magazines called for closer accounts of working lives and the means for workers themselves to record them. Edwin Hoernle's 'no camera without a Proletarian eye' marked a moment of self-affirmation which, whilst short lived, would advocate approaches that went beyond the checks and balances of the industrial photography more usually deployed, towards a vernacular, a place of self-determination and a kind of photography capable of speaking from the interior.

The very potential for a more immersed, emotive rendering of working lives seems better served in recent years. Perhaps this was what Bruce Bernard was doing when he included Toby Glanville's portrait of a plasterer's young mate in his Phaidon survey, *Century*. A young man, paused, plaster-speckled and shirtless in a part-renovated house had been photographed in such a way that, for Bernard, the picture had the reach of an X-ray. If you looked closely enough, he seemed to infer, you'd see the boy's very make-up—even his future. Good photography can suggest where we're heading long before we reach there.

In the mid 1990s I heard Paul Reas introduce his photographs by first showing a photograph of himself as a bricklayer. Taken decades before and standing by a low wall, the picture must have provided a rare interruption from a working life that would see him work in the north of England before following the itinerant trails of his contemporaries

Building site, Burgdorf, Hannover Germany. Paul Reas, second from left. 1979. Photo courtesy of Jane Reas.

build and earn in a new Europe. To move towards photography must have led to a recalibration on so many levels. Leaving the dialects of the building site, with its noise, its physicality and abrasions, Paul Reas would draw on his own experiences, share affinities with the heavy industries he made work about and engage with the craft of storytelling at a time when the orthodoxies and dynamics of documentary itself were being rattled, rejected and revised.

And change isn't easy. How do you come to terms with what happens when the foundations you've laid in life no longer mean enough, when working for the Friday pay packet is just the drag it is and all the bold talk in the portacabins you thaw out in wear down to the frustrations and surrenders they so often are? Stale biscuits, stale news and spilt milk on stained tables, with each scrawled mark and blemish so familiar because you take the same seat at every break time. It can't be easy, as you sit with men who started as young apprentices and who are now weeks from pensions, to feel all this is taking us nowhere fast. God knows, the anger it can fuel, and perhaps the spirit it can kill. But some find the strength to step out of routines that tire our minds, that prematurely age us, that can even maim us—and to do all this after Thatcher and her *look after your own* selfish vision broke down all it could in regions that resisted her callous dismantling of manufacturing industries and their workforces—all this, in a time in which it would be easier to do nothing, to say nothing, to be nothing.

Paul Reas was moved to do something, to make something of worth and he and his contemporaries consciously exploited the subjectivity implicit in documentary practices. They dismissed the played out subservience of earlier picture stories in favour of multi-vocal authorship and narratives that were as complicated and layered as the worlds they were responding to were themselves. When Peter Mitchell visited Quarry Hill in Leeds to photograph the last days of the housing estate as workers began its dismantling, he moved door to door to gather the cuttings and family pictures kept by residents who would eventually leave. In doing so, he created a rare and tender archive that, by proxy, grew to be an account as imperfect and beautiful as our lives can be. How different the joyful birthday picnics at the foot of the tower block looked from so many of the gratuitous accounts of working class lives that gathered over the last century. Mitchell knew the value of these kept fragments—so remote as they were from the official designs and aspirations against which he placed them when consolidating his book *Memento Mori*. Perhaps because they show the details, the breaths instead of the screams, the embraces instead of the breakdowns, the life affirming instead of the newsworthy, they mark a territory so underplayed in photography that, when they do appear, they become precious, magnificent appreciations of a working-class life we have all but lost in this age of moral panics, civil fracture and suspicion.

At the threshold of an era of digital development, Paul Reas was photographing with the kind of insight that had moved him from the sure but well accounted structures of the Welsh coal fields to the communities who peopled the component parts industries that now precariously sat upon them. In recognising such changes, his photographs have built a bridge between the work of the hand—with its craft and industry, its learning and evolution, to the work of the head, with an emphasis on surface, profit, brand and the short-lived technologies that circle around cheap labour forces only to close and relocate with the slightest breeze. How do we photograph work now that what we once recognised as such is hardly there? As Paul Reas migrated from the black and white Valleys to the new-build monotony of out of town retail parks, he would begin to make pictures that conveyed something about new dreams being sold, the retail opportunities and aspirations, the quick fixes and final days of sales. The regions he was moved to photograph in had seen skills replaced with service and security with, well, don't they call it *flexibility*?

Promises were harder to fulfil than proclaim in the new-start new-dawn new-towns, populated as they were with residents from the faltering inner cities. Through the late 1980s and 90s, as regions like my own resisted the 'managed decline' that was planned for them, Paul Reas photographed the carnival of heritage that created pantomimes across former regions of industrial labour. We can all sing the song now—industries close, redundancies bring insecurities, new jobs and uncertain months veer from fallow to feast, short contracts, privacy clauses and corporations shepherding photographers away from their peripheries because they tell us they even own the views now. The photographers who engaged with such worlds had to find a new language to articulate the very quiet breakdowns and tensions that were as much psychological as physical and find a response to signs that—if you're busy making repayments, or if you're anchored to the malevolent docility of cable TV packages—it would be all too easy to miss and probably impossible to feel.

I believe Paul Reas felt things. As he photographed former miners in their reconstructed landscapes, the shuffling sightseers in the Beamish heritage park and spat fire with his camera at the likes of us who paid our money, were told how things used to be and then went to look for cheap cuts of meat and ready meals in the supermarket freezers on the way home. He must have felt it too in the life sentences passed on middle-aged men and women selling endless cheap furniture in soulless stores near the ring roads of so many Raintowns. Britain was already fucked and the chattels we were encouraged to sign up for and keep close came at us with the honey of advertising and the tripwires of credit. How angry must you feel; how clear must your intentions be, to be wary of the lucrative majesty of industrial assignments when it's so easy to perpetuate a kind of photography that simply applauds and flatters? And how clear minded must you be, to make observations as gauche, as perplexing and as cautionary as responses to those worlds should be? Paul Reas went on to make sustained series of photographs about declining industries and their consequences that have few close parallels. Julian Germain's remapping of Consett and Bart Sorgedrager's relentless archive of European factories and workers in the last months before closure seem fitting company in a shallow pool. Each are purposeful, singular, forthright and clear sighted and each made by photographers relating something they found impossible to ignore at a time when it would have been so easy to look the other way.

Perhaps more will eventually be understood about this immersion and the formative experiences that sensitised Paul Reas to make the work that he did at a moment when working processes in Britain were changing right in front of him. When the potter Emmanuel Cooper came to see me in the early 1990s, he was progressing his book *People's Art* around the same time. He was looking for work shaped by the rituals, languages and preoccupations of the regions that had compelled them. If he had lived to see the success of his book he may have thought to add a chapter that included the likes of Paul Reas and I—mid 20th century nomads in a land that isn't Eden, helplessly shaped by our homes and labours, by the revelations that came with an escape to college and, as ever, the urgencies of money and work — along with the nous that gets us by when sometimes it would be easier to fail. He might have thought of how we're wilfully burdened by our adolescence, by the experience of work, by upbringings that are imperfect yet well-meaning and by the abrupt awareness we share that this is not a rehearsal or an entitlement, it's a second chance and one that comes with a hunger to build on, but never quite temper, the earlier lives we moved away from.

These are the thoughts I sometimes work through on a Friday as the twilight turns the North Welsh hills indigo through the pub's southern window and I try and work out what I recognise in these men as they talk each other through what really matters. Paul Reas would recognise something too and know the rhythms of work and release that those sitting in front of me are close to putting behind them for another week He would eventually decide to leave behind the uncertainty of a world we both knew for the uncertainty of life as a working photographer and, with the integrity, anger and hope of a man who knows how to build the foundations of a new life, he would make a ritualistic trip to the Yorkshire coast, cast his tools into the North Sea and start all over again.

The deindustrialisation of Britain effectively started in 1971 with a series of industrial actions which would eventually target the trades union movement and systematically dismantle its base power. This started when the Conservative Government, under the Leadership of Ted Heath, tried to curb the power of the trades unions with the introduction of the Industrial Relations Act of 1971, which effectively imposed a 'no strike' clause into individual contracts of employment. The 1972 miner's strike, and in particular the 1974 National Union of Mineworkers (NUM) strikes over pay, resulted in the implementation of a three-day working week throughout the UK, in an attempt to conserve energy as the nation's power stations were starved of coal. The huge social and industrial disruption caused by the frequent 'blackouts' led to the collapse of the Conservative Government in the 1974 General Election, which made way for a Labour minority government.

Ironically the Labour Party Governments of 1974–79, under the Leaderships of Harold Wilson and James Callaghan, further soured the relationships between the trade unions. The Winter of Discontent was the winter of 1978–79, the coldest in the United Kingdom for sixteen years. During this period there were dozens of strikes by public-sector trade unions, following the imposition of the Labour Party's pay caps in an attempt to control inflation. Strikes by refuse collectors resulted in uncollected rubbish piled high on the streets of the country and National Health Service workers blockaded hospital entrances, meaning many hospitals were only able to take emergency patients.

The Winter of Discontent had a profound effect on the voting intentions of the British public, and in the 1979 General Election, Margaret Thatcher—Conservative—became Britain's first female Prime Minister. Prior to the election, Thatcher delineated her proposals for curbing trade union influence in a political broadcast occurring during a lorry drivers' strike. She believed that trade unions were harmful to both 'ordinary' trade unionists and the public, a belief which would eventually lead her to refer to the striking miners of 1984 as 'the enemy within.' Bruised by the miners' role in the collapse of the Tory government in 1974, Thatcher was determined that her government would not suffer the same fate. In an act of vengeful vandalism, she embarked on a process of dismantling the heavy industries which employed, as she saw it, some of the 'radical' factions of the trade union movement. This process began with the national steel strike in 1980 and would culminate with the bitter dispute of the miners' strike of 1984.

South Wales, with its long history of heavy industry and political unrest, was hit particularly hard. I graduated college in July 1984, four months into the miners' strike against pit closures, and by March 1985 the strike was over, Thatcher was victorious and the miners made a reluctant but dignified return to work. What followed was a wholesale closure of pits and the jobless miners of South Wales joined the dole queue with the redundant steel workers from the 1980 dispute.

The Welsh Development Agency (WDA) was a government organisation established to help regenerate the region and find a solution to the problems of high unemployment. Via a process of tax breaks, free rents and an available pool of labour, the WDA began to attract a new generation of industry to the region. On the sites of former collieries and on new industrial parks on the edges of towns, huge tin shed factories began to appear. Their purpose? To house the manufacturing processes for the newly emerging computer industry. But this was an industry for a new age, with different ideas about who made a good employee. They wanted to employ mainly women (who they claimed were best suited to the intricate assembly of electronic circuit boards) and they also wanted a workforce with no previous experience of work, one which had not been unionised. Thatcher's emasculation of the trade union movement made this not only possible but increasingly desirable to employers.

Paradoxically, an industry created to solve the unemployment of a predominantly male former workforce resulted in the employment of the wives and daughters of redundant miners and steel workers. The men, who had historically been the breadwinners, were staying at home and the women of the household were going out to work. At the time

1985–86

The Valleys Project

this was a large sociological shift in the region. In addition to the changing sociological patterns, there were also distinct changes to the landscape occurring, as areas were levelled in preparation for the construction of factories and new roads introduced to improve communication routes from the M4 motorway to the valleys. All of this was a part of my interest in the subject and would form the basis of my work for 'The Valleys Project' (1984–79).

My interests in photography had begun to change. Having been introduced to the more subjective works of Lee Friedlander and Garry Winogrand, I was also developing a taste for the quietly understated, seemingly objective photography of Robert Adams, Lewis Baltz, Joe Deal and other practitioners of the New Topographics movement. These would be important influences upon my work for 'The Valleys Project,' as would the experience of my own mother, who had worked on an assembly line in a television manufacturing company in Bradford during my early teens. 'The Valleys Project' was a Ffotogallery series of photographic commissions and was instigated by then gallery director Susan Beardmore. In the early to mid-1980s these kinds of commissions, which were mainly documentary, were very popular and they provided a small income stream for independent photographers to explore a subject over a sustained period of time.

'The Valleys Project' was modelled on the important work being created in the North East of England by the Amber collective, under the stewardship of the late Murray Martin. They were committed to documenting working-class and marginalised lives and landscapes in the North East and helped enable important works by Chris Killip, Sirkka-Liisa Konttinen, Graham Smith, John Davies, Isabela Jedrzejczyk, Julian Germain, Peter Fryer and many more.

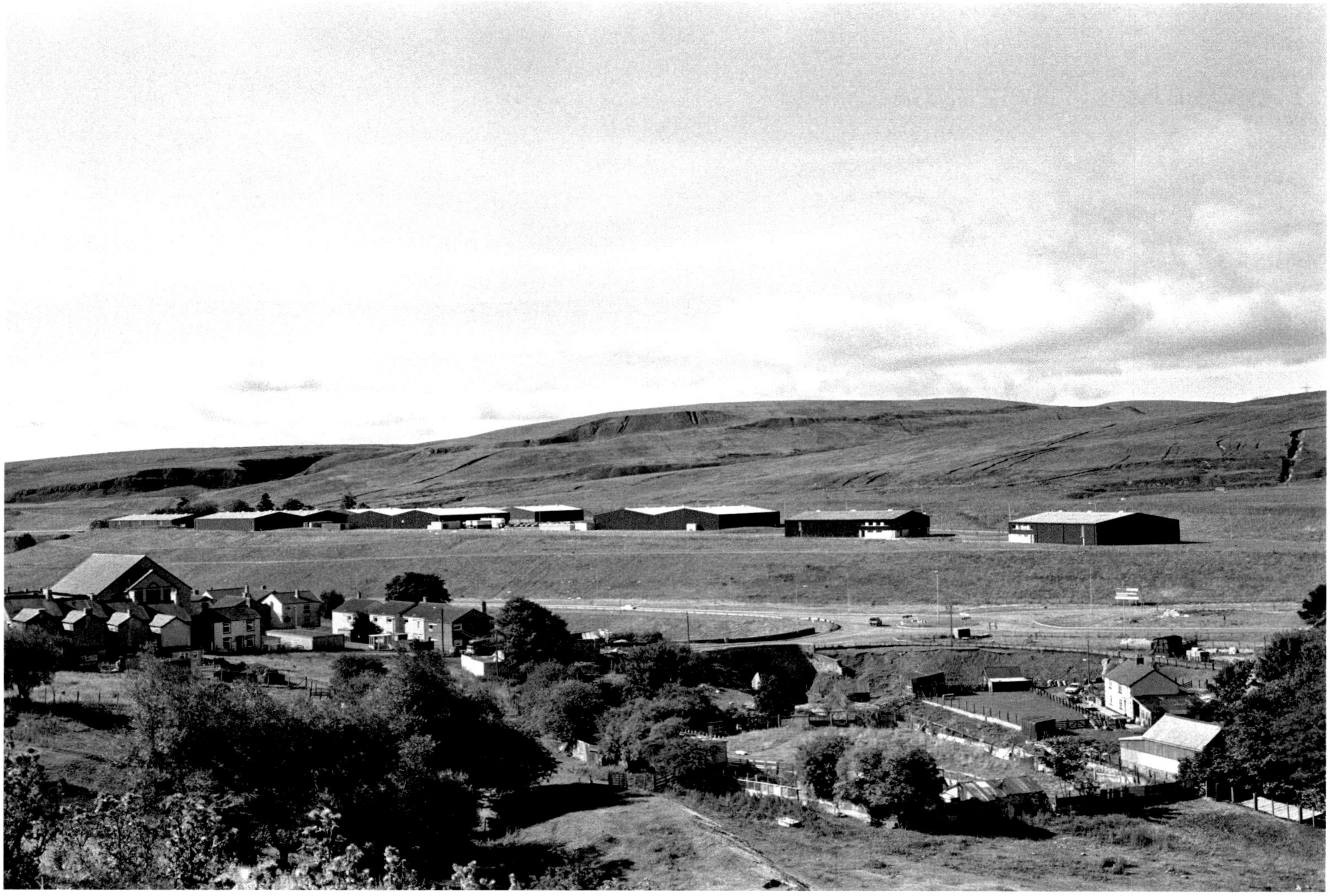

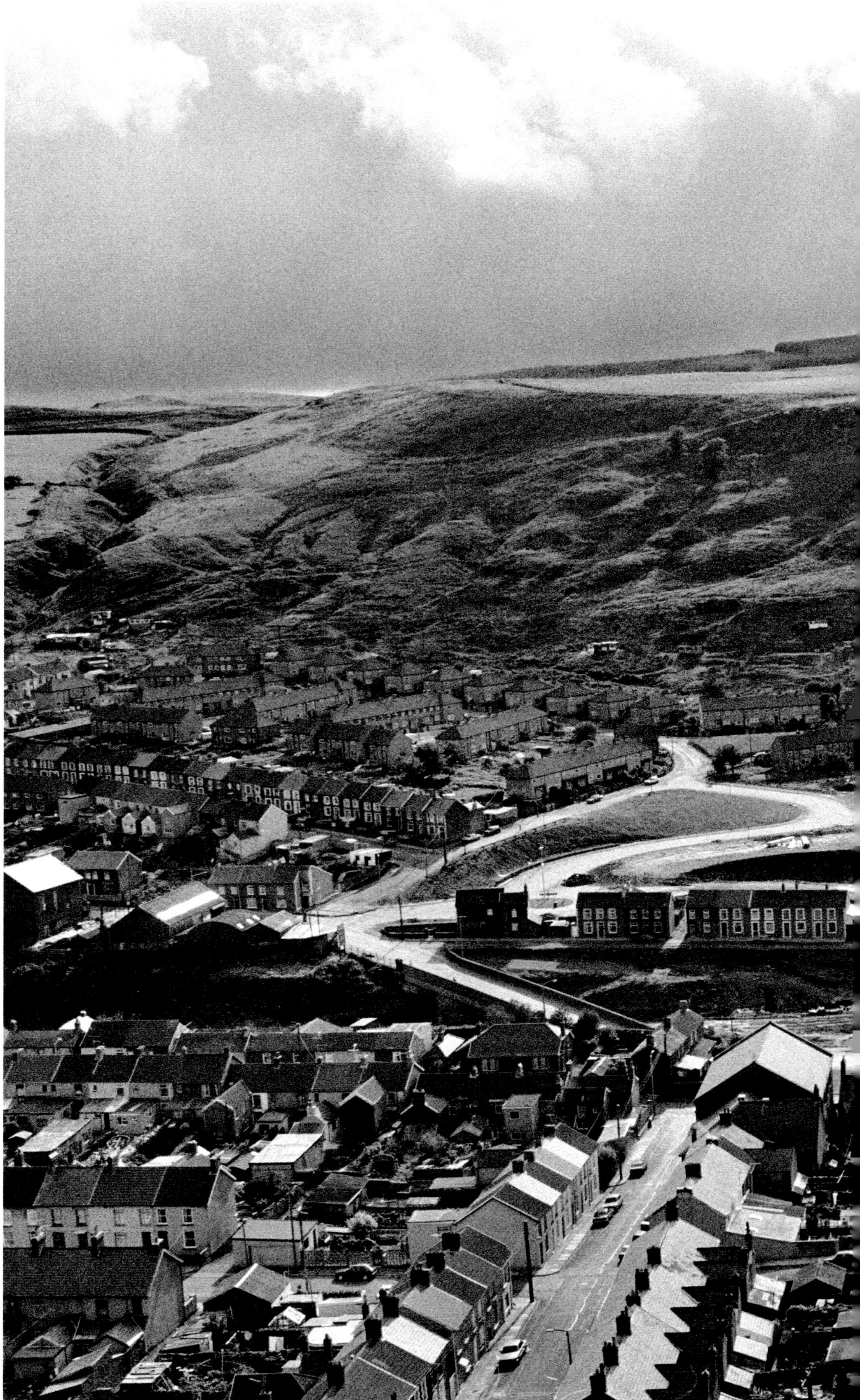

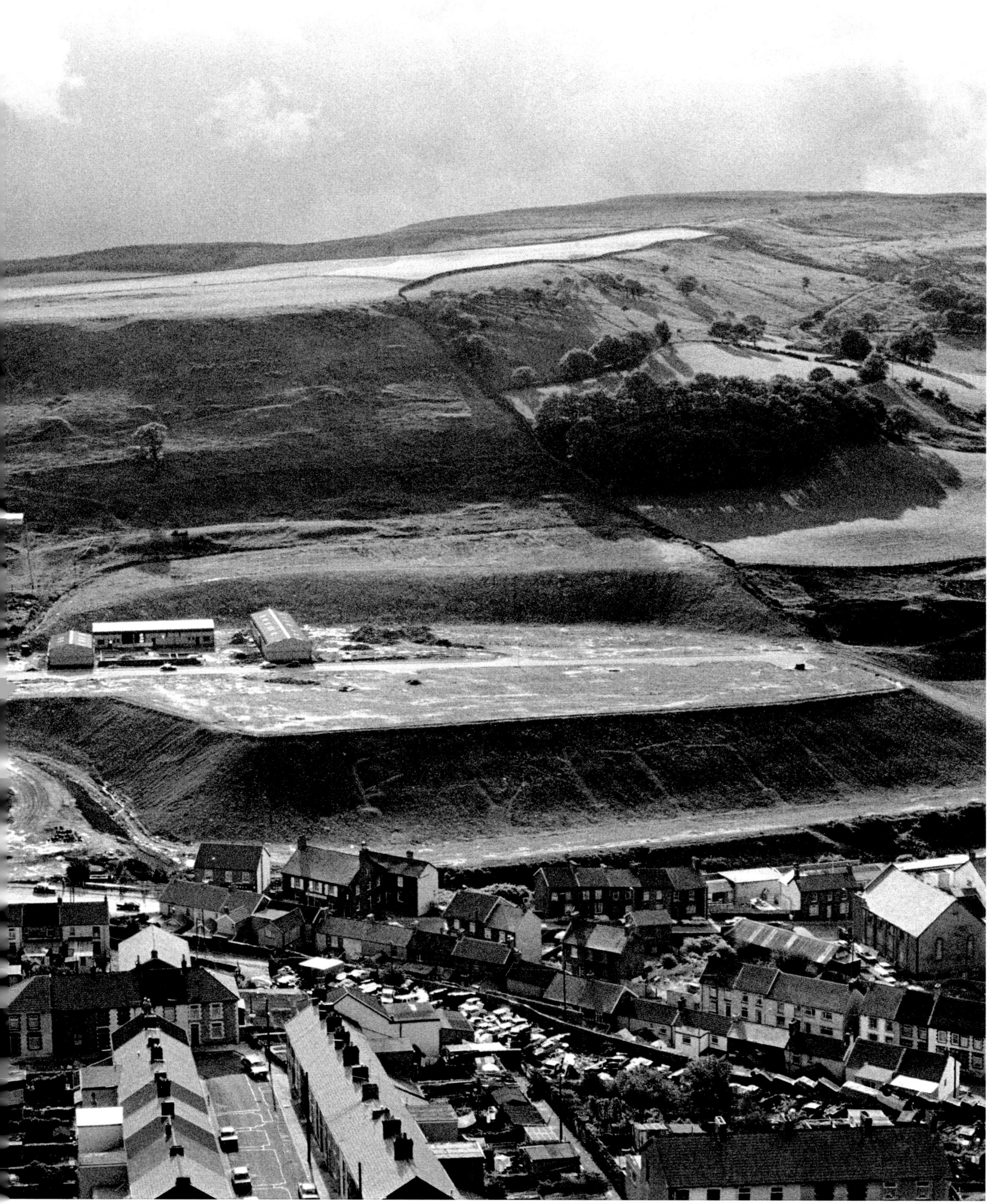

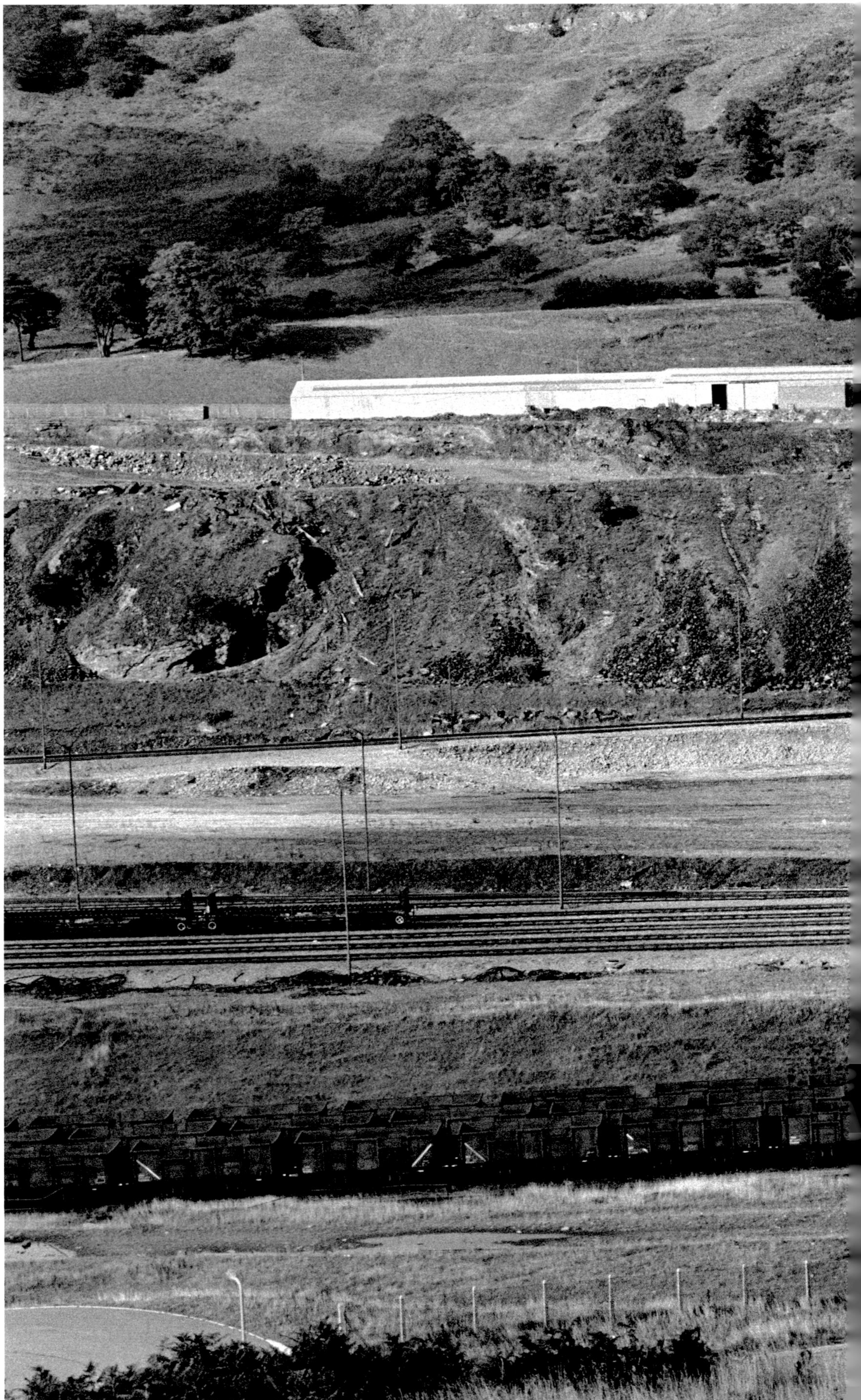

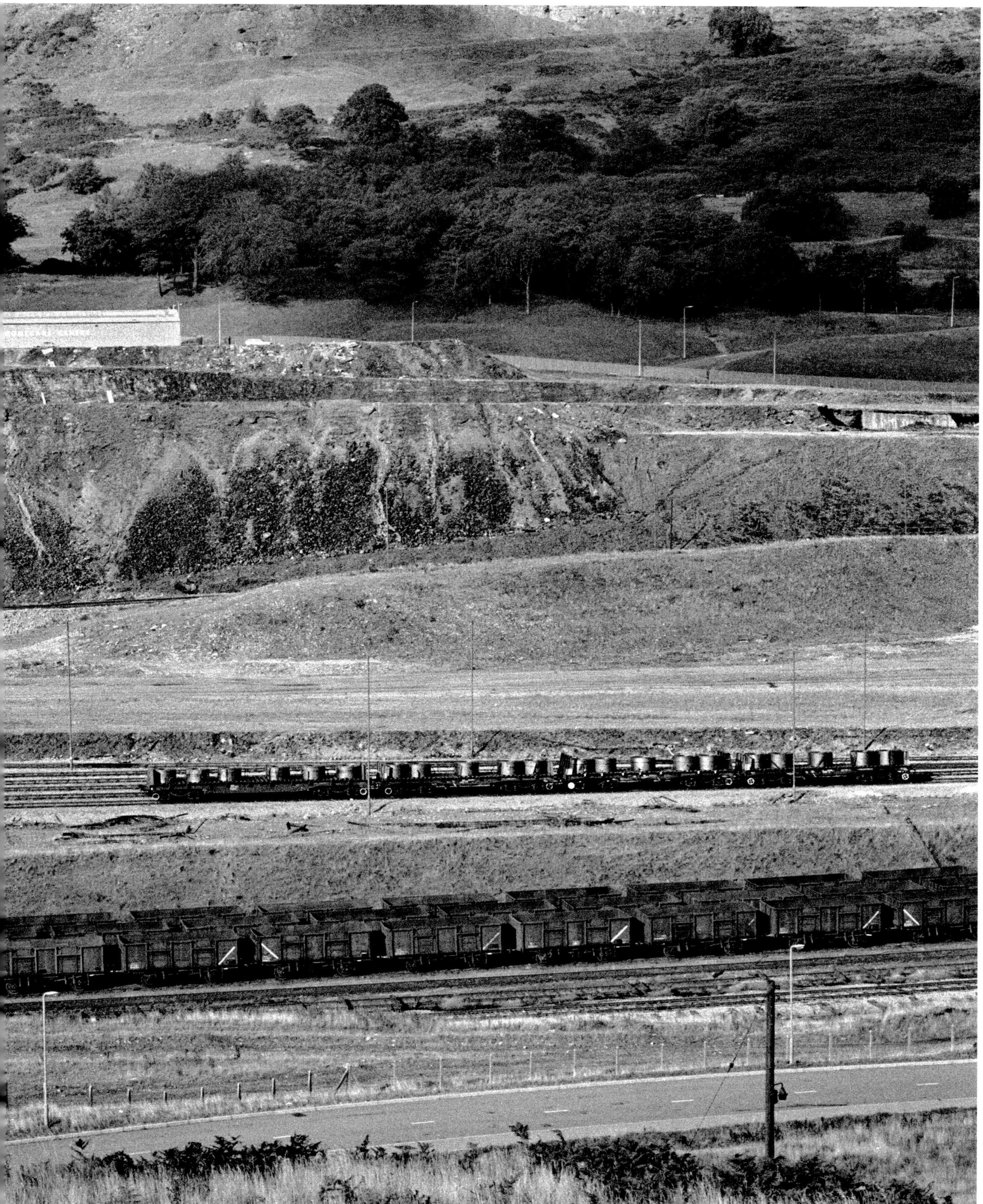

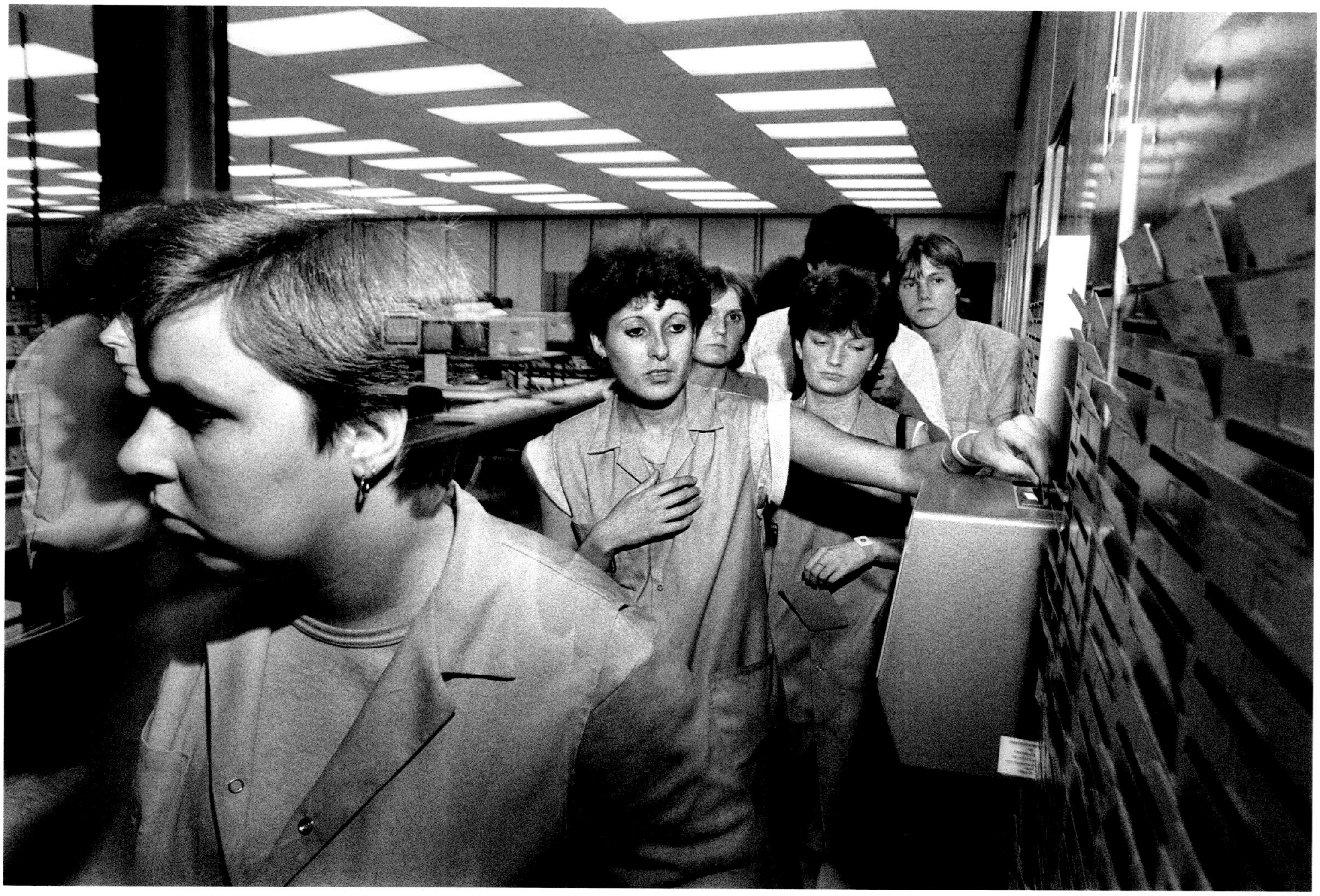

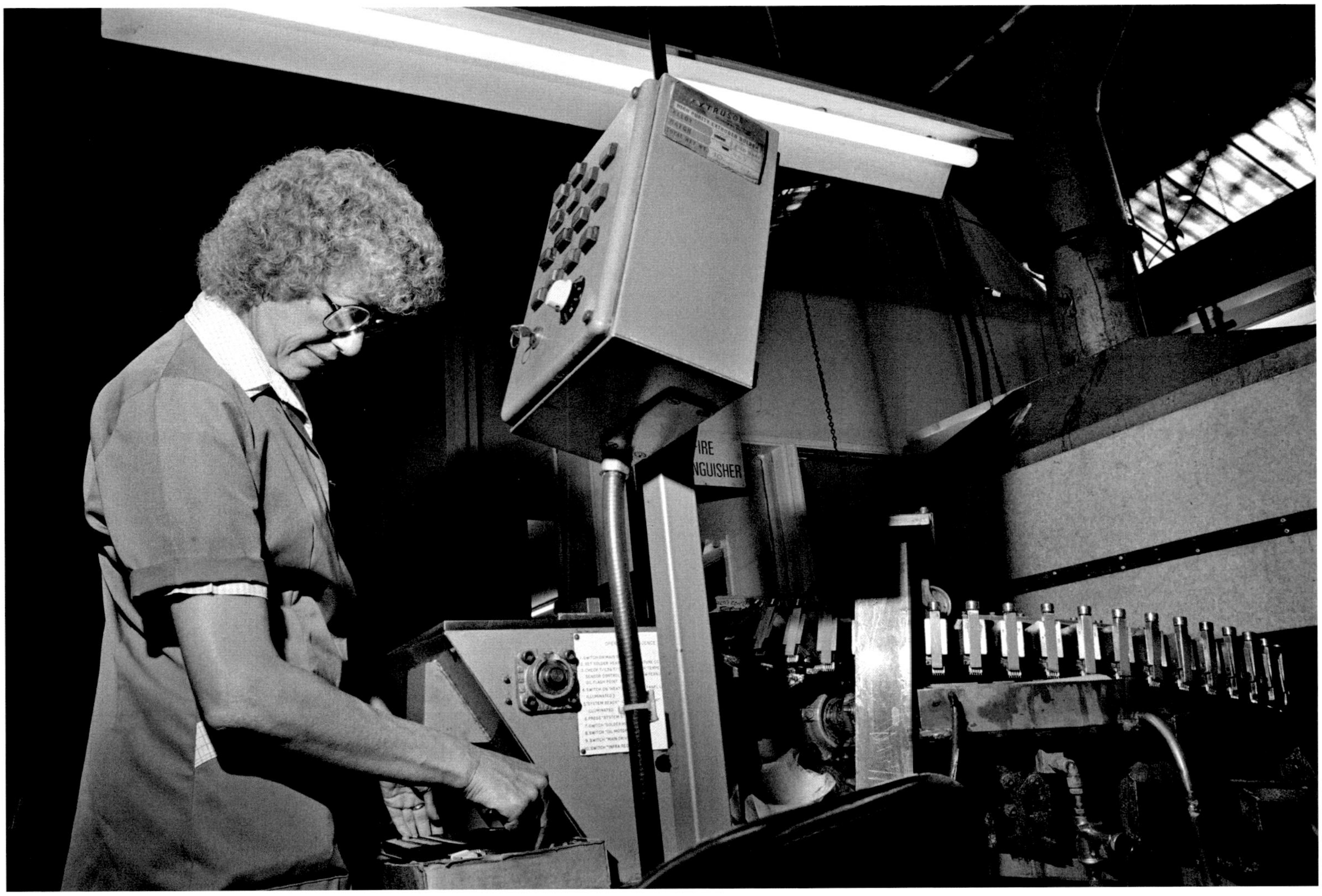
FIRE
NGUISHER

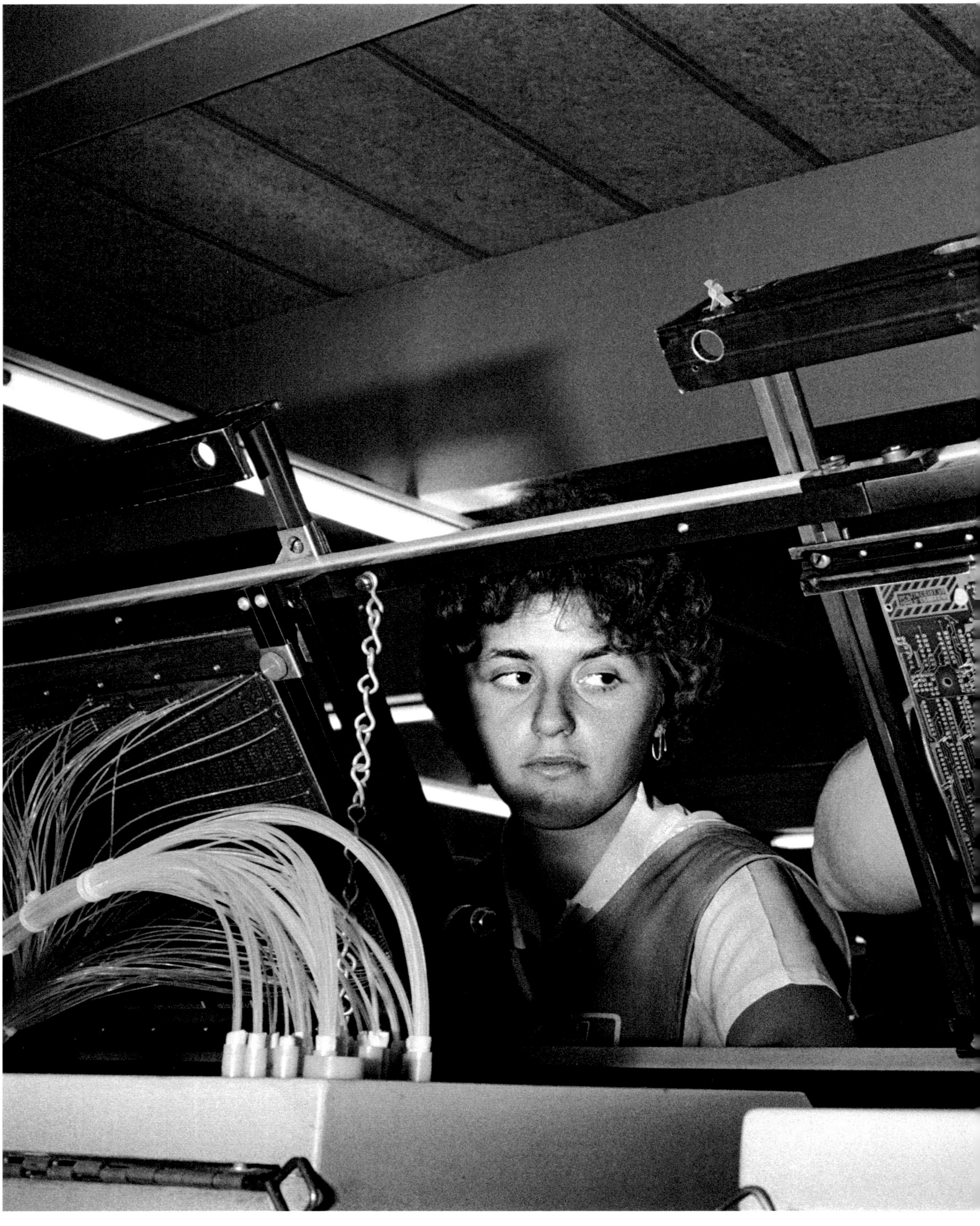

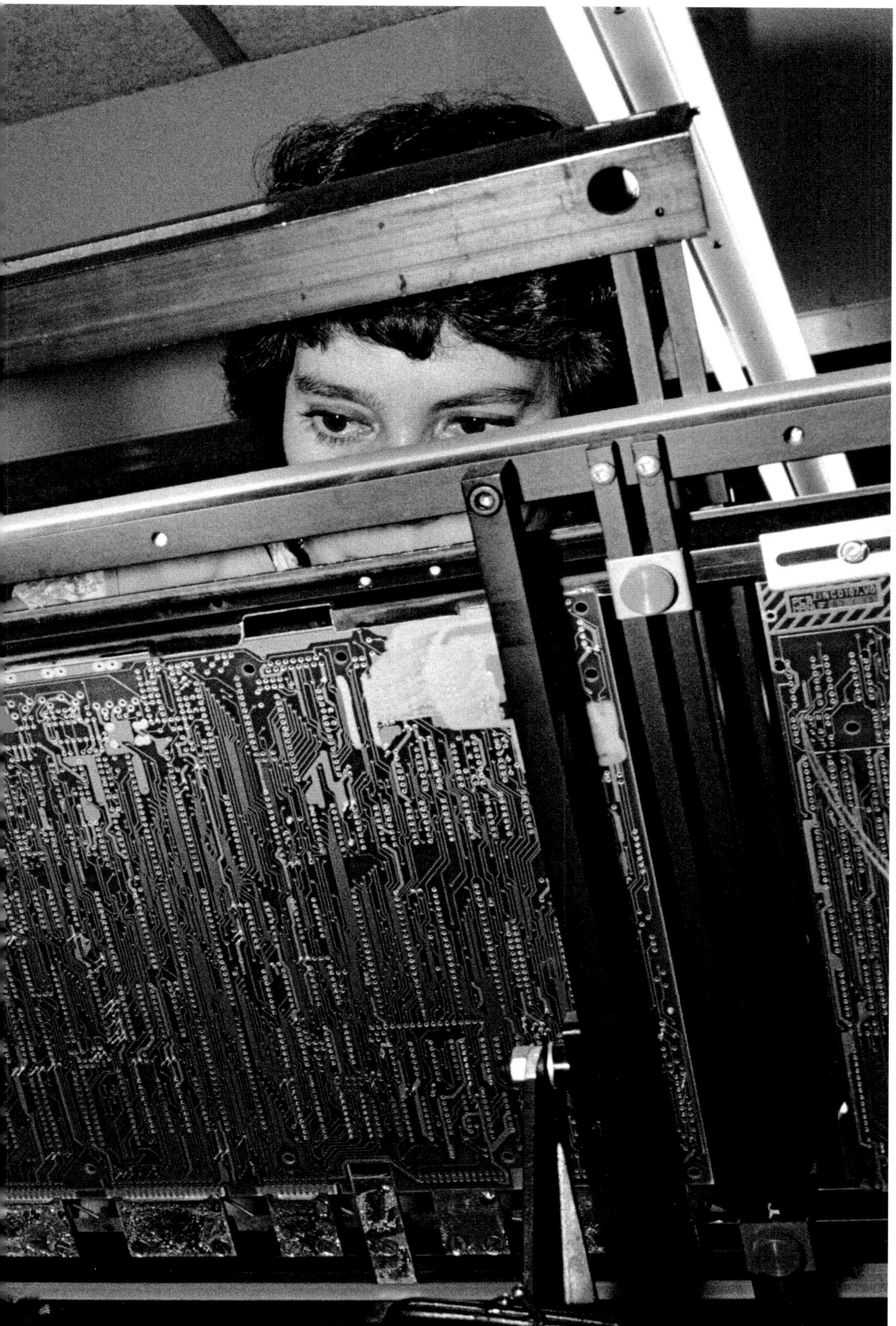

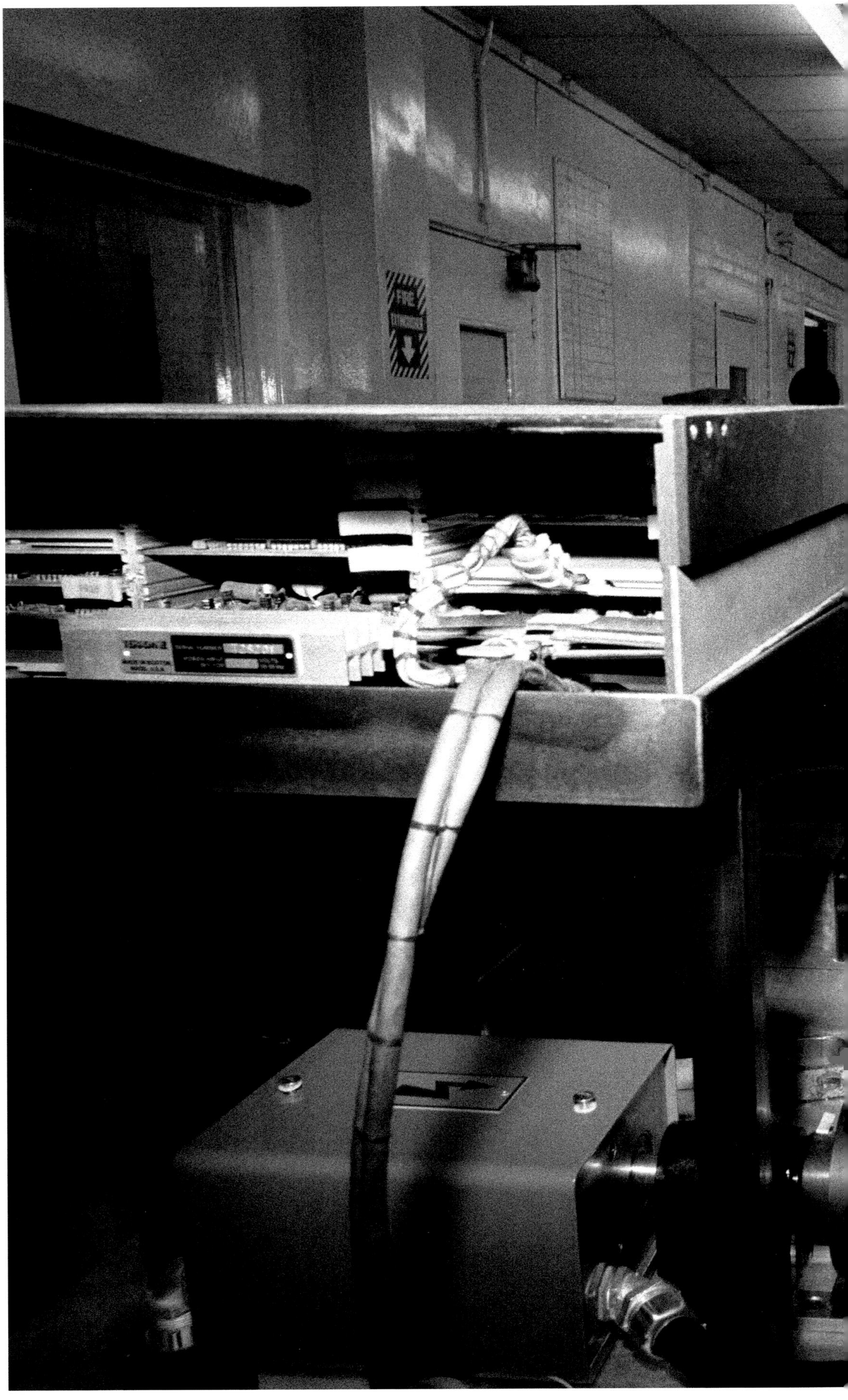

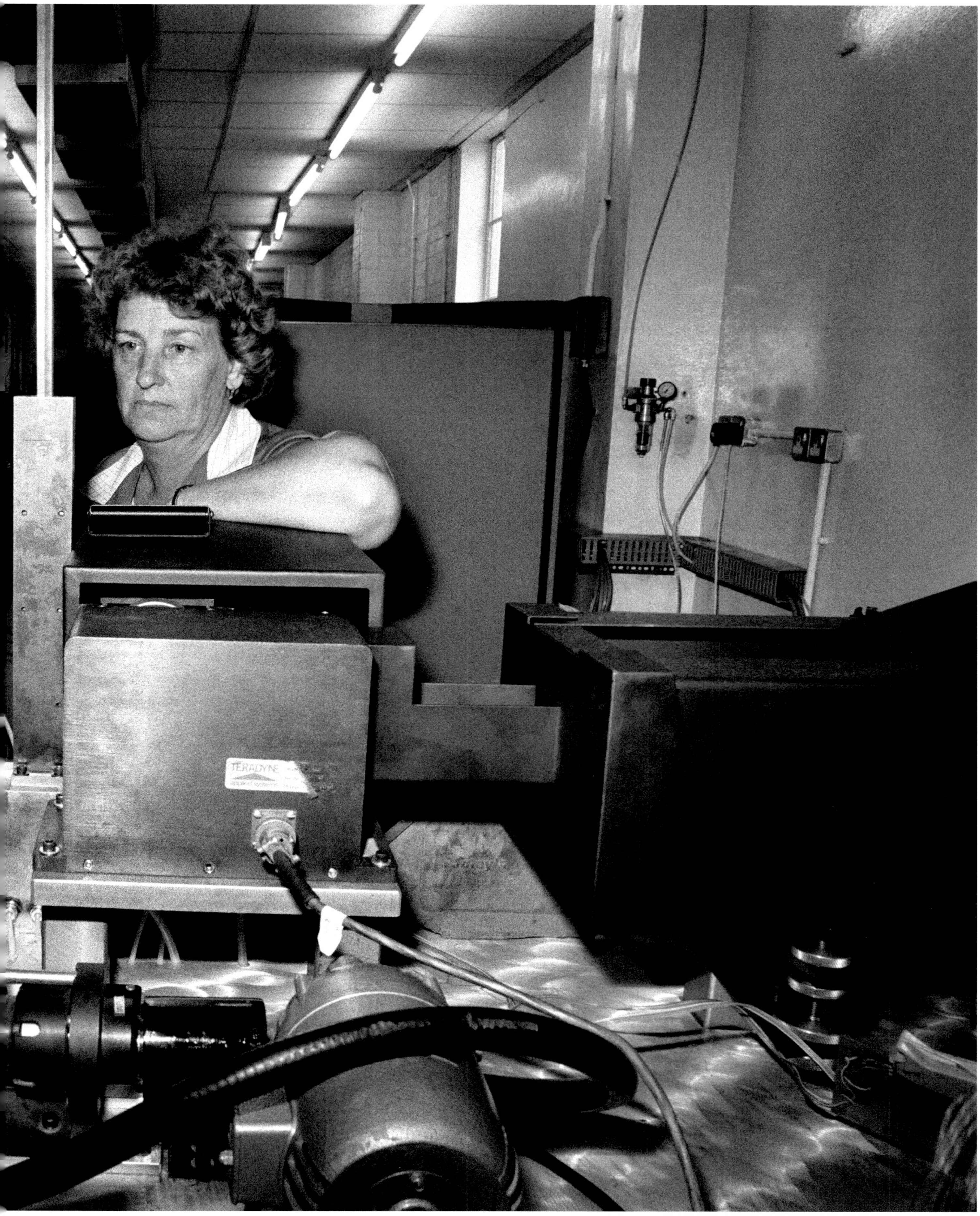
TERADYNE

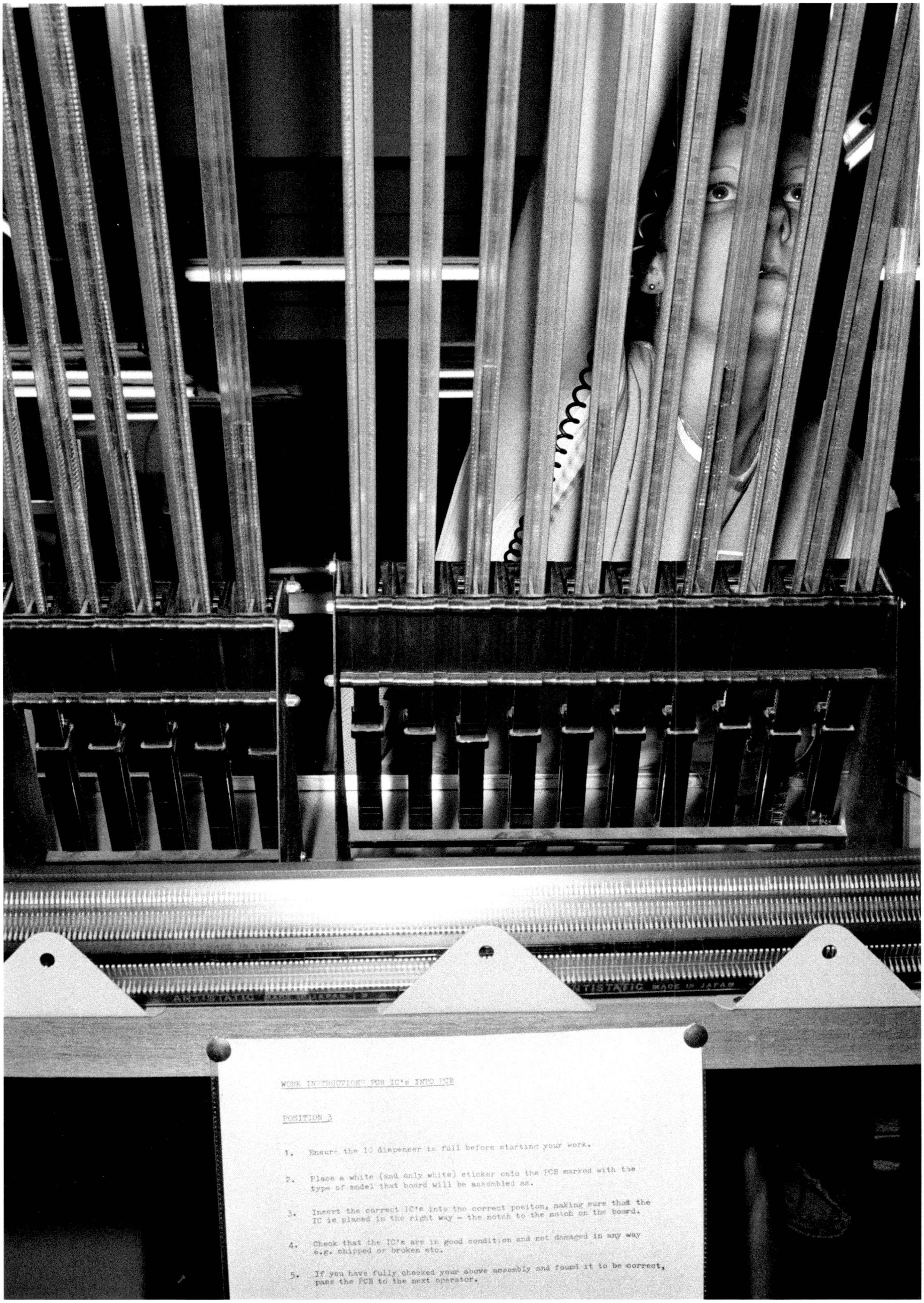
WORK INSTRUCTIONS FOR IC's INTO PCB
POSITION 3
1. Ensure the IC dispenser is full before starting your work.
2. Place a white (and only white) sticker onto the PCB marked with the type of model that board will be assembled as.
3. Insert the correct IC's into the correct positon, making sure that the IC is placed in the right way - the notch to the notch on the board.
4. Check that the IC's are in good condition and not damaged in any way e.g. chipped or broken etc.
5. If you have fully checked your above assembly and found it to be correct, pass the PCB to the next operator.
ANTISTATIC MADE IN JAPAN

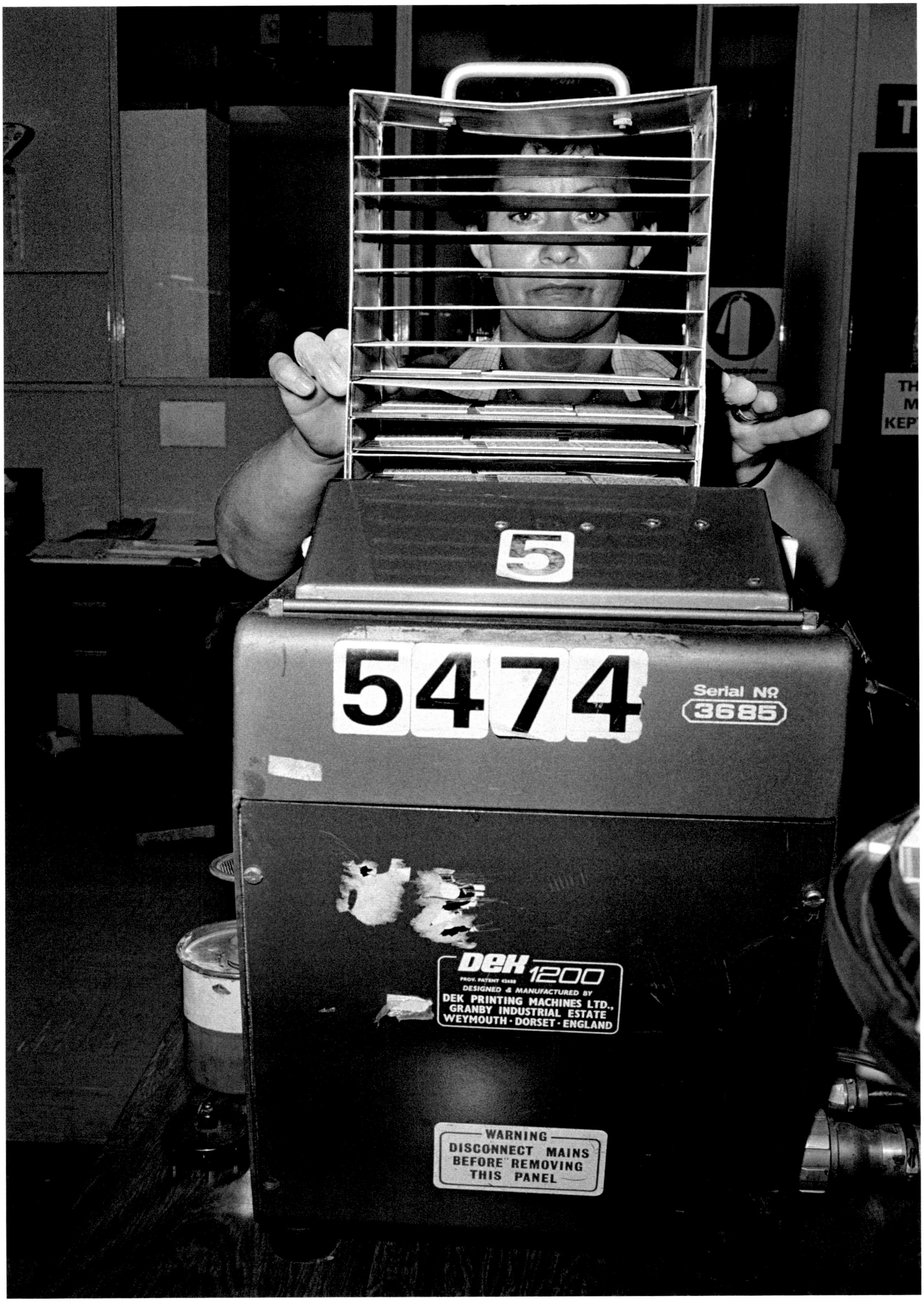
5
5474
Serial Nº
3685
DEK 1200
DESIGNED & MANUFACTURED BY
DEK PRINTING MACHINES LTD.,
GRANBY INDUSTRIAL ESTATE
WEYMOUTH · DORSET · ENGLAND
WARNING
DISCONNECT MAINS
BEFORE REMOVING
THIS PANEL

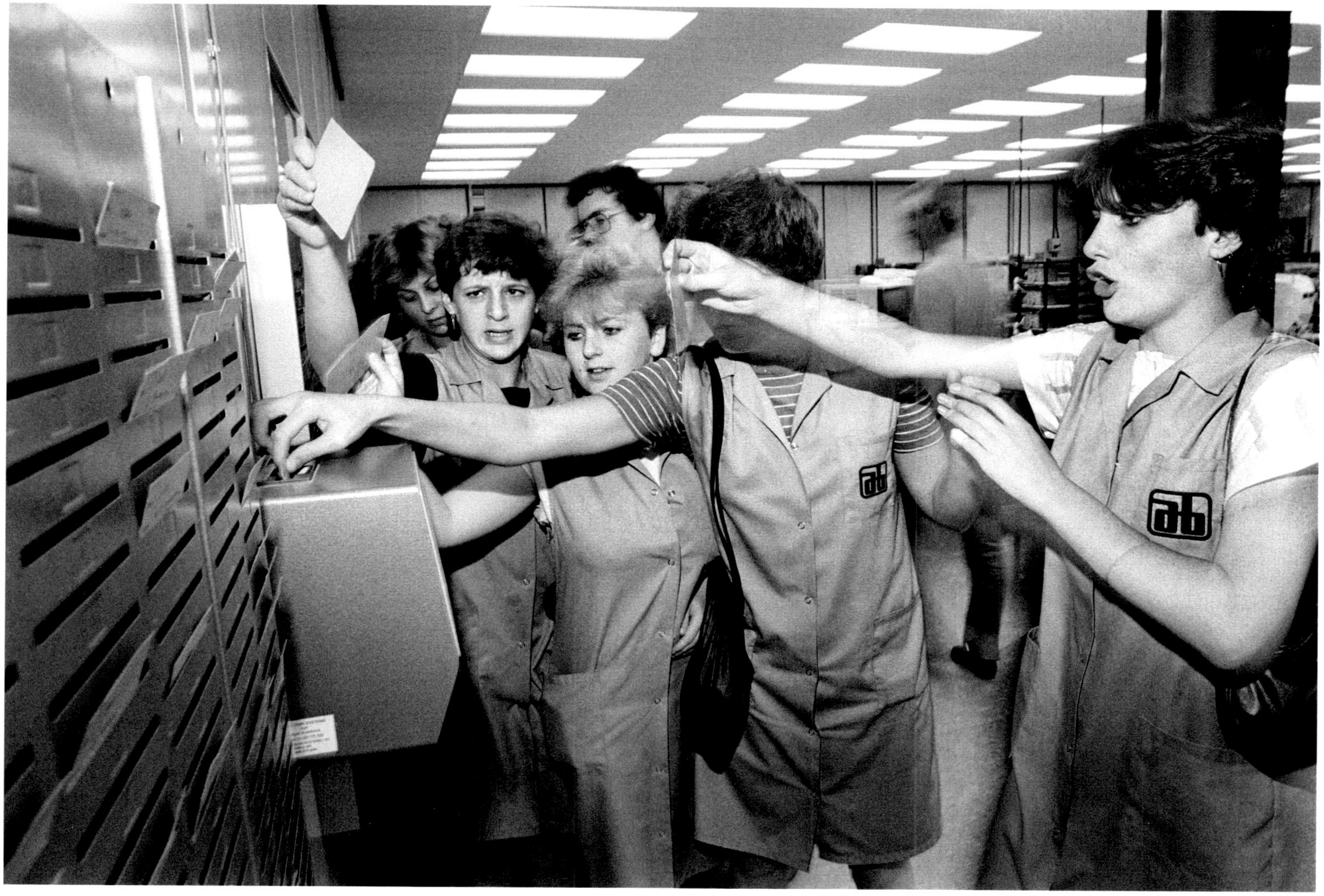

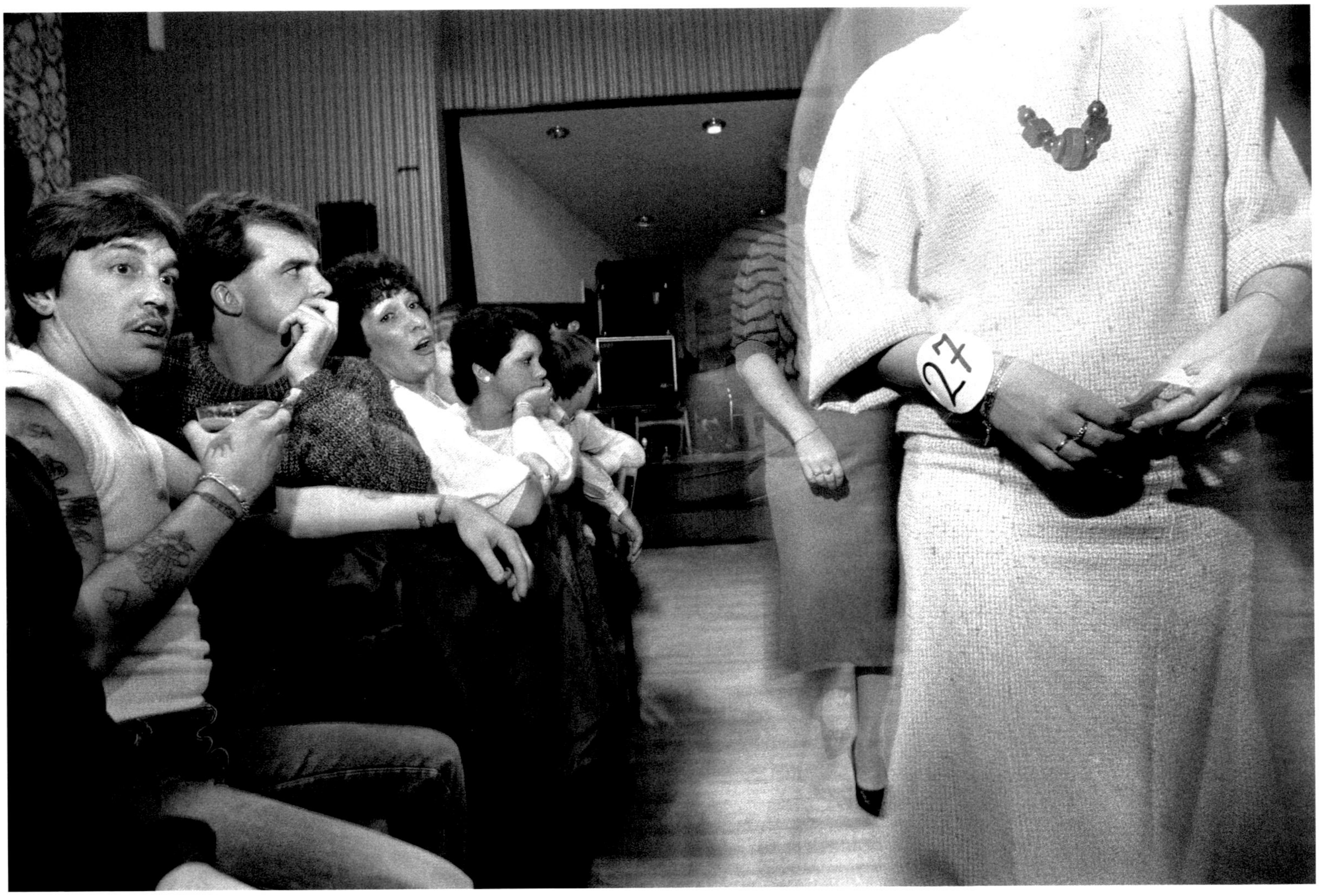
27

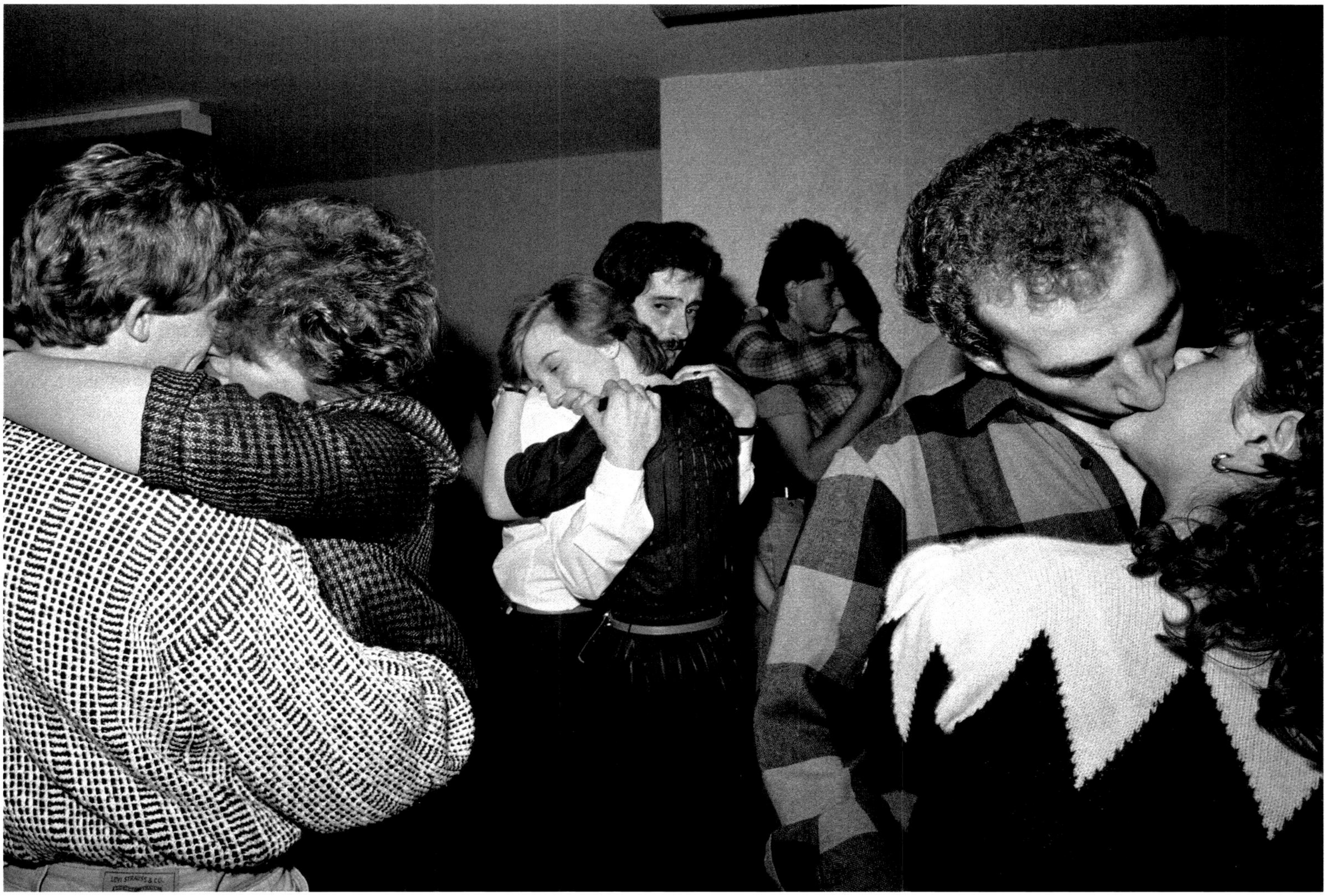

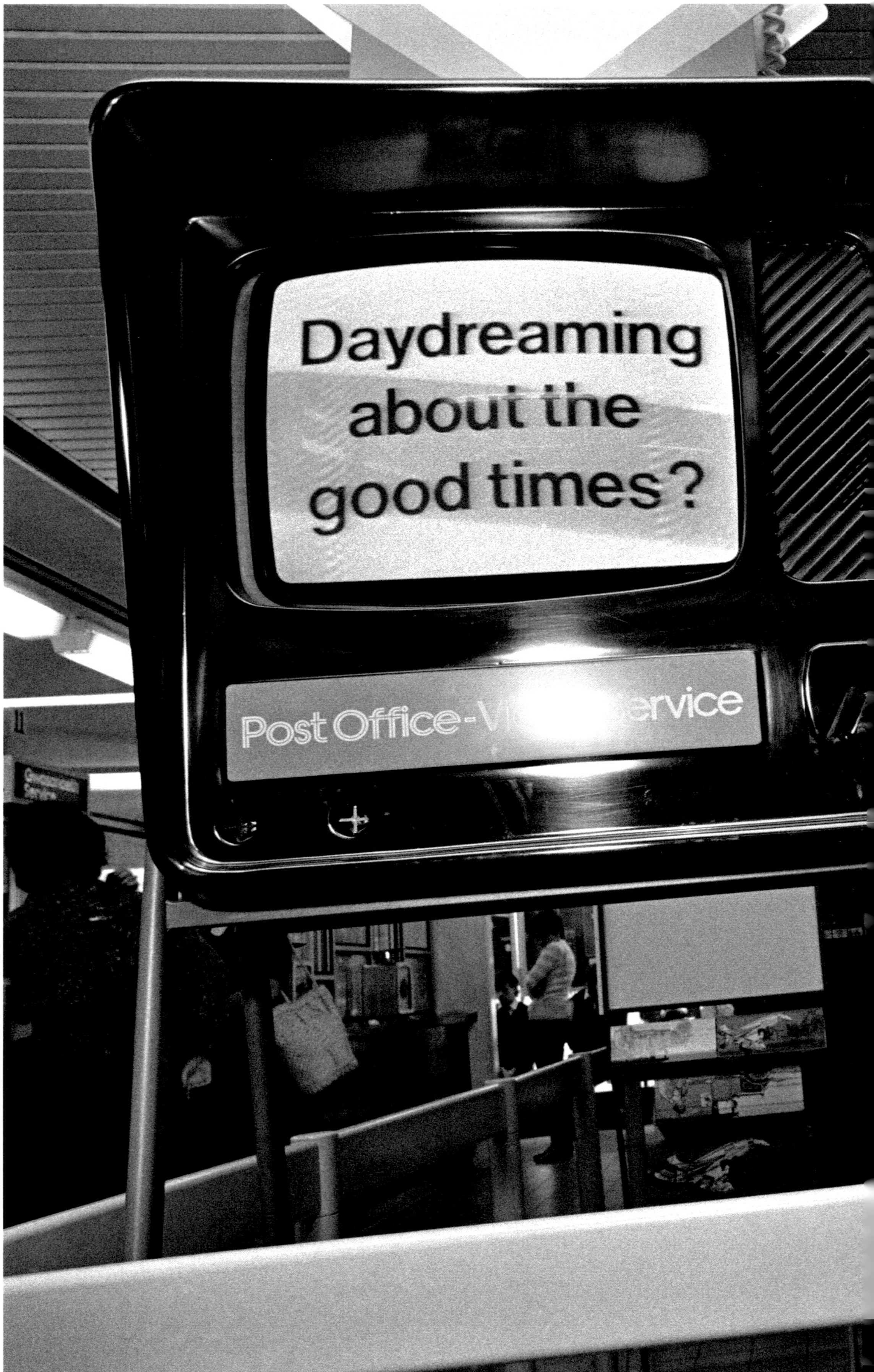
Daydreaming
about the
good times?
Post Office-

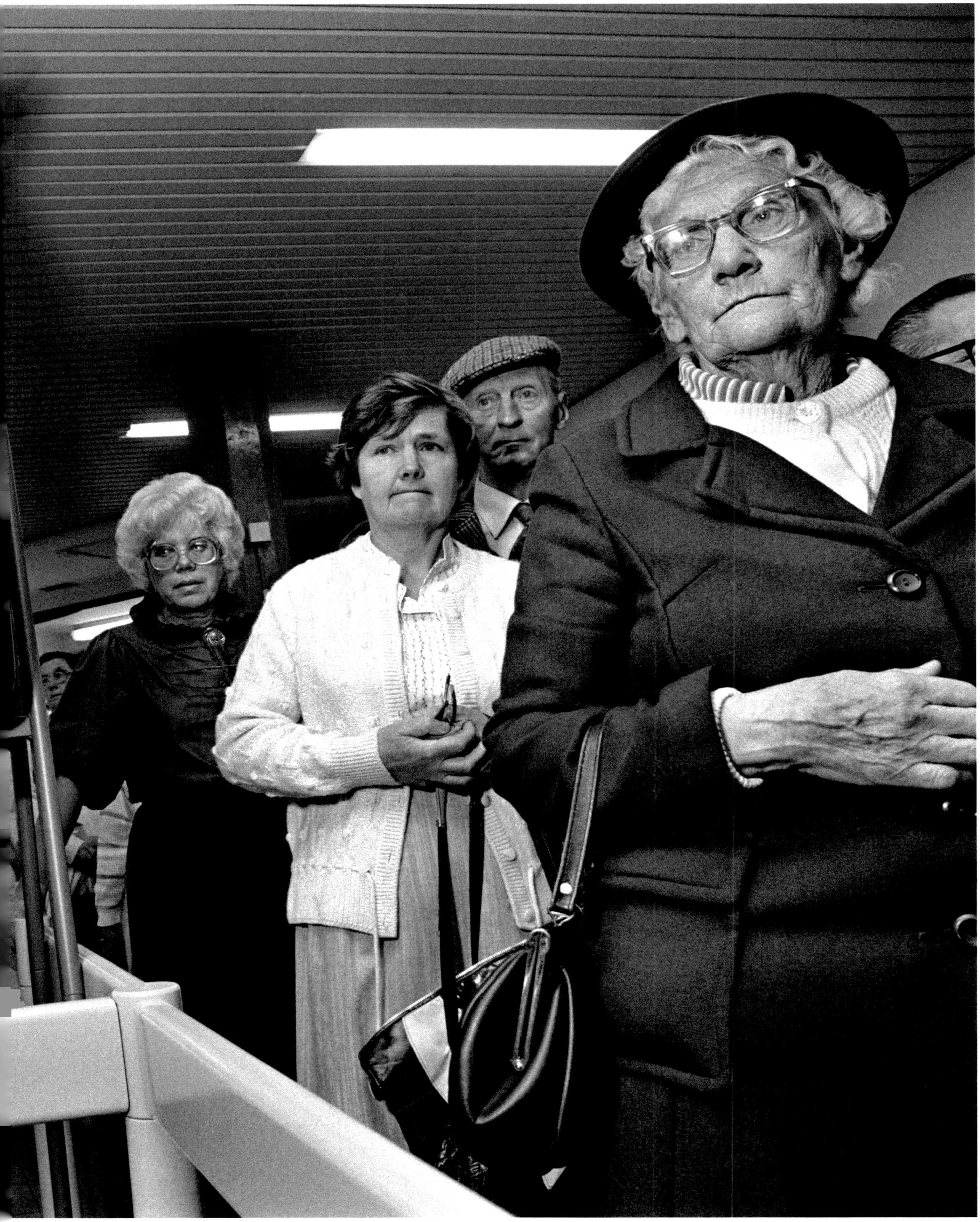

Val Williams

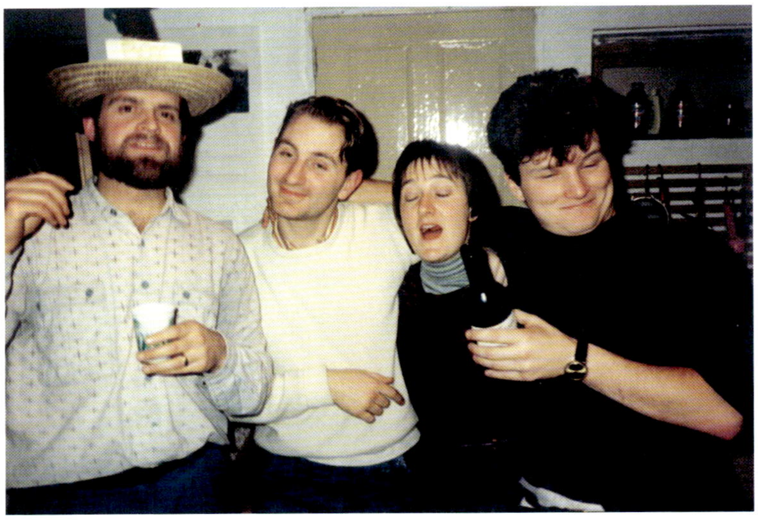

From the Supermarket to the Elephant.

In April 1988, Paul Reas held a solo exhibition at Ffotogallery in Cardiff of his series 'I Can Help' which explored the rise of consumerism in the 1980s.

It was one of a number of photo series appearing in Britain during this time which explored aspiration, lifestyle and shopping. Anna Fox's 'Basingstoke' (1986) looked at retail parks in the South of England commuter belt, Martin Parr's 'Point of Sale' (1986), explored small shops and supermarkets in Salford. The retail park was a phenomenon of the late 1970s, as planning laws were relaxed under the Thatcher government. Many of the parks were built on land previously occupied by industry, which became vacant as the UK deindustrialised in the 1980s.

For emerging photographers of the 1980s—many working in colour—this new landscape offered opportunities to make socially engaged work without necessarily embracing the humanitarianism which had become de rigeur in traditional photojournalism. Reas invited journalist Stuart Cosgrove, who had written and edited for the *New Musical Express* (*NME*) and *The Face* to write an essay to accompany the photographs. Cosgrove's piece was energetic and eccentric, and included a small section on the Hungerford mass murderer Michael Ryan, a set of alarming facts about meat and a fantastical construction around the idea of selling orphans in supermarkets. The text set the scene for Reas's photographs: a series of images which not only explored, via photodocumentary, the ways in which the British consumed in the 1980s, but also experimented with the ways that the photographic image could be constructed from the 'real.'

Paul Reas came to photography after some years spent working in the building trade. He grew up on a Bradford Council Estate and became interested in photography in the mid 1970s. He began to take photographs, and was interested in the black and white documentary work of Martin Parr, which he had seen at Impressions Gallery in York. He had also visited the Side Gallery in Newcastle to see 'Survival Programmes,' the survey work of the Exit Group, which included the work of Nicholas Batty, Paul Trevor and future Magnum photographer Chris Steele-Perkins.

When Paul Reas graduated from the documentary photography course at Newport in 1984 (fellow students included Paul Lowe and Simon Norfolk), he was 'very dissatisfied with the work' he had produced. 'It was romantic and nostalgic, produced in a particular mould. We were all seeking out the marginalised and whimsical, the obscure, dying crafts etc. I wanted to try and make work which was more contemporary.'

The Valleys Project was established by Ffotogallery in 1984. Together with photographers Ron McCormick and John Davies, Reas produced work for the commission in 1985, with David Bailey joining in later that year. The Valleys Project was described by Ffotogallery as 'a unique undertaking to document what has to be one of the most beautiful yet industrialised landscapes of Northern Europe.' For Reas, it was an opportunity to change both methodology and subject matter, as he decided to photograph the introduction of new technology industries to South Wales: 'They were industries which employed mainly women and these women were manufacturing small electrical components for the newly emerging computer industry. I wanted to photograph it in a way that wouldn't pull any punches.'

'The Valleys' series was an intimation of the work which would emerge from 'I Can Help.' Like the later series, it concentrated on the choreographies of bodies, hands, arms, faces. One photograph, where women are jostling to slot time cards into a clocking-in machine, has a kind of ecstasy, as arms implore and faces shine. Reas was determined to make a more 'felt,' subjective piece of work. The photographs are imbued with powerful ideas about the politics of labour—Reas's mother had been a piece worker at Thorn Electrical in Bradford, who often had to bring her work home with her. He was shocked by the repetitiveness of women's work in the new hi-tech factories. Before studying at Newport, Reas had worked on many construction sites in the UK and abroad, and was a skilled bricklayer. Manual work was at the centre of many of his early projects. From his time at Newport, series included 'Working Men' (1982) and 'Desmond's Mine,' a series on a small independent coal mine in Pantygasseg (1983).[1]

'I Can Help' was very different—where 'Working Men' and 'Desmond's Mine' could be easily placed within a long-established tradition of international photojournalism which was still influential in the 1980s, this new colour series was raw and performative. In supermarkets and retail parks across the land, customers implored and grasped, faces set in the ecstasy of consumption.

The photographs from 'I Can Help' were set in a number of locations across Britain, from Tesco's to MacDonald's to Barratt Homes. In the shopping photographs, the colour red is everywhere, leisure time is more pastel, mirroring Reas's experience of MFI furniture stores in the 1980s where, he said, 'the showrooms were full of energy and primary colours, but the collection rooms, where the self-assembly furniture was collected were like a doctor's waiting room, all cool pastel-ey colours, like a depressurising chamber.'[2] Meat, red, signs that

Paul Reas (left), Simon Norfolk, Jane Reas and Paul Lowe, Newport, 1987

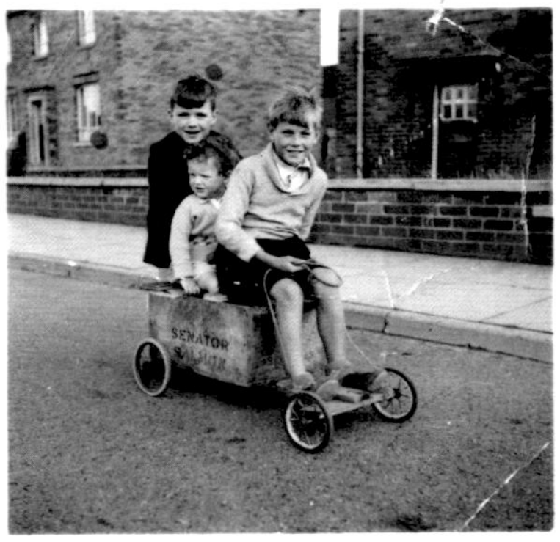

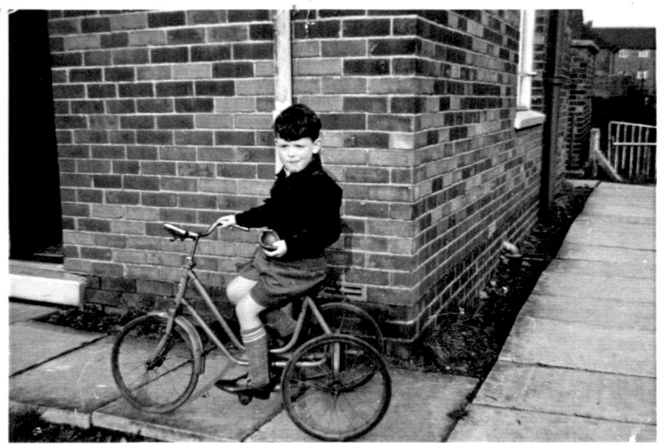

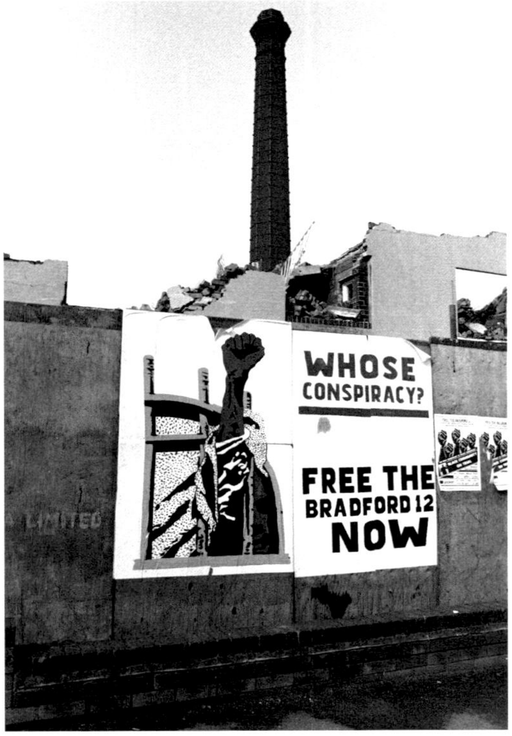

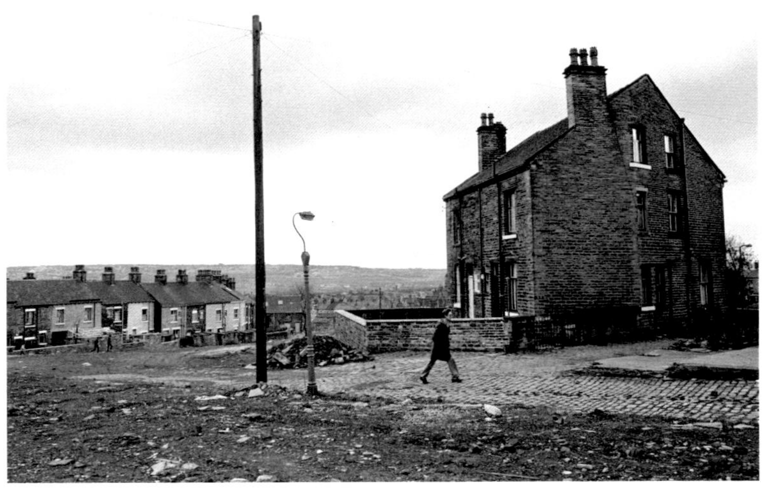

Clockwise from the top:
Reas (centre) outside the Brafferton Arbor family home, Buttershaw estate, Bradford, 1959
Reas outside the Brafferton Arbor family home, Buttershaw estate, Bradford, 1963
© Paul Reas/Bradford, 1975
© Paul Reas/Bradford, 1975

Clockwise from the top:
Daniel Meadows and Martin Parr, Newport College of Art and Design, Newport, 1984
Documentary Photography seminar at Newport College of Art and Design, with David Hurn (left), John Charity, Keith Arnatt and students, c. 1970s
© Paul Reas/Coney Beach, Porthcawl, South Wales, 1982
© Paul Reas/Weston-Super-Mare, Somerset, 1982

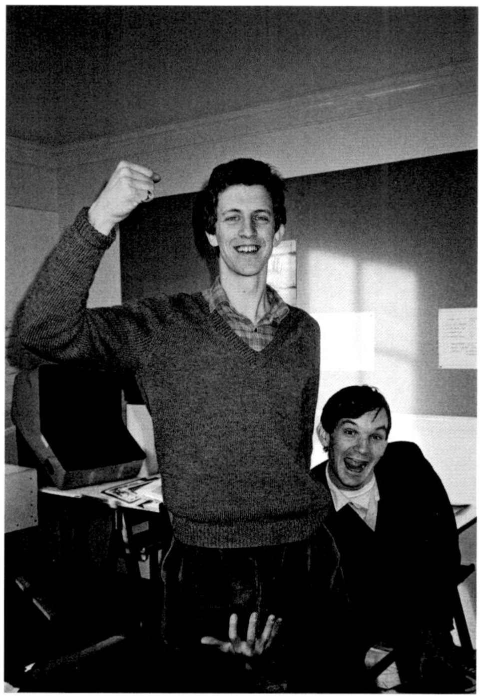

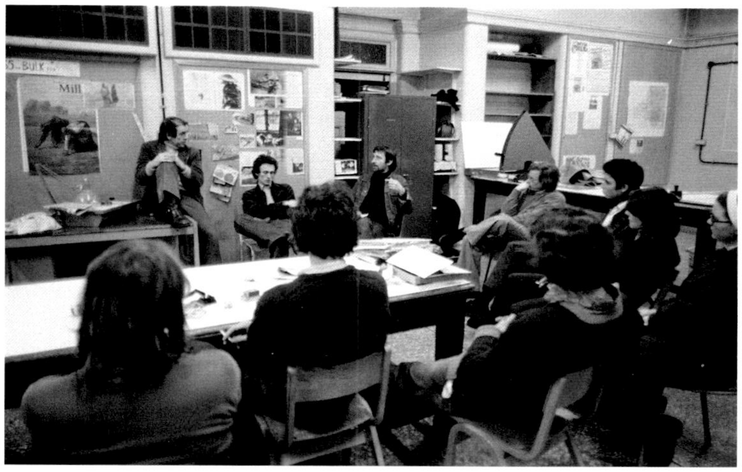

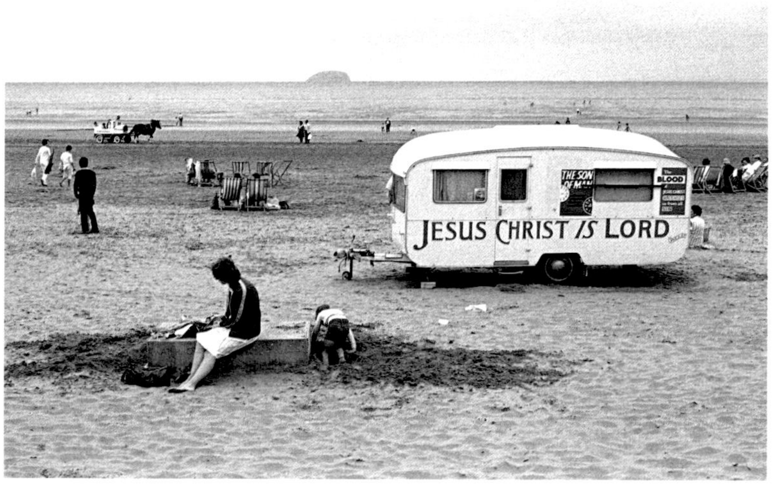

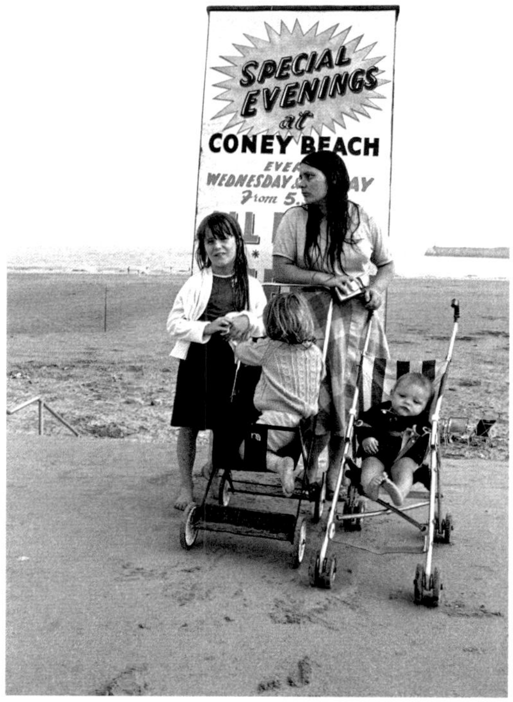

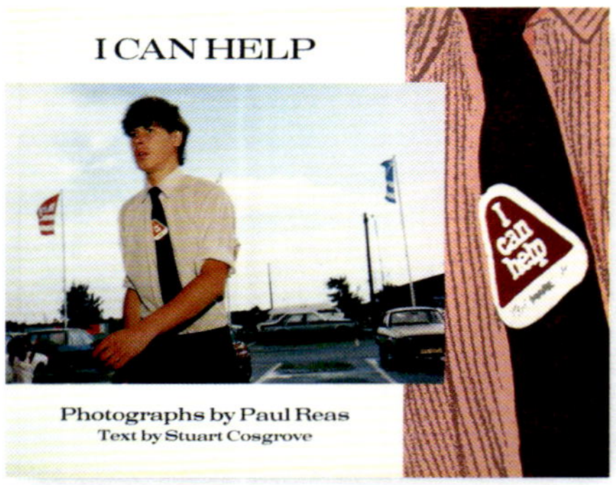

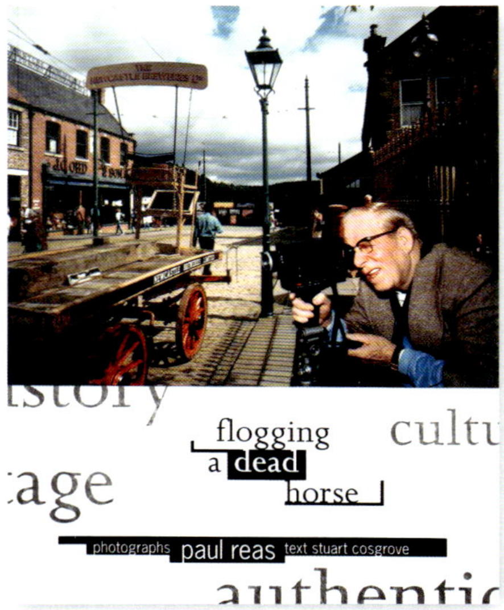

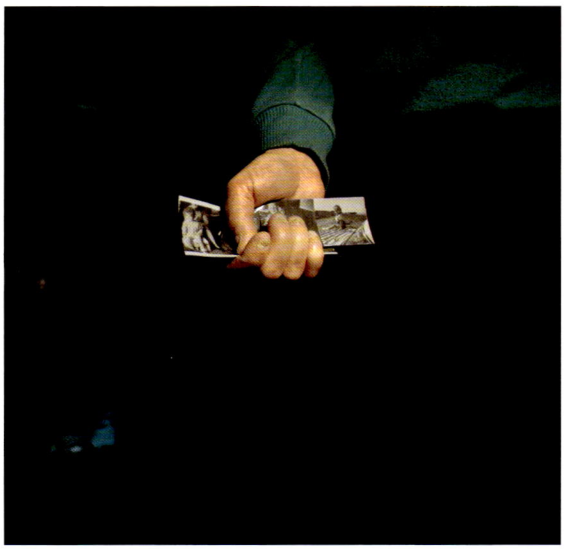

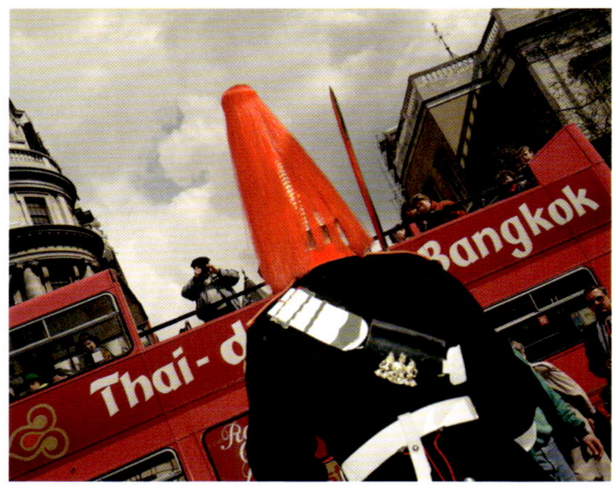

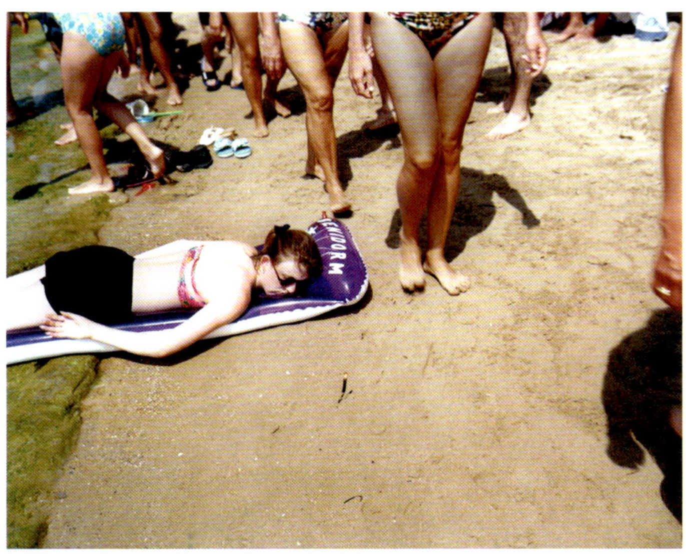

Clockwise from the top:
I Can Help (Cornerhouse Publications, 1988)
Flogging a Dead Horse (Cornerhouse Publications, 1993)
From The *Sunday Times Magazine* assignment on tourism in London, 1992
From The *Sunday Times Magazine* assignment on British tourism in Benidorm, Spain, 1993
From the series 'Portrait of an Invisible Man,' 1993–94

screamed offers, exhausted patrons, the brightness of flash illuminating scurrying customers—'I Can Help' was brazen and without the irony or the whimsy that Reas had kicked against within the new British photography of the late 1970s and early 1980s.

If 'I Can Help' put Paul Reas at the centre of the new British colour photography of the 1980s, *Flogging a Dead Horse*, published in 1993, proved his photography had not settled into a set of photographic norms, but was rather segueing into a sharp, political dialectic using photography's range and precise subject matter to make its point. Growing up in a working class family and working for some years in the building trade, Reas was fascinated by the idea of manual work. 'Flogging a Dead Horse' explored the rise of the heritage industry, and took issue with the re-writing of the past of working people by the burgeoning leisure industry. Throughout the 1980s, Reas had been interested in the changing face of work: 'I felt heritage was a big project bobbling over, we'd gone through a boom and were entering a depression. Mining museums were a travesty; they weren't making a serious attempt to explore the realities of what mining was.'[3] The project took him from Lands End in Cornwall to Beamish in the north east. Visiting the disused Lewis Merthyr Colliery in South Wales, he noted how it would soon reopen as 'a total mining experience.'[4]

The photographs in 'Flogging a Dead Horse' are more phantasmagorical than earlier projects. While the supermarkets and stores that Reas had photographed for 'I Can Help' were theatres of action and anxiety, the heritage sets he chronicled were dead spaces, brown and murky. In the supermarkets, everyone knew what to do, but in these museums of heritage and labour, they were unsure as the real collided with the imaginary. Was that a real pit pony? A real miner? Or a simulacrum dreamt up for marketing?

In 1989, three works by Reas were included in 'Through the Looking Glass: Photographic Art in Britain 1945–1989,' a group exhibition at the Barbican Art Gallery in London, which explored the growth of British documentary and photojournalism, and touched on feminist and conceptual photography. This show was important, in that it acknowledged the work of the new British colour photographers, including Paul Graham, Anna Fox and Paul Reas, as a significant grouping in British photography. Though ways of thinking about photography have changed substantially since then, the importance of the colour documentarists of the 1980s is still widely acknowledged. Reas's work was popular from the beginning. In 1988, 'I Can Help' was shown at The Photographers' Gallery in London, subsequently toured, and his work was included in group shows in the UK and in Europe. Photographs from 'I Can Help' were also included in Mark Haworth Booth's *British Photography: Towards a Bigger Picture* published by Aperture in 1988. A wave of interest in the new British colour photographers meant that British photographers were increasingly shown in Europe and further afield. He was also included in the British Council touring exhibition 'Documentary Dilemmas' in 1994, and in the same year in the Barbican's 'Who's Looking at the Family?,' with his new series about his father 'Portrait of an Invisible Man.'

'Portrait of an Invisible Man' was a rare departure into the autobiographical. It revealed the story of Reas's father, who had a second, secret family. 'Invisible Man' became part of a growing movement to use photography to explore personal history. Other projects on the topic would include Anna Fox's *My Mother's Cupboards and My Father's Words* (2000), Larry Sultan's *Pictures from Home* (1992) and Richard Billingham's *Ray's a Laugh* (1996). Reas's father is never fully seen in the series, but there are traces of him everywhere. 'Invisible Man' was a departure, and although Reas continued to work on the project until 2003, he did not return to the autobiographical over the years to come. It was, nevertheless, a significant development in his photography. There is a fascination with the object as metaphor—the clues in the story are scattered around the house. When we see Reas's father, he is headless, disembodied by photography, always mysterious, never visible.

During a successful decade spent working in the editorial and advertising sector in the 1990s, Reas produced many memorable campaigns for Volkswagen, British Telecom and was on assignment frequently for magazines such as the *Sunday Times* and *The Face*. Like many of his contemporaries, he was courted by media groups eager to incorporate the new documentary into their campaigns and editorials, marking a significant shift in attitudes to photography from the corporate world. At the same time, new magazines such as *Dazed & Confused* blurred the lines between fashion and documentary, and graduates from critical documentary photography courses, such as Farnham's Robert Wyatt, were making groundbreaking editorial fashion shoots which soon led to international campaigns for major designers. Reas's anti-consumerism was taken up by an industry keen to distance itself from selling and to create a theatre of the absurd around major products. 'I've always had a very pragmatic view of photography—I've always had to make

Top to bottom:
From the *Sunday Times Magazine* assignment on Center Parcs, 1990
From the *Sunday Times Magazine* assignment on Roswell, New Mexico, 1997
British Telecom advertising campaign, 2001
Volkswagen advertising campaign, 1999
Fujifilm advertising campaign, 1999

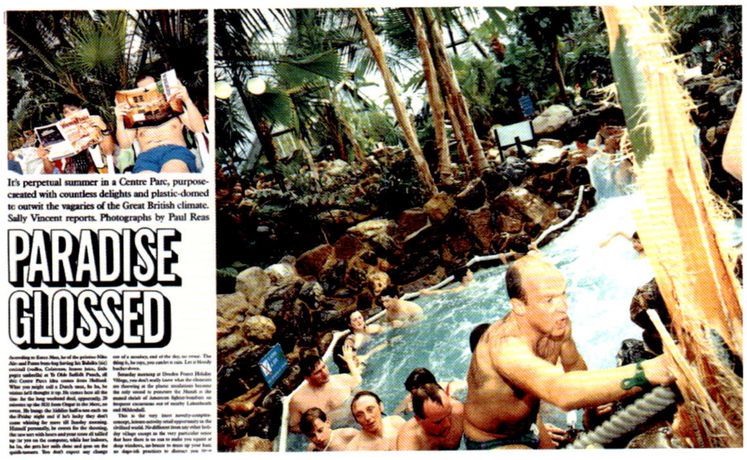

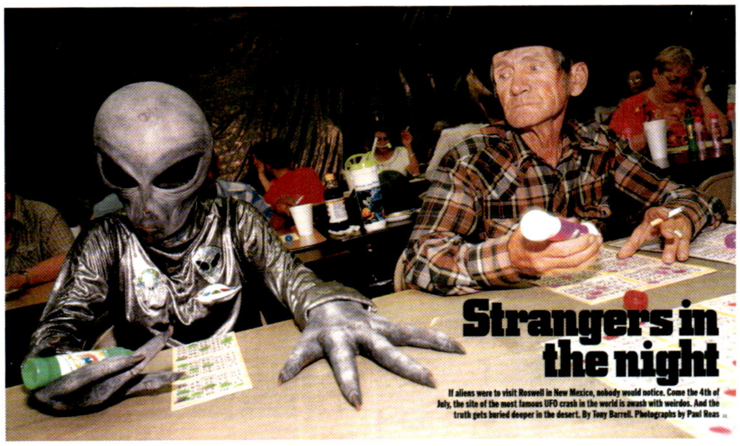

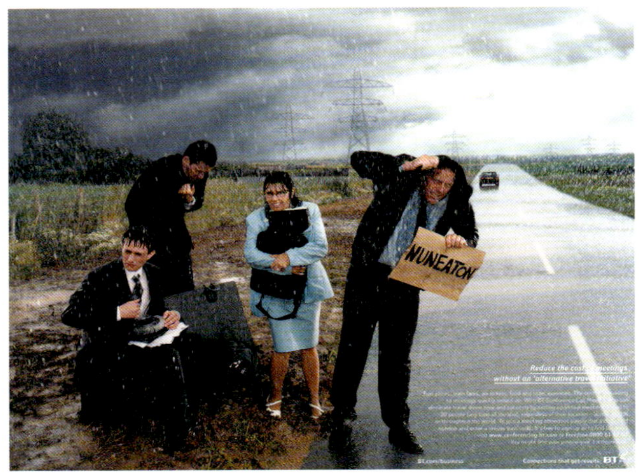

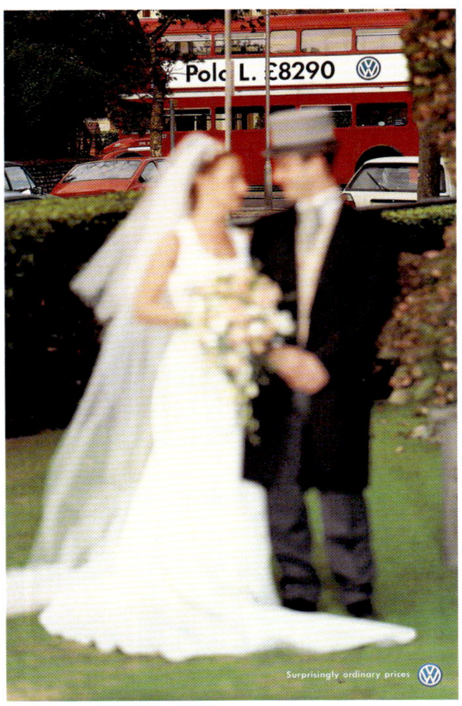

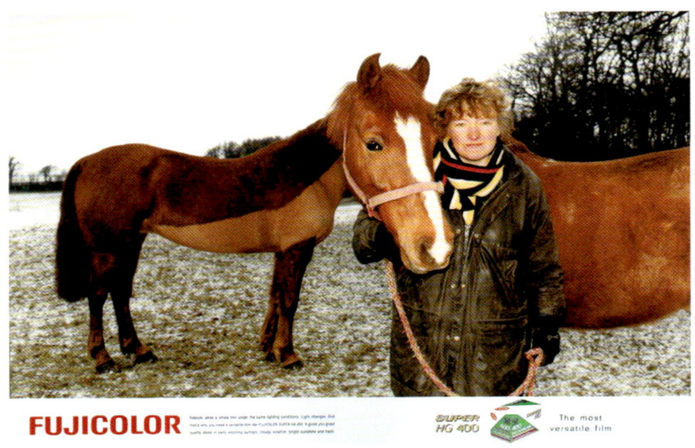

a living...'[5] he said, 'I thoroughly enjoyed it. In my personal work I would spend a lot of time convincing museums, supermarkets etc. to grant me access to photograph. Within the commercial world, everything was in the service of the picture; you could get access to anything you needed, but I lost sight of what motivated me initially about photography. I had no time left to make work for myself, or to be involved in the world of photography, where I'd started. I didn't go to festivals or private views.'[6] Reas's advertising photographs were remarkable—dramatic and subversive—revealing our human vanities and frailties.

In 2010, he was approached by Patrick Sutherland, who was then directing 'The Elephant Vanishes' project at the London College of Communication, to make new work about the Elephant and Castle which was facing major regeneration, during which many residents would be relocated and large blocks of flats demolished. 'It was a big strong working class community and also very diverse ethnically. That really interested me. The house that I grew up in in Bradford was demolished to make way for a private housing estate. I deliberately wanted to make photographs on the streets—things that I came across on the street... If you photograph people a lot you get to understand body language. I'm very honest about how I make photographs, I've got a very big camera with a flash gun so I don't snatch photographs.'

The photographs from The Elephant Vanishes commission were both raw and ethereal and a selection of the work was exhibited at the London College of Communication in 2012, titled 'From a Distance.' It was accompanied by an issue of *Fieldstudy*, published by Photography and the Archive Research Centre. 'From a Distance' was produced as poster prints glued to the wall and lit so each image would be highly illuminated against a dark background. The exhibition was moving, dramatic and theatrical. For the area in and around the Elephant and Castle, it was highly relevant. For Reas, it was a return to the critical documentary that he had used in 'I Can Help' and 'Flogging a Dead Horse.' It was also a return to photography as a purely personal practice. Although the Elephant and Castle work was a commission, Reas was left free to develop it as he saw fit. It was, in the end, very modern work. Shorn of the ironies of 'I Can Help' and 'Flogging a Dead Horse,' it expressed a new sensibility, a way of looking at the world which was closer to Lee Friedlander than to Gary Winogrand. Making something monumental out of everyday life, Reas paid tribute to ordinary people by making them extraordinary.

1 Exhibition Guide: 'Day Dreaming About the Good Times'. Impressions Gallery. c 2013.

2 Paul Reas in conversation with Val Williams, Oral History of British Photography British Library National Sound Archive c.1993.

3 Ibid.

4 Williams, Val. Afterword. 'Flogging a Dead Horse.' Cornerhouse Publications. 1998.

5 Paul Reas Gallery talk, Impressions, Bradford 2014.

6 Ibid.

Buoyed by her defeat of the miners, victory in the Falklands War of 1982 and the survival of an assassination attempt in 1984, Margaret Thatcher increasingly saw herself as invincible and on the right side of history. Her neoliberal policies, faith in a free market economy and a firm belief in individualism turned British culture from a 'we' to a 'me' generation. The deregulation of the banking system meant that credit was easy to come by and consumer spending was rising fast. This growth in consumption was becoming more and more evident in Britain in the mid-1980s. The then new shopping malls, situated on the edges of cities, were the new cathedrals of consumption, and the new 'retail parks,' with their supermarkets and furniture stores, were the parish churches. Shopping and the purchasing of an off-the-shelf lifestyle were becoming new leisure activities.

In addition, 'Thatcherism' also encouraged home ownership. Fundamental to her idea was that government, which had built between a third and half of all homes for the previous three decades, should step back. Councils could no longer build council housing. The market would provide. Houses would be built by housebuilders. As a result, new large private housing estates, aimed at newly aspirational individuals, were rapidly becoming a feature of most towns and cities.

It was this consumer culture which became the subject for my first book, *I Can Help*, published by Cornerhouse Publications in 1988. This would also be my first work in colour. I had been aware of the important colour work of British photographers Paul Graham, Martin Parr, Charlie Meecham, Peter Mitchell and others, but it was whilst at a talk at Chapter Arts Centre in Cardiff by Sally Eauclaire, author of *The New Color Photography* (1981), that I started to appreciate the real possibilities of colour. It was at this talk where I saw the work of Stephen Shore, William Eggleston and Joel Sternfeld for the first time.

1986–88

I Can Help

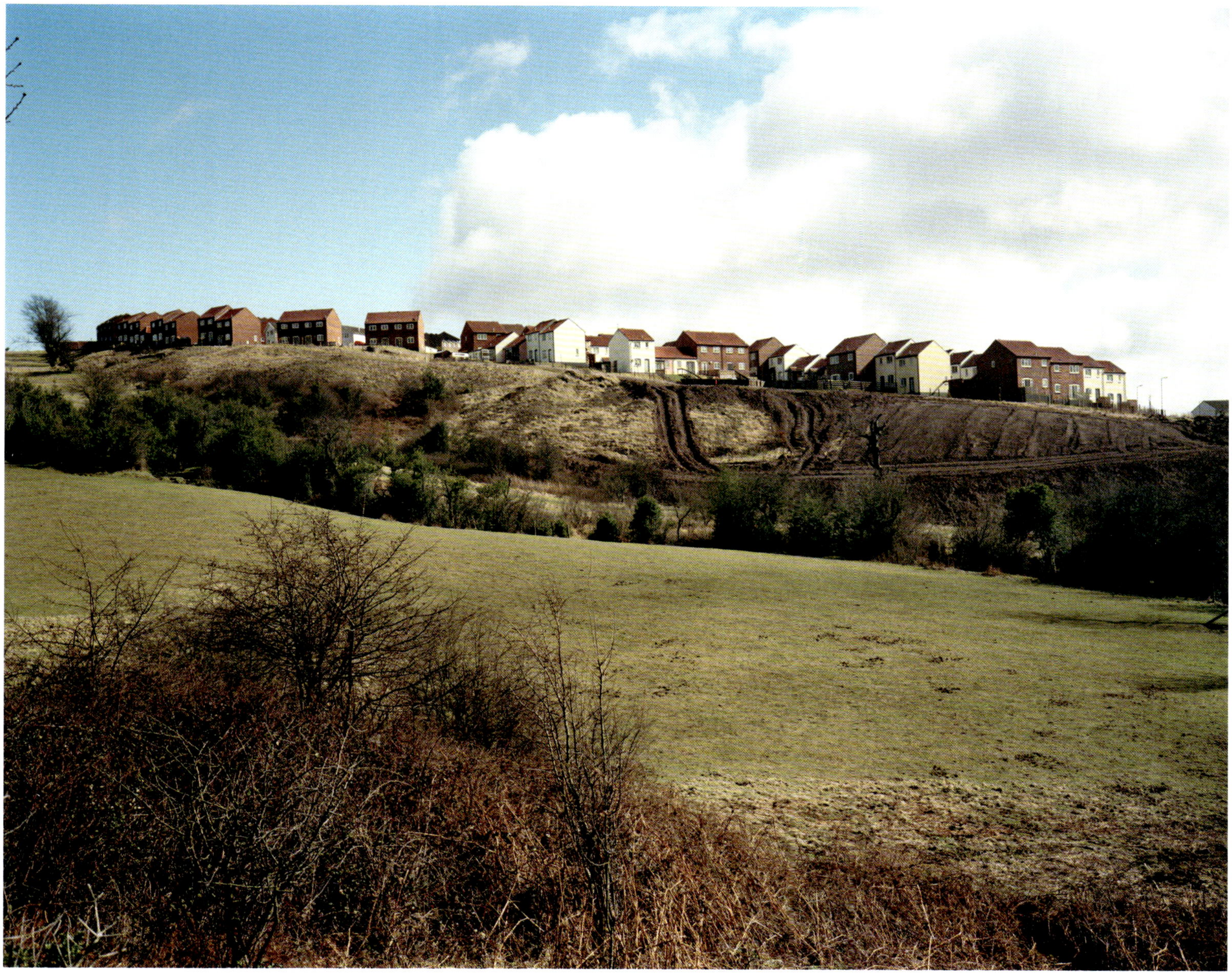

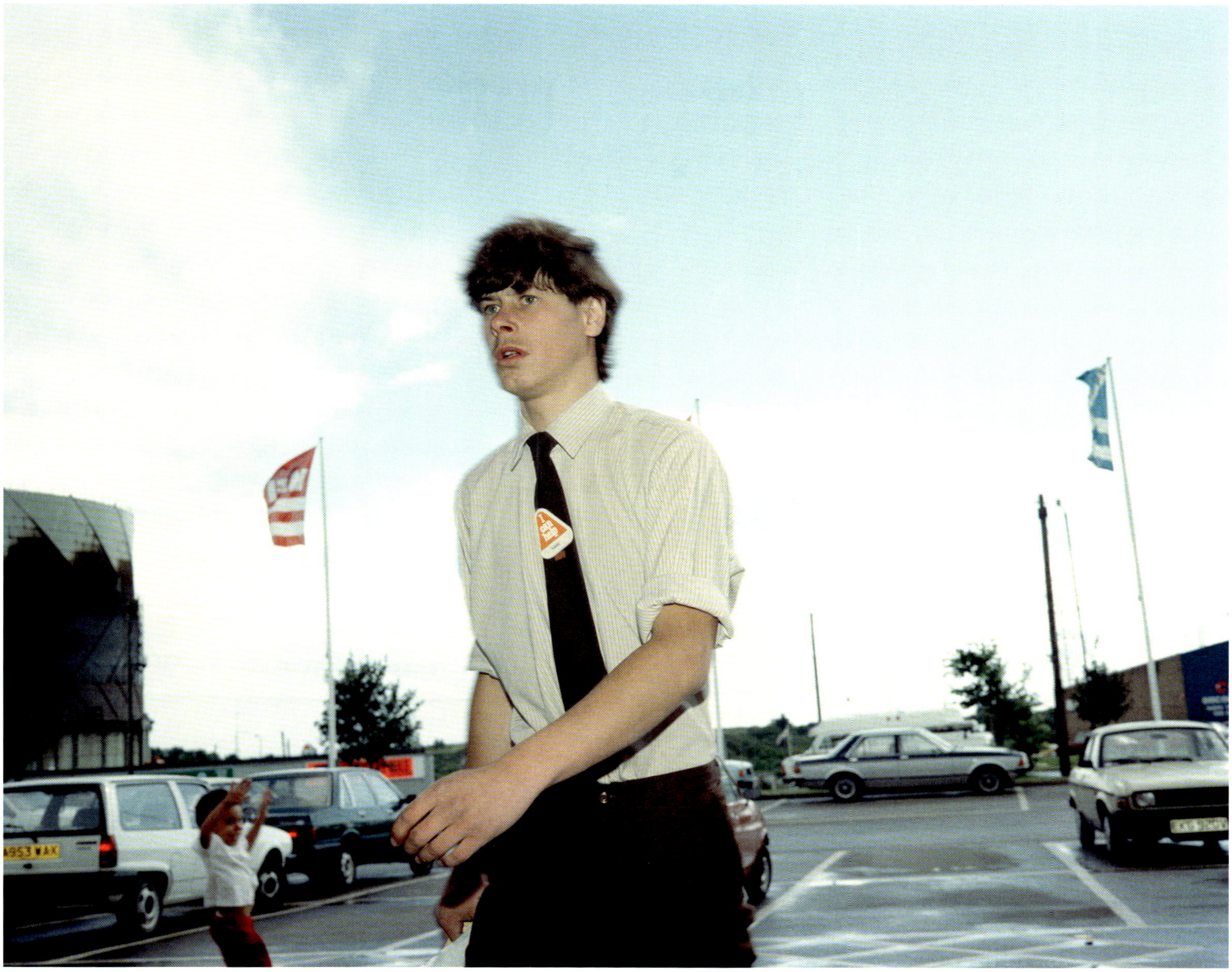
A953 WAK

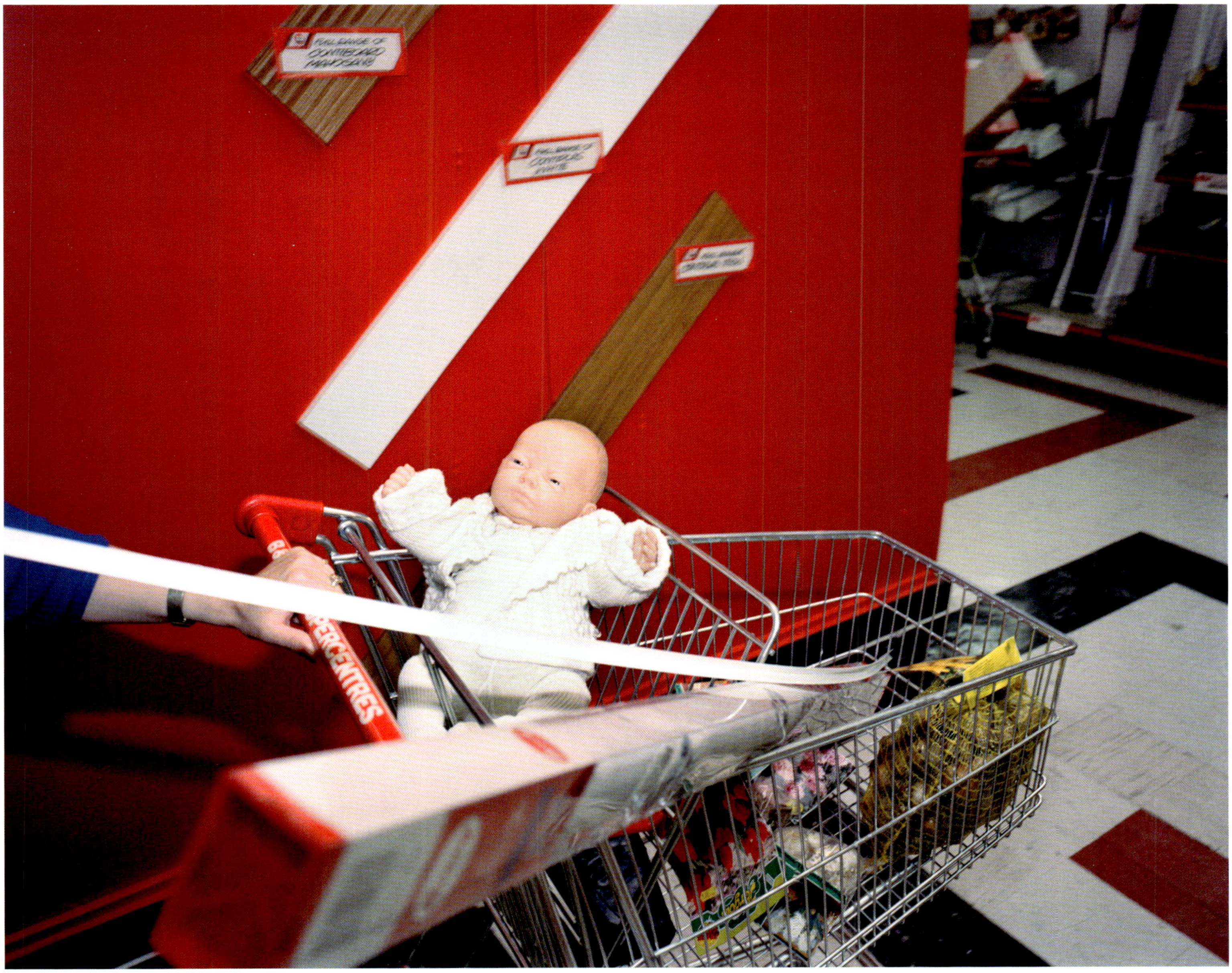

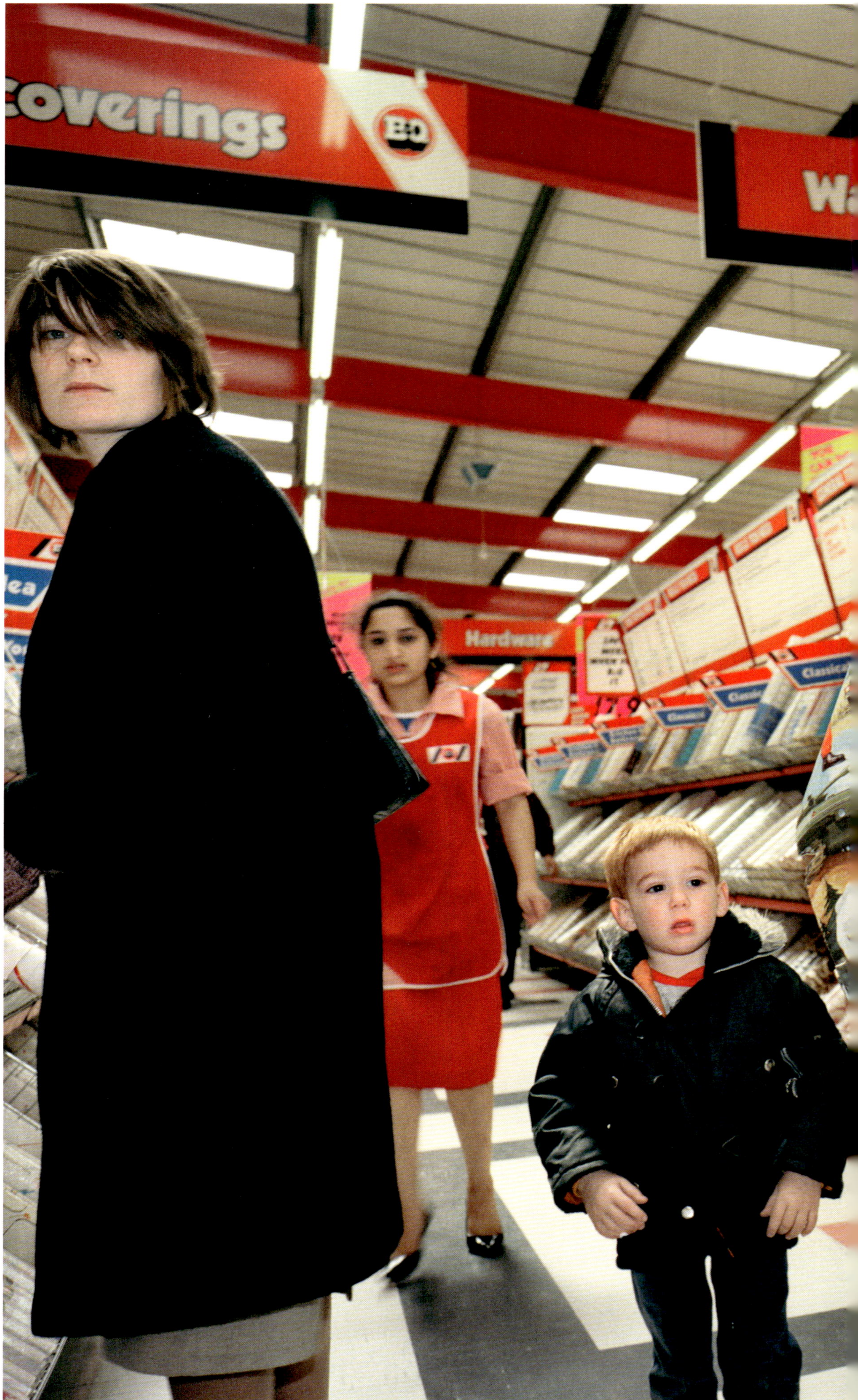
coverings
Hardware
Classics

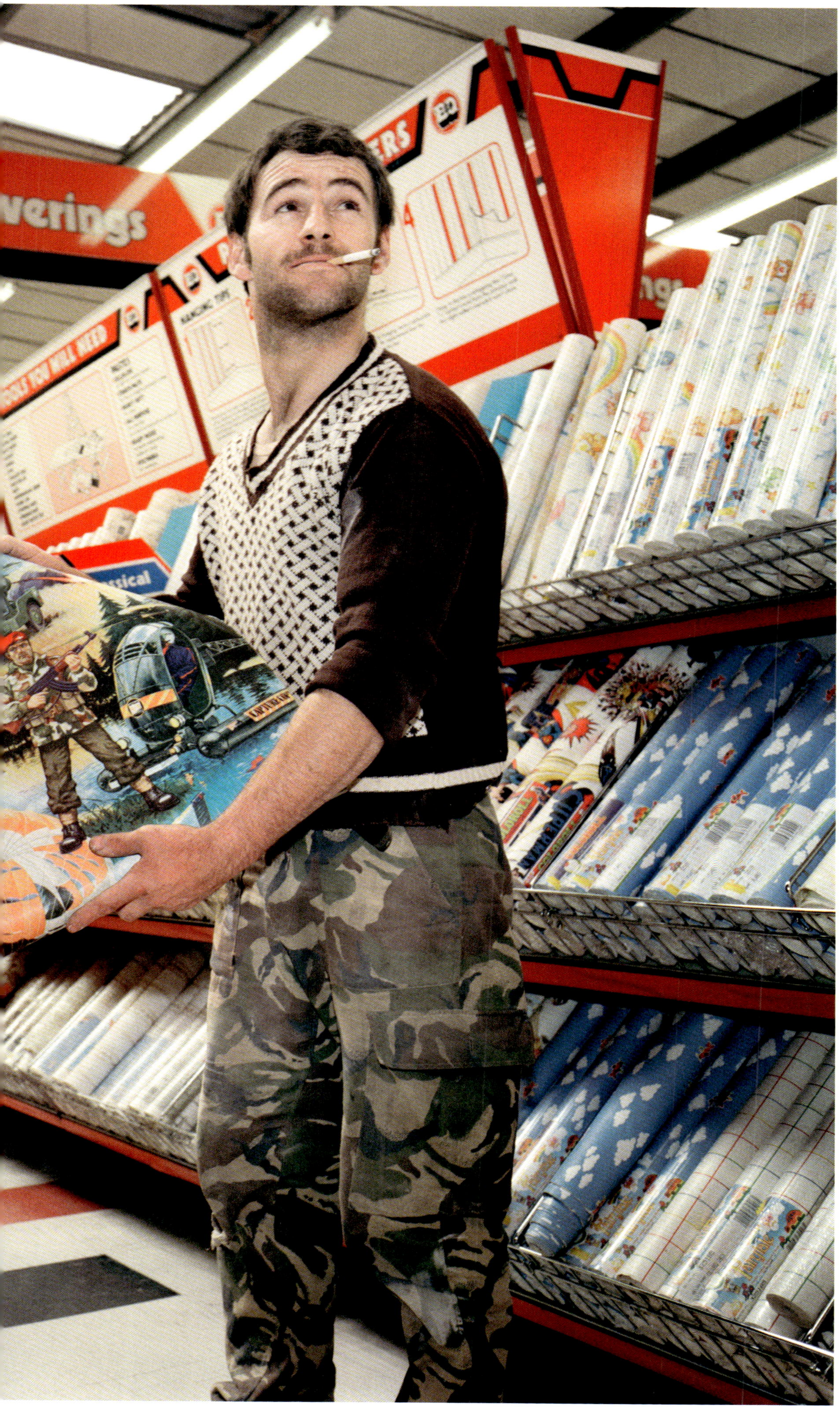

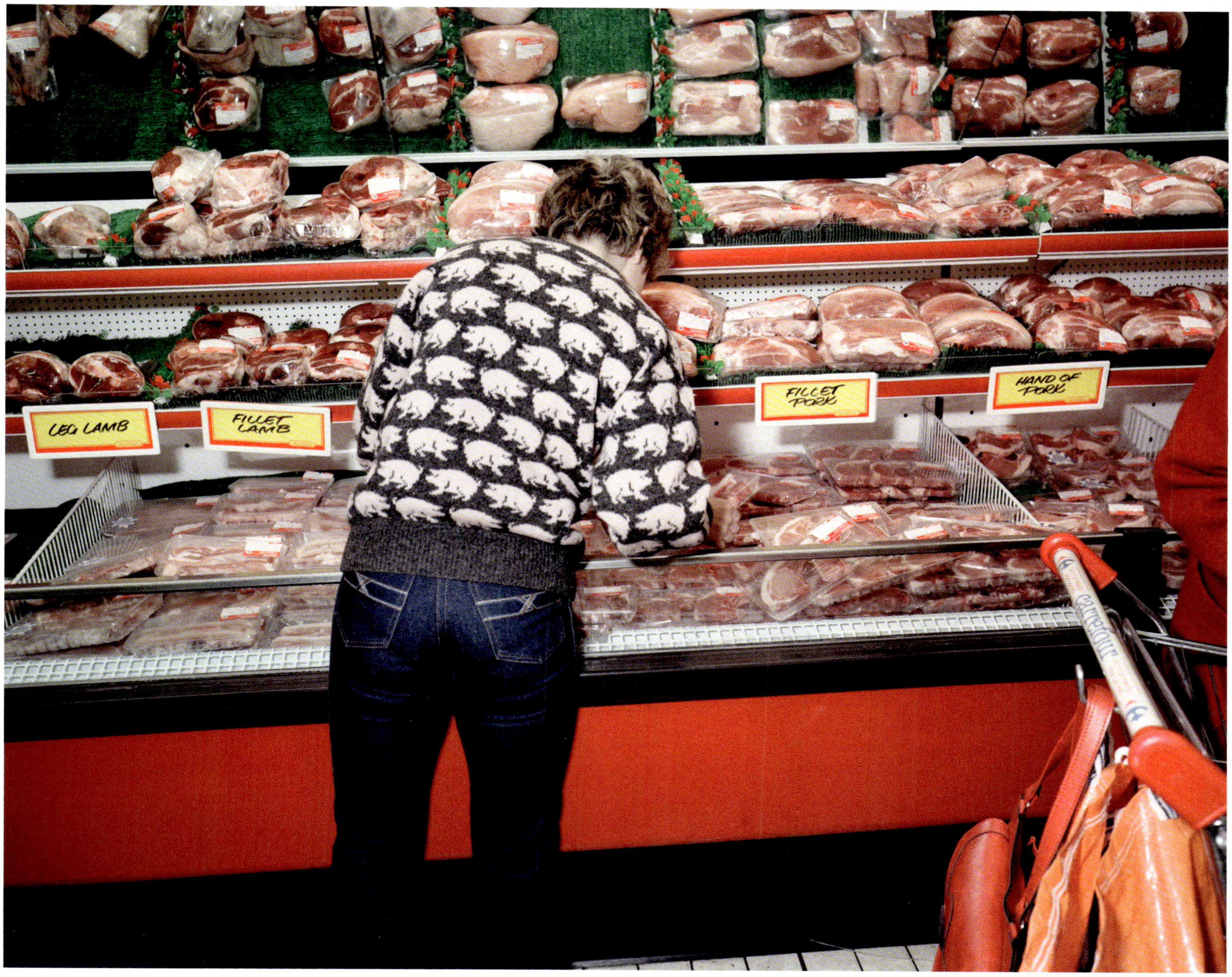
LEG LAMB
FILLET LAMB
FILLET PORK
HAND OF PORK

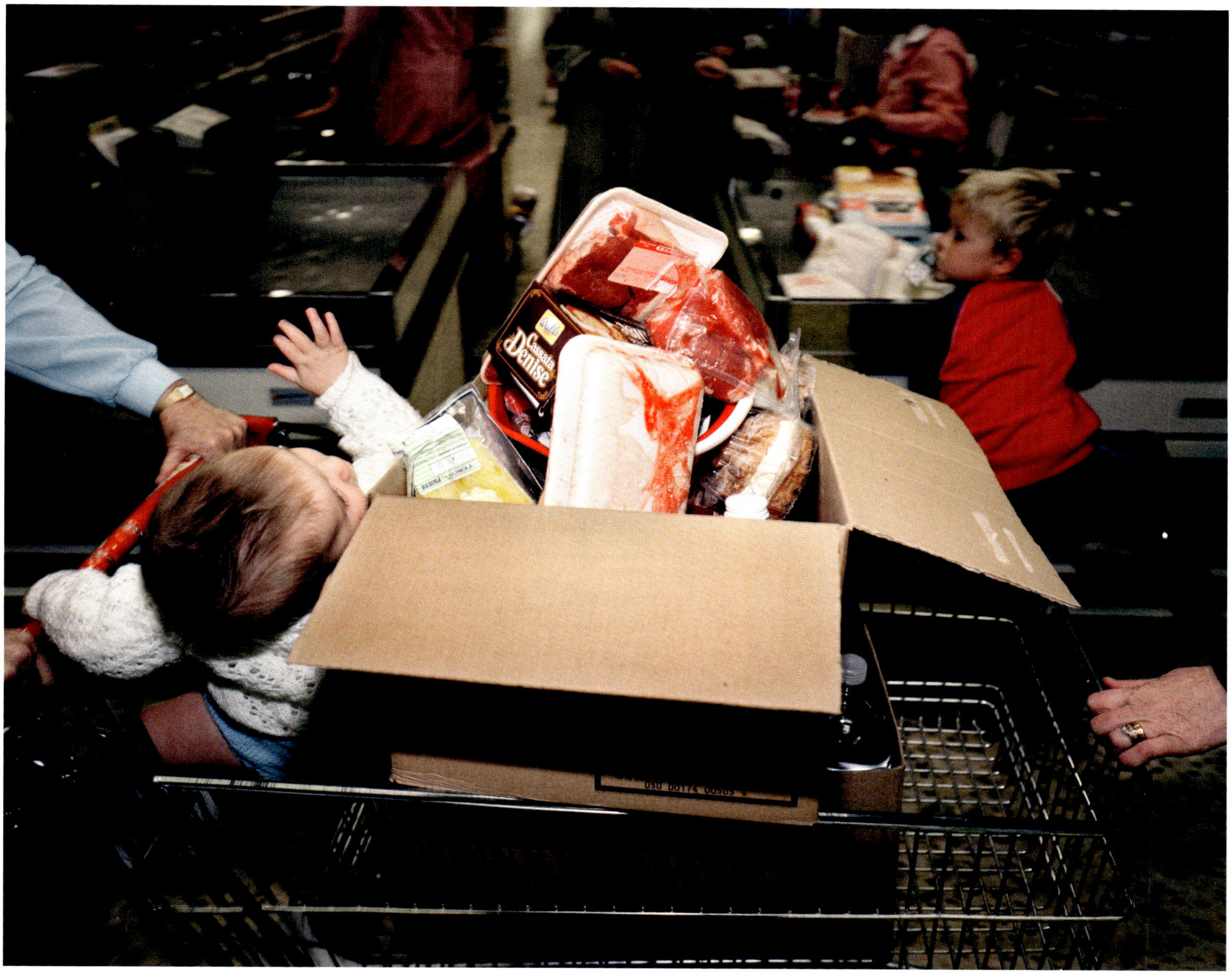
Cassata
Denise

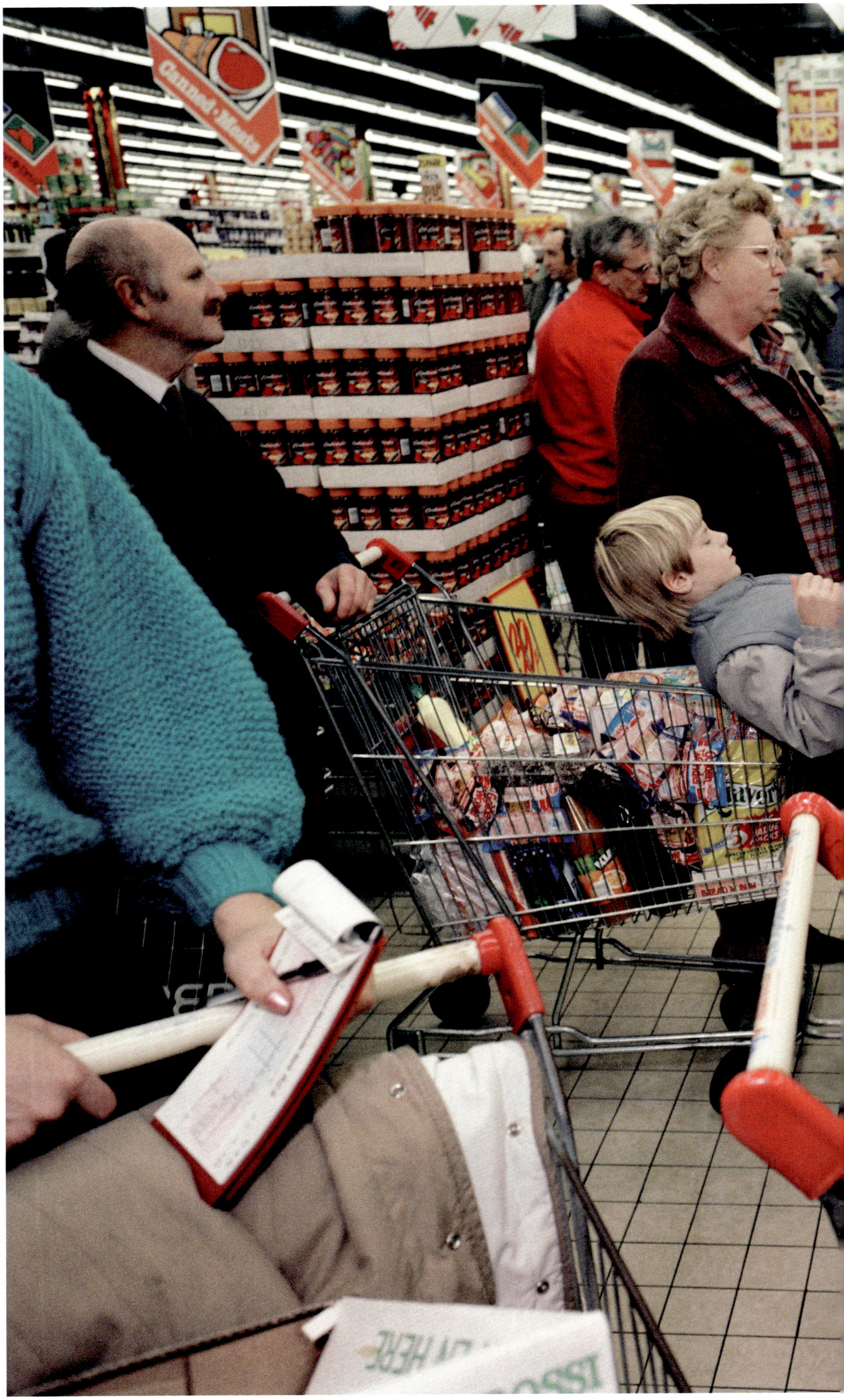

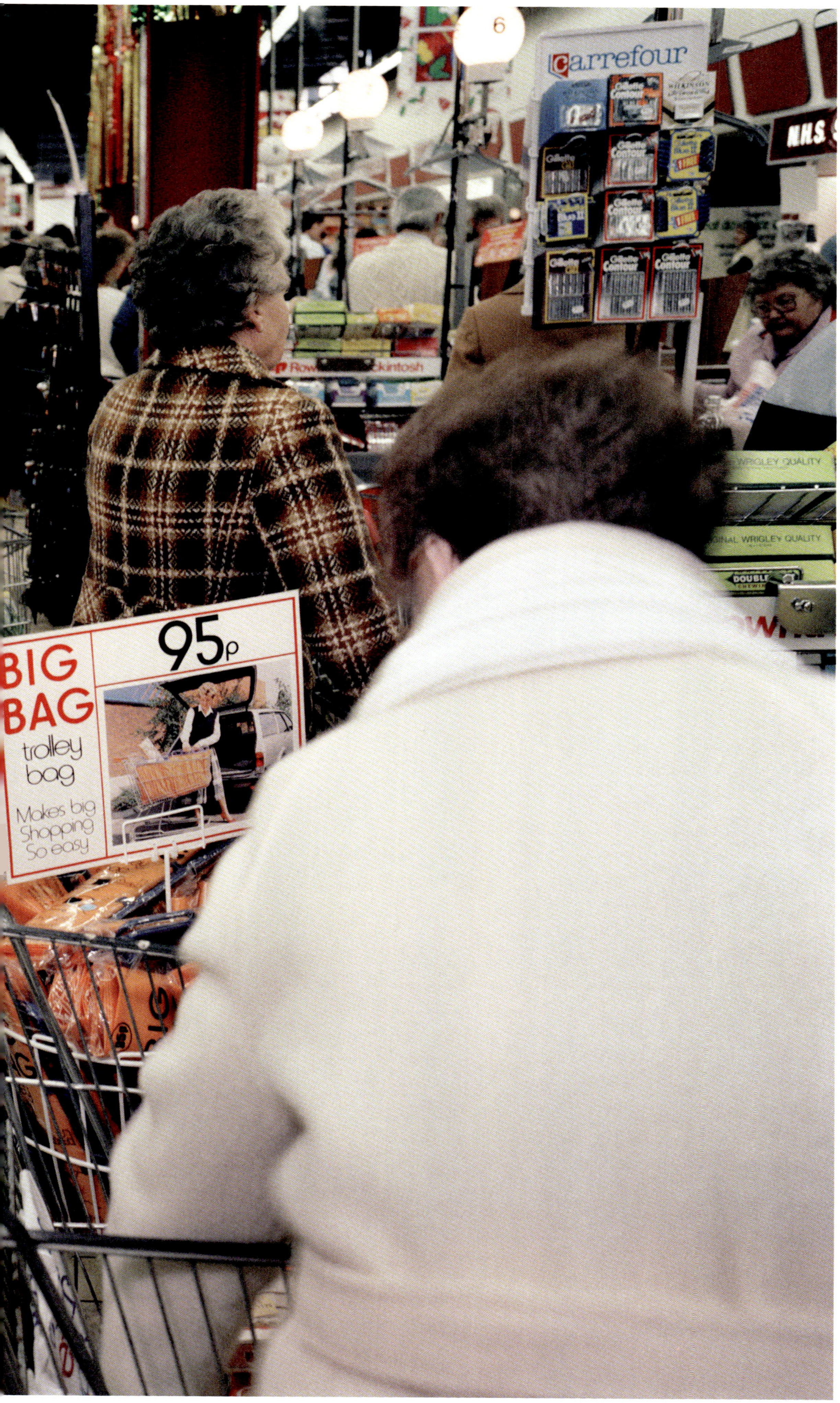
Carrefour
Gillette Contour
95p
BIG BAG
trolley bag
Makes big Shopping So easy
WRIGLEY QUALITY

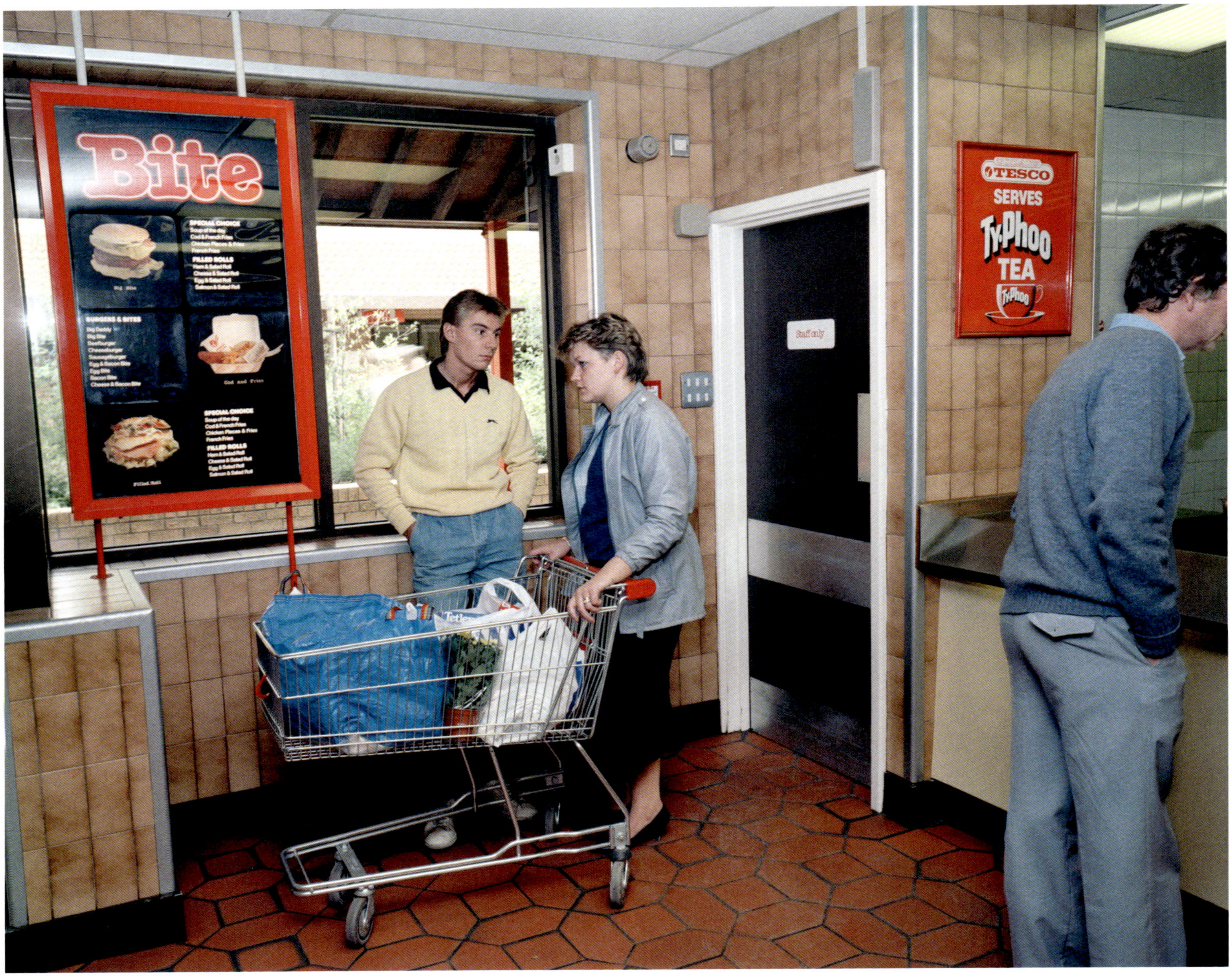
Bite
TESCO
SERVES
Ty·Phoo
TEA

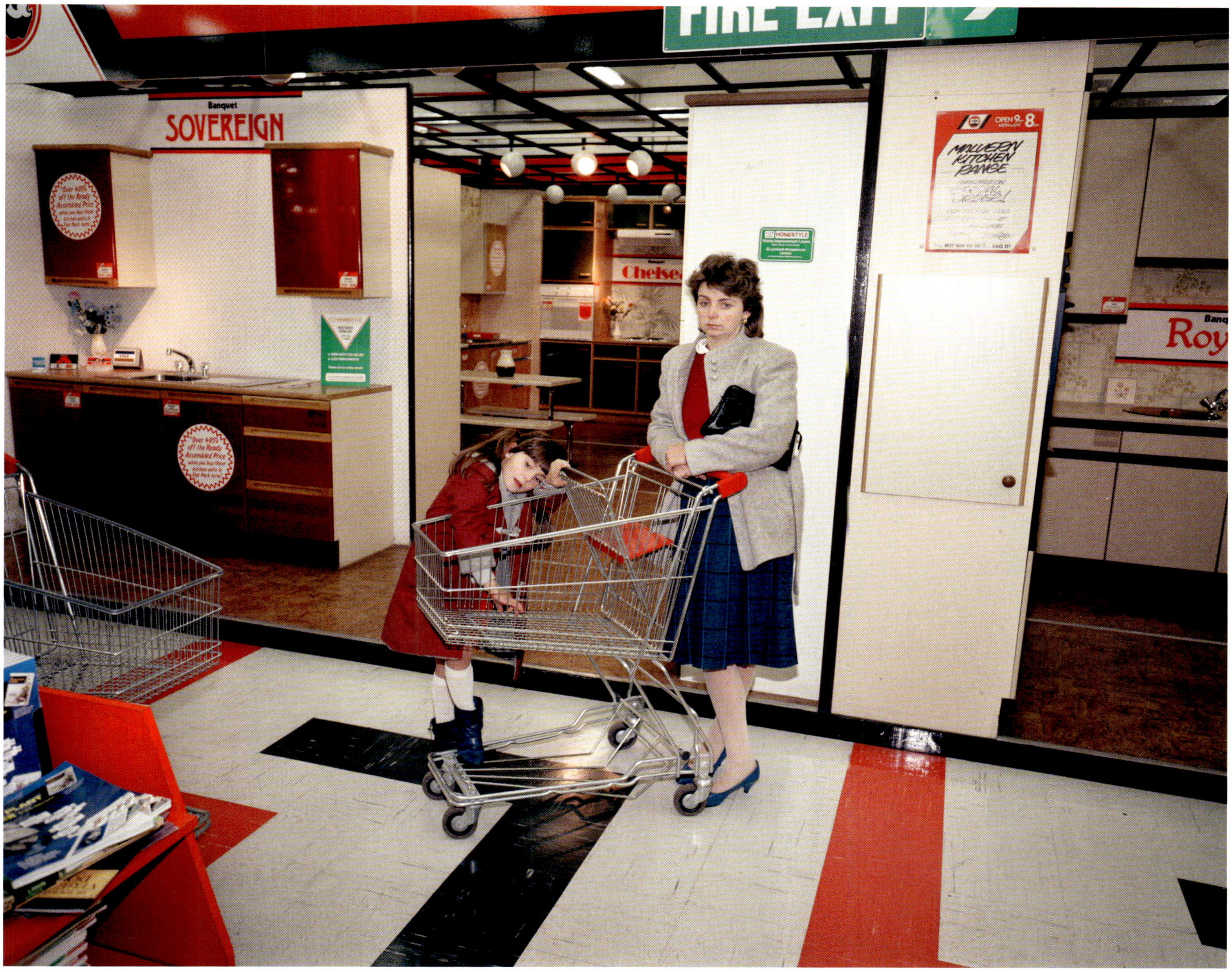
FIRE EXIT
Banquet
SOVEREIGN
HOMESTYLE
MALVERN KITCHEN RANGE

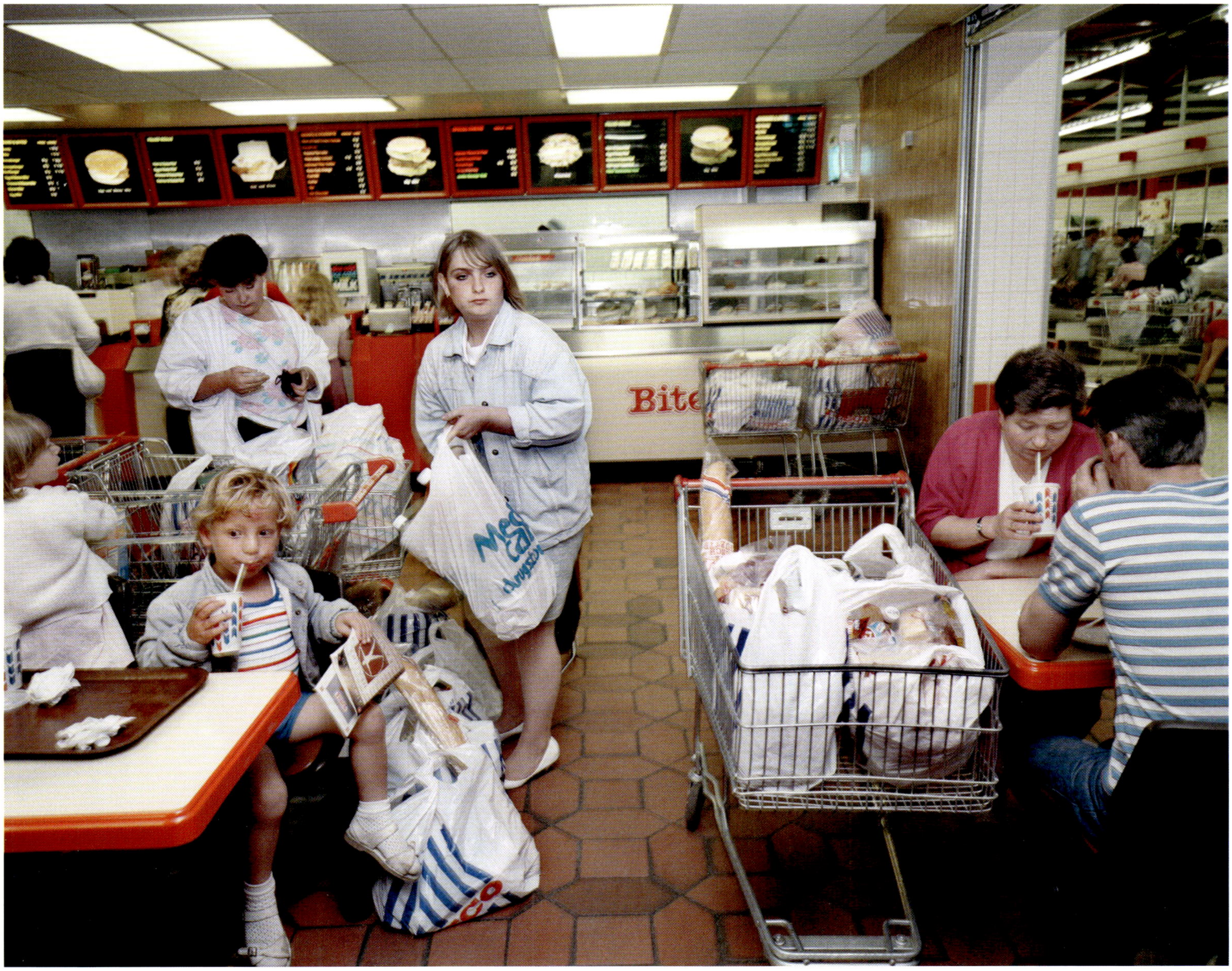
Bite

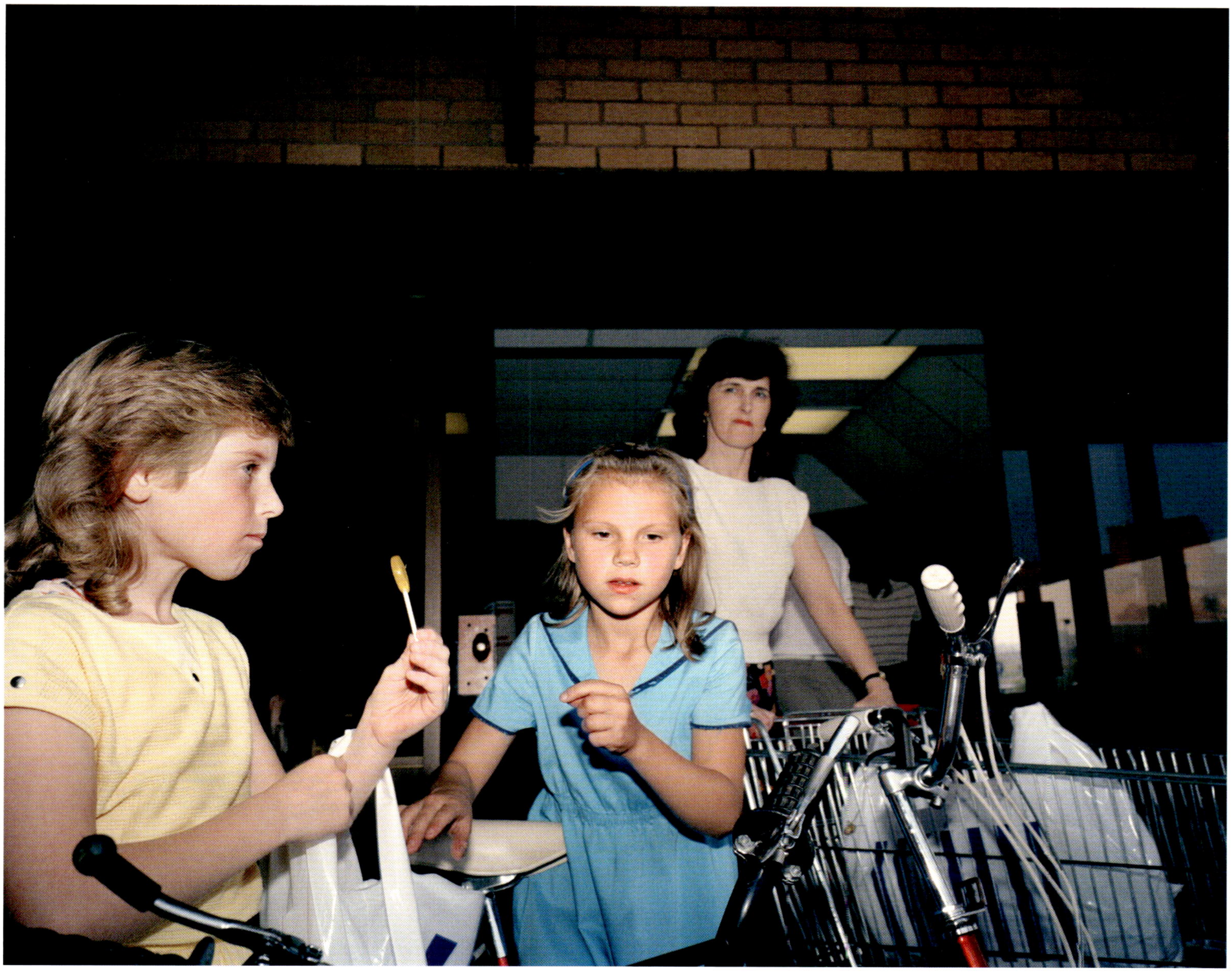

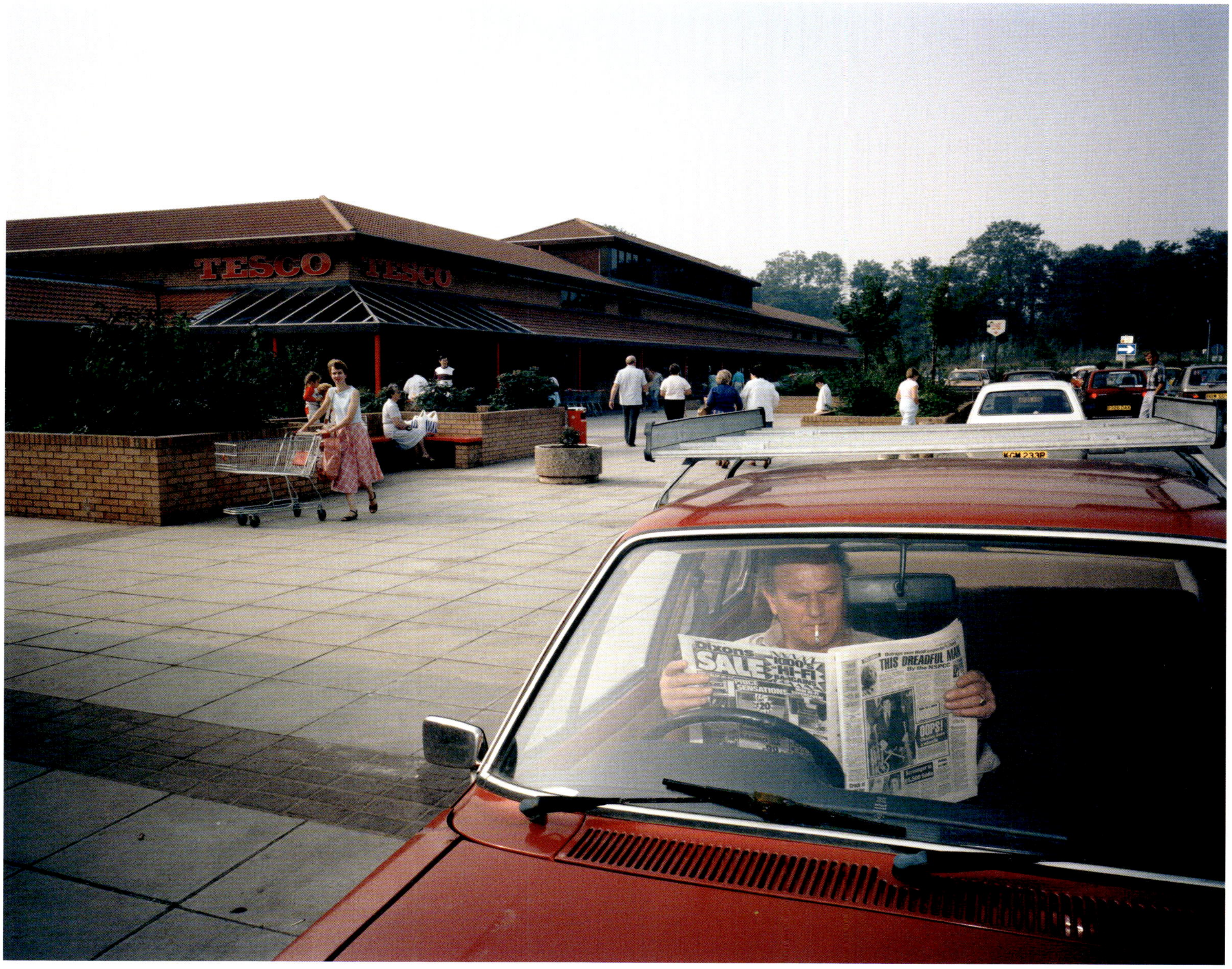
TESCO
TESCO
Dixons
SALE
THIS DREADFUL MAN

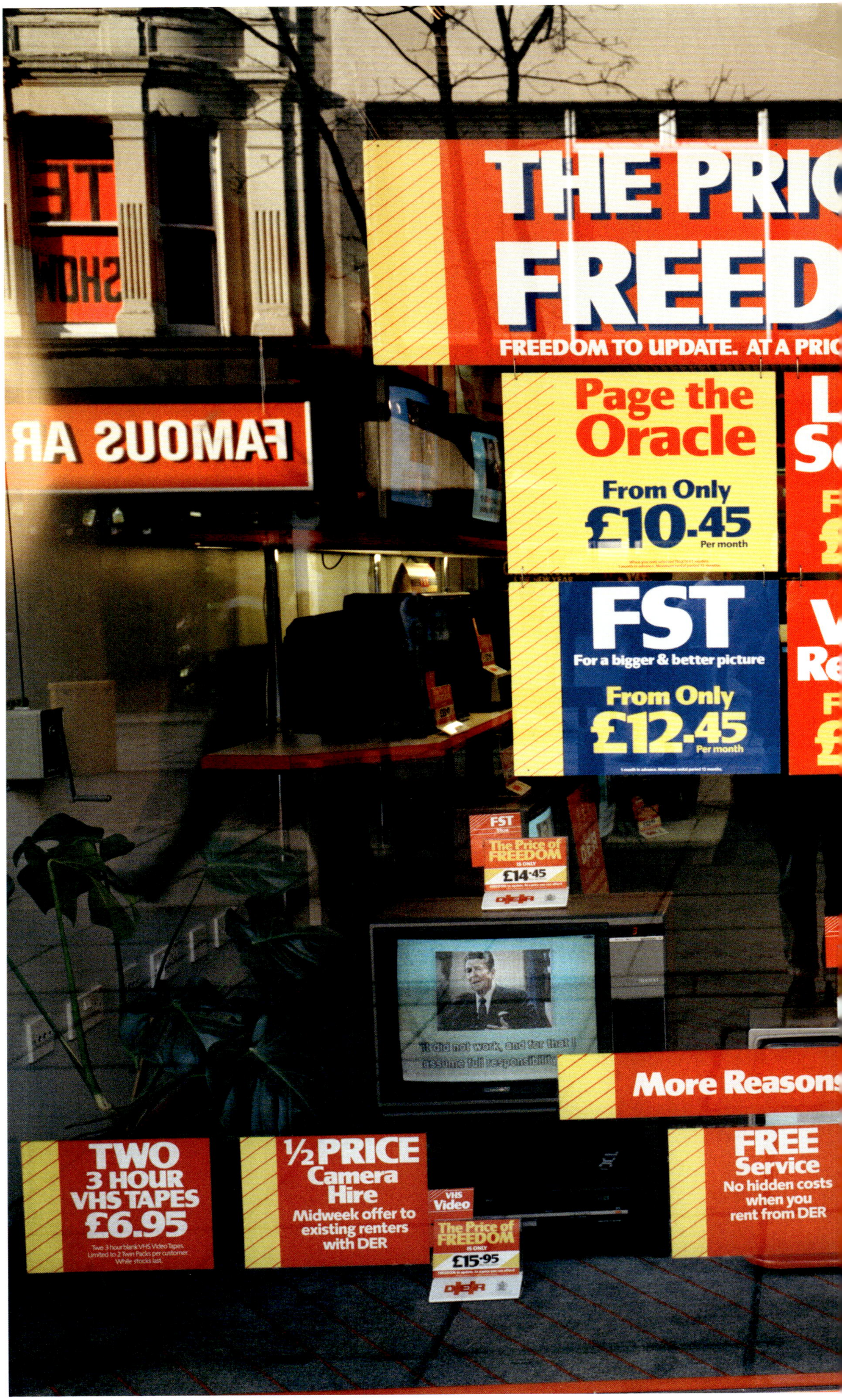
THE PRIC
FREED
FREEDOM TO UPDATE. AT A PRIC
Page the Oracle
From Only
£10.45
Per month
FST
For a bigger & better picture
From Only
£12.45
Per month
FST
The Price of FREEDOM
IS ONLY
£14.45
DER
'it did not work, and for that I
assume full responsibility
More Reasons
TWO 3 HOUR VHS TAPES £6.95
Two 3 hour blank VHS Video Tapes.
Limited to 2 Twin Packs per customer.
While stocks last.
½ PRICE
Camera Hire
Midweek offer to existing renters with DER
VHS Video
The Price of FREEDOM
IS ONLY
£15.95
DER
FREE Service
No hidden costs when you rent from DER

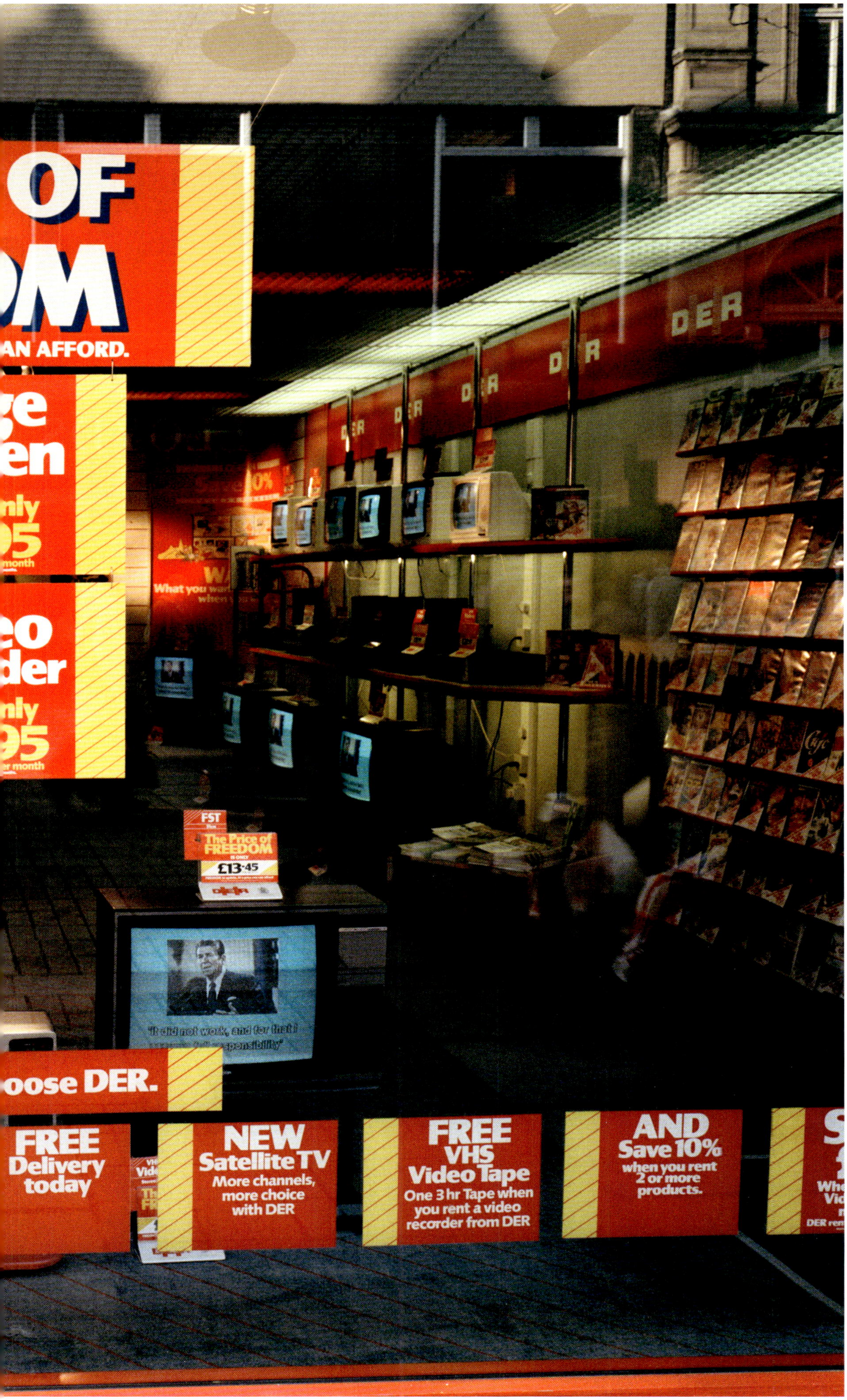
OF
AN AFFORD.
DER
The Price of FREEDOM
£13·45
oose DER.
FREE Delivery today
NEW Satellite TV
More channels, more choice with DER
FREE VHS Video Tape
One 3 hr Tape when you rent a video recorder from DER
AND Save 10%
when you rent 2 or more products.

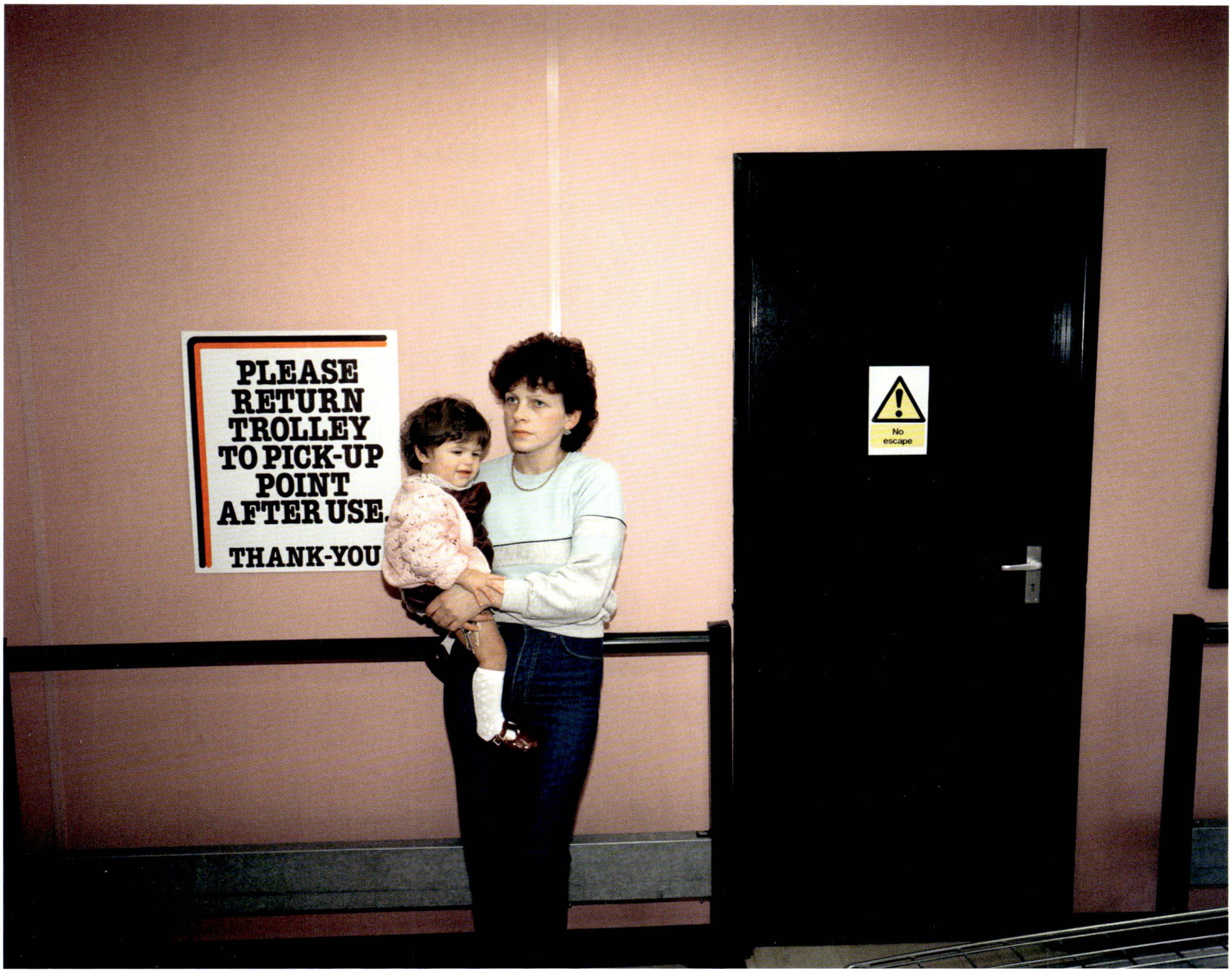
PLEASE
RETURN
TROLLEY
TO PICK-UP
POINT
AFTER USE.
THANK-YOU
No
escape

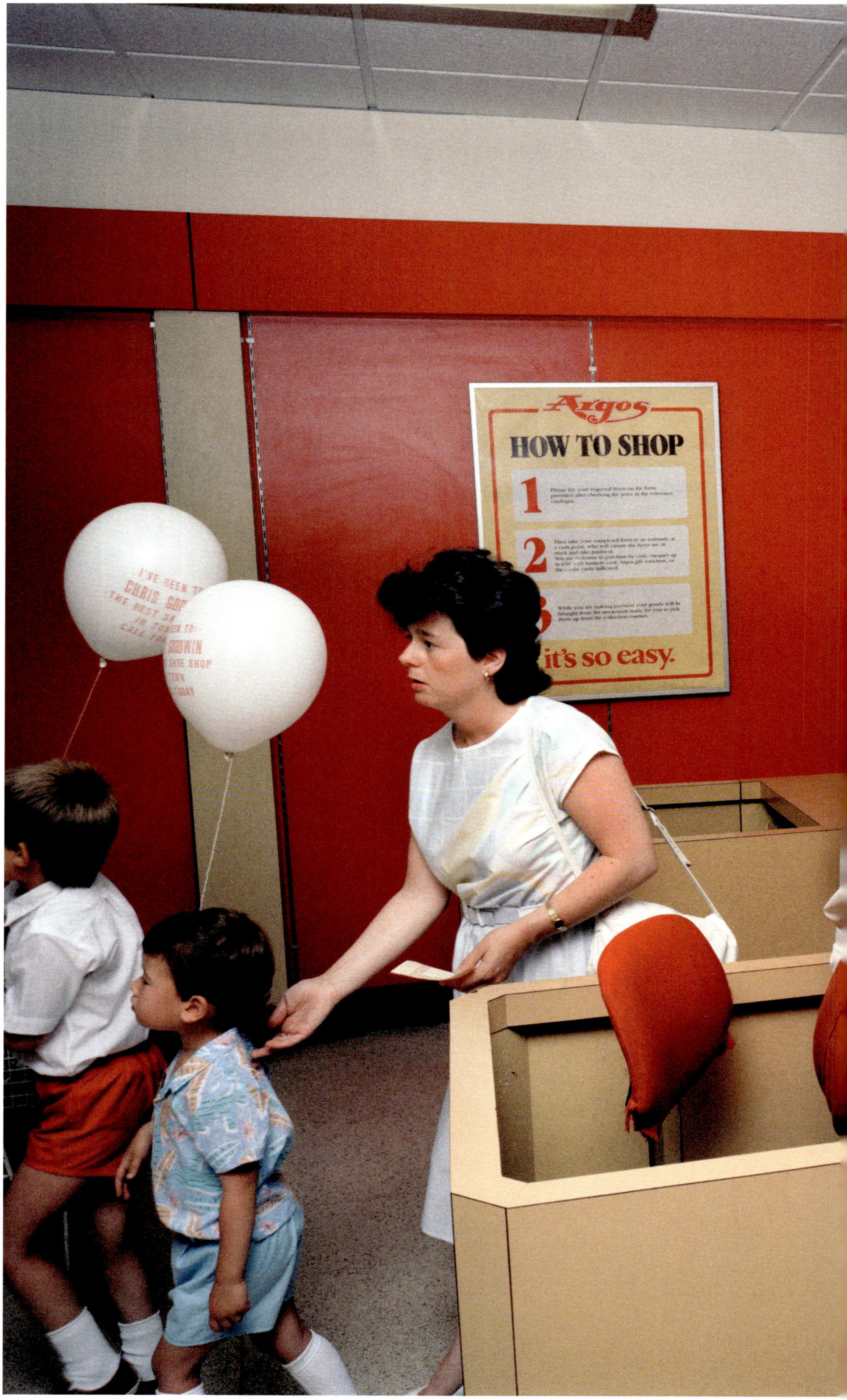
Argos
HOW TO SHOP
1
2
it's so easy.

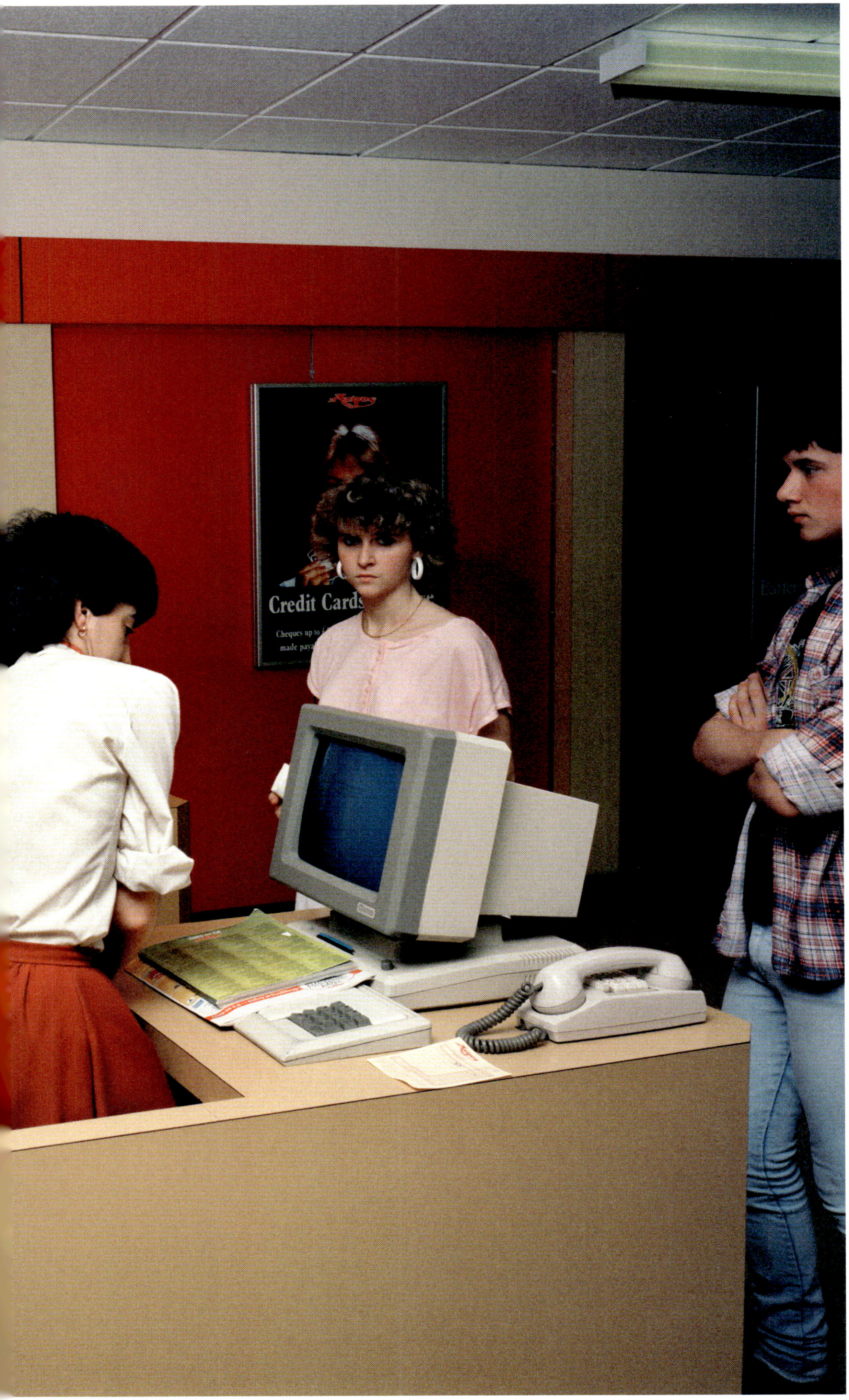
Credit Cards

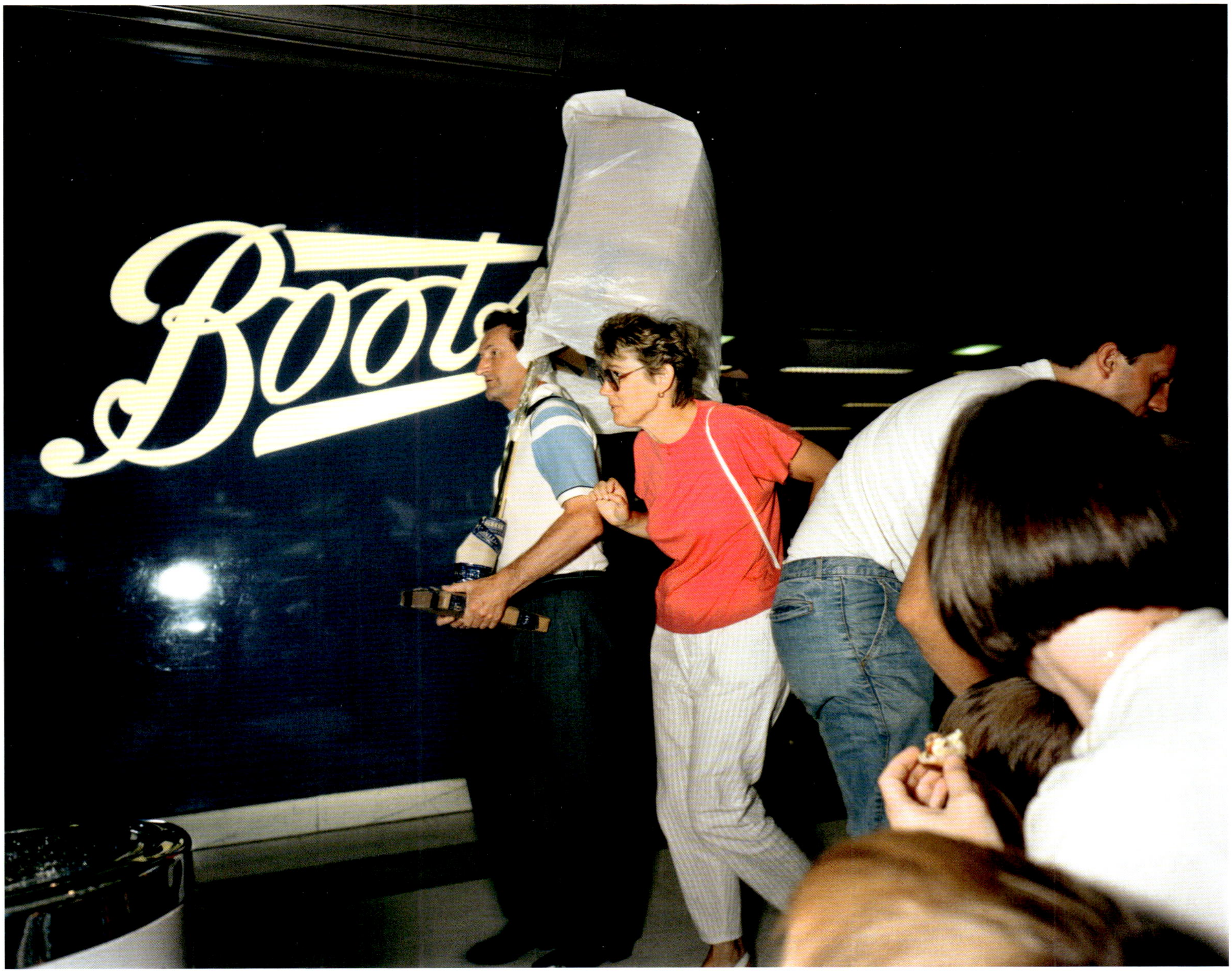

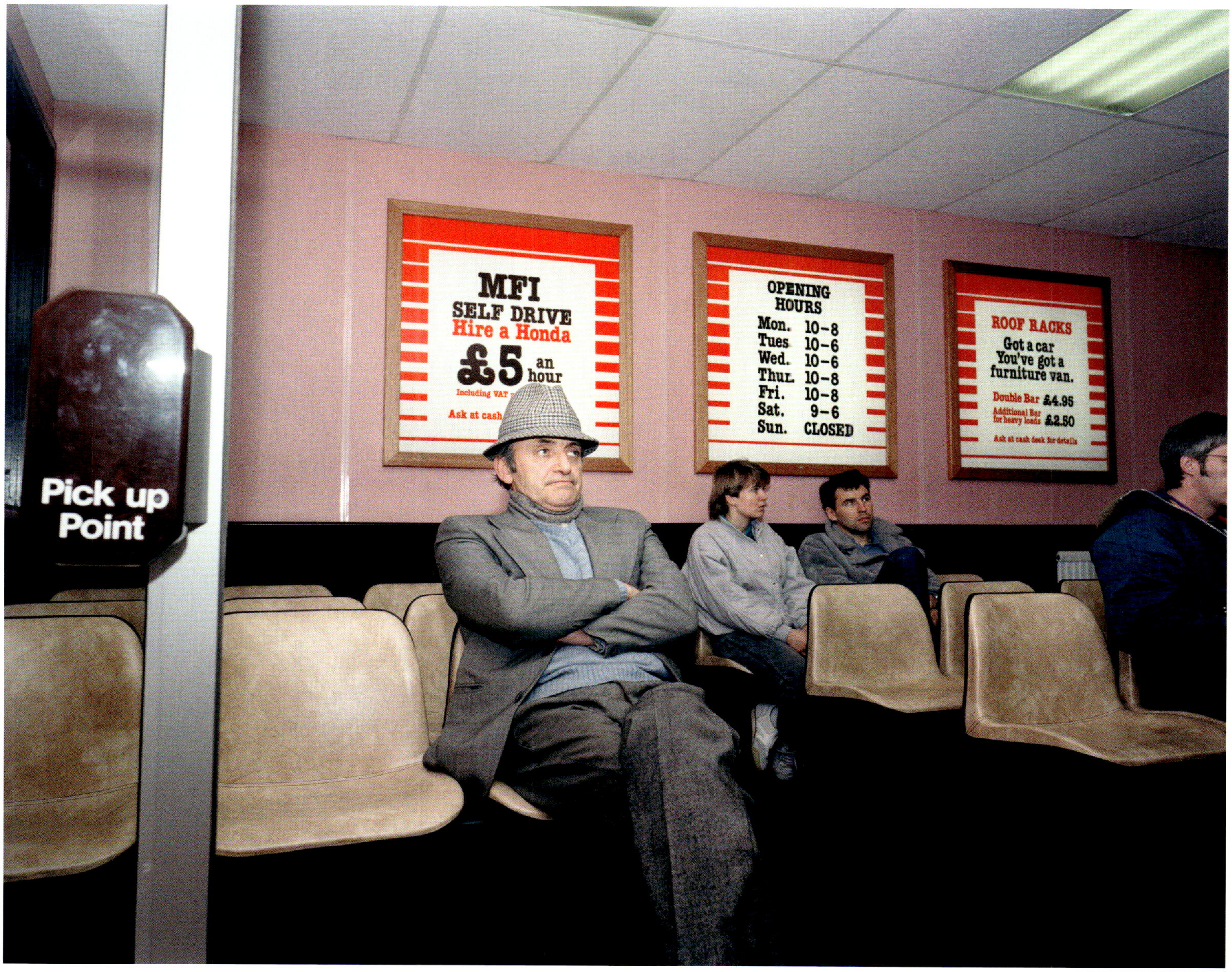
MFI
SELF DRIVE
Hire a Honda
£5 an hour
OPENING HOURS
Mon. 10–8
Tues. 10–6
Wed. 10–6
Thur. 10–8
Fri. 10–8
Sat. 9–6
Sun. CLOSED
ROOF RACKS
Got a car
You've got a
furniture van.
Double Bar £4.95
Additional Bar for heavy loads £2.50
Ask at cash desk for details
Pick up
Point

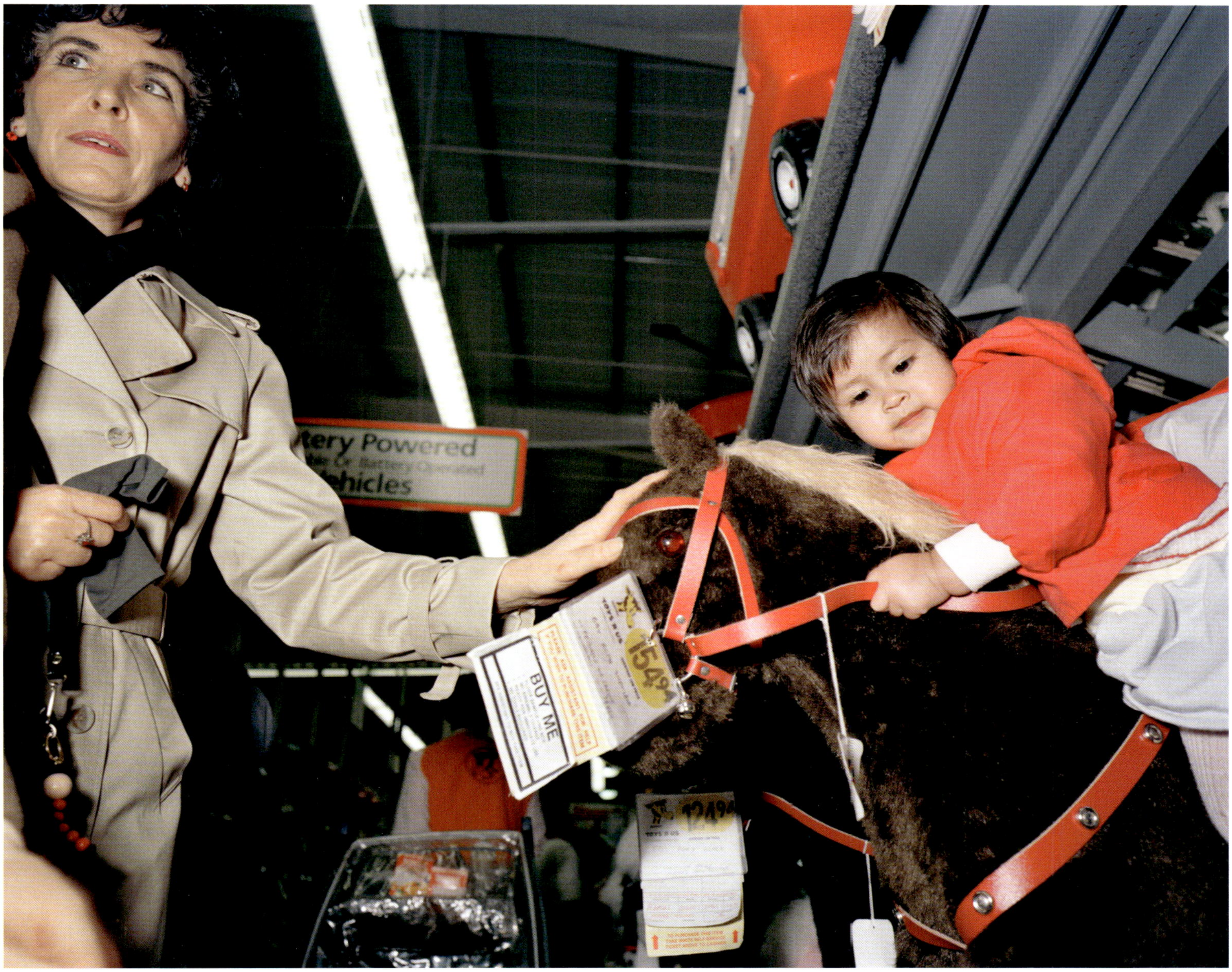
tery Powered
hicles
BUY ME

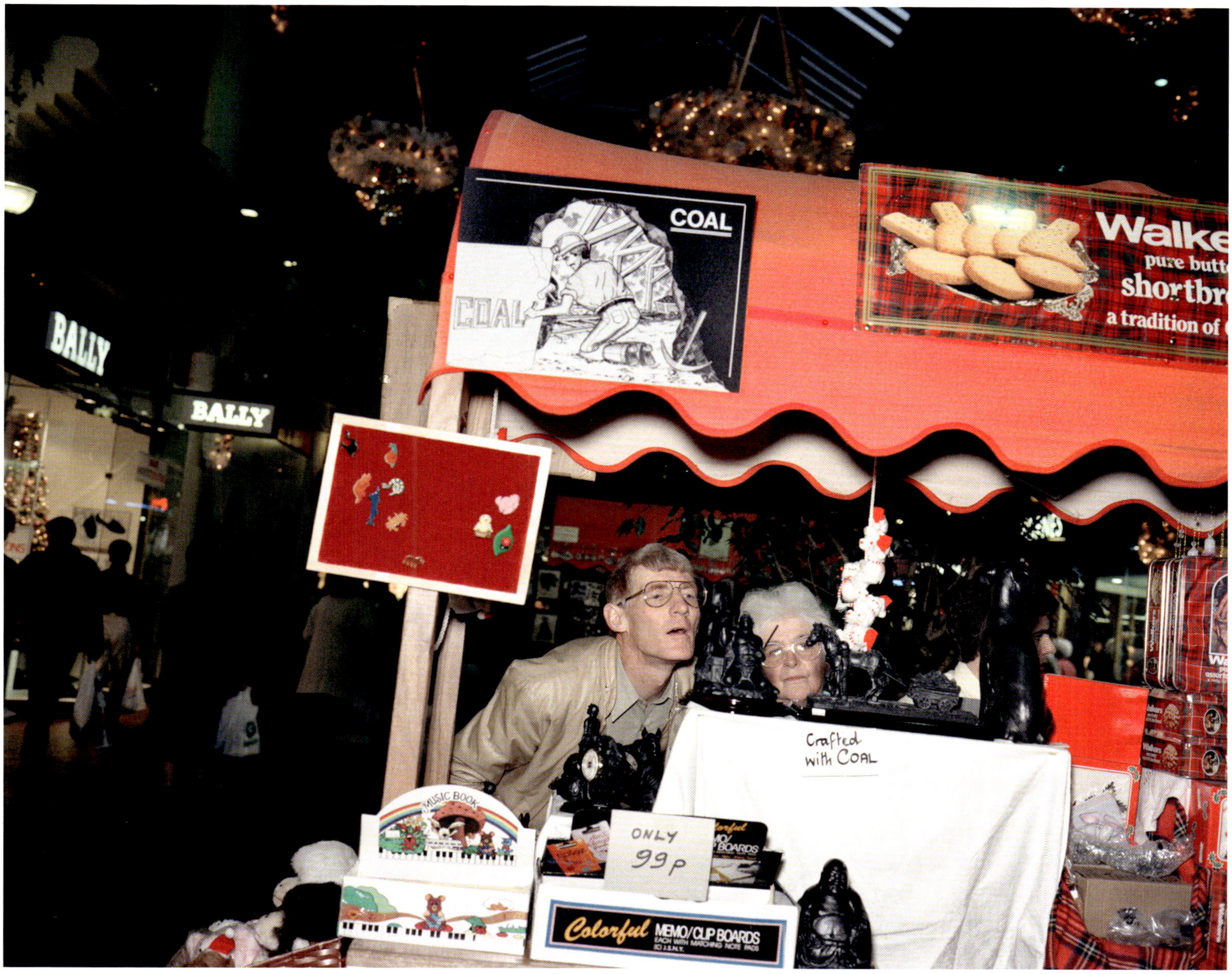
COAL
COAL
BALLY
BALLY
Crafted with COAL
ONLY 99p
MUSIC BOOK
Colorful MEMO/CLIP BOARDS

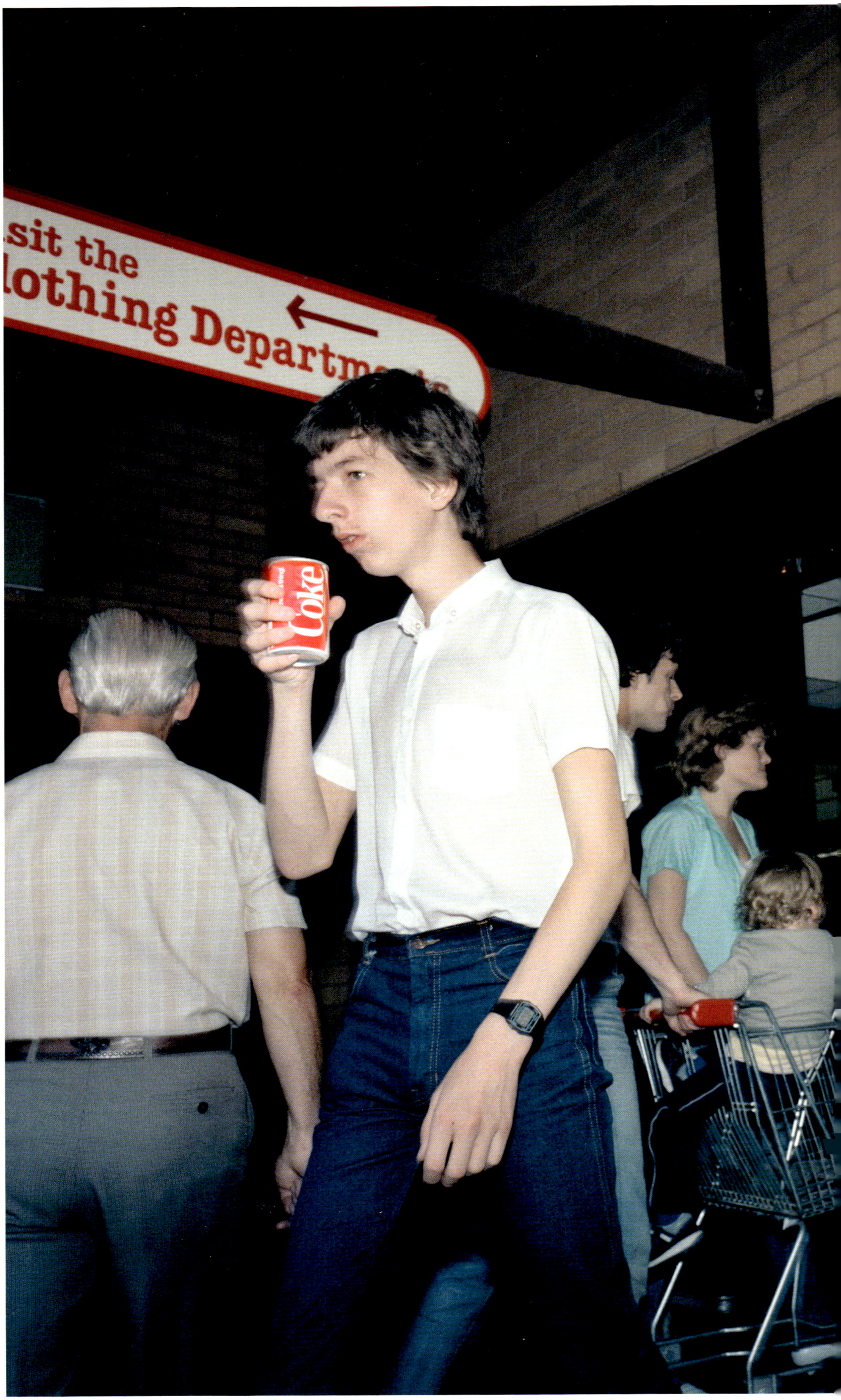
sit the
lothing Departm

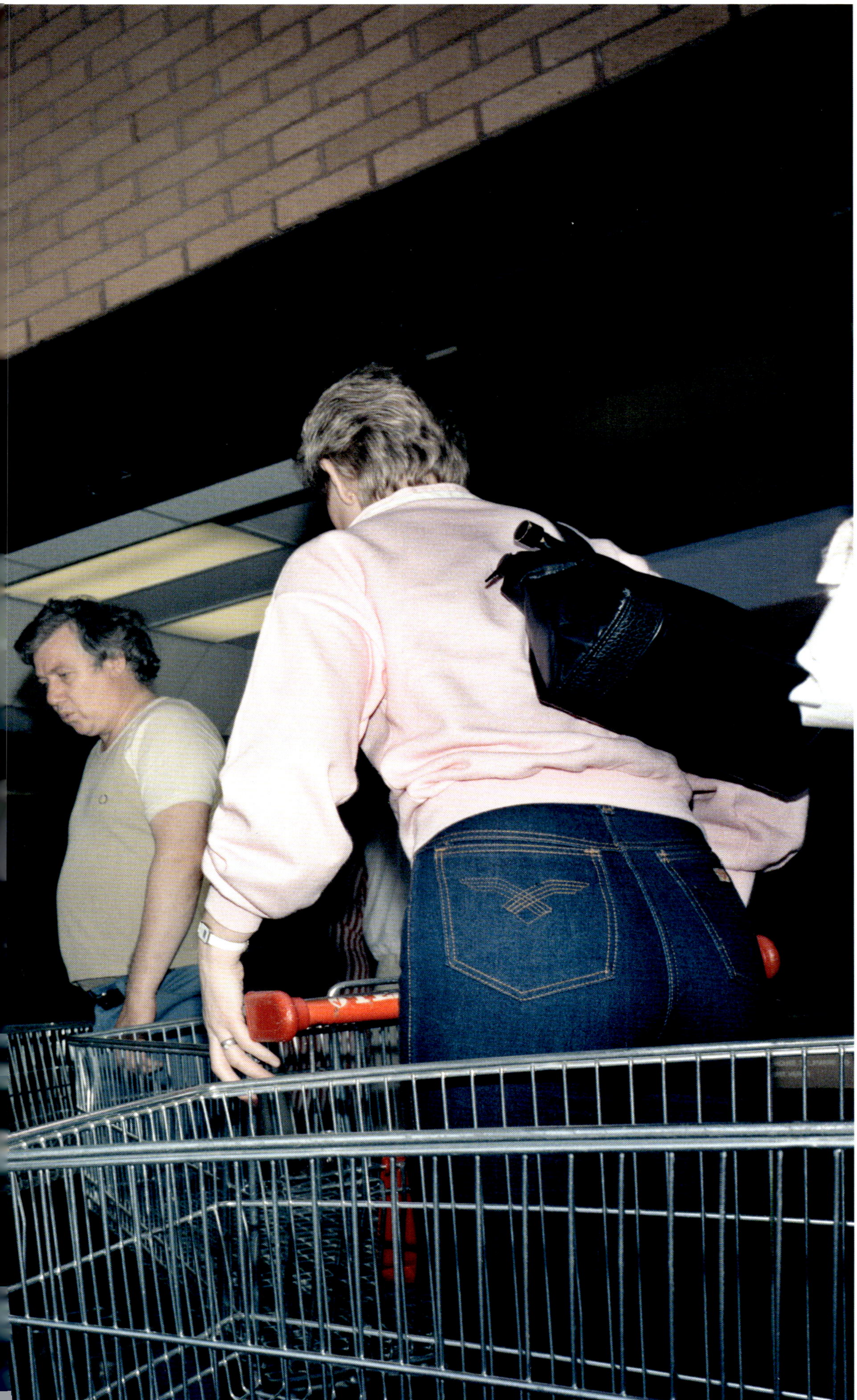

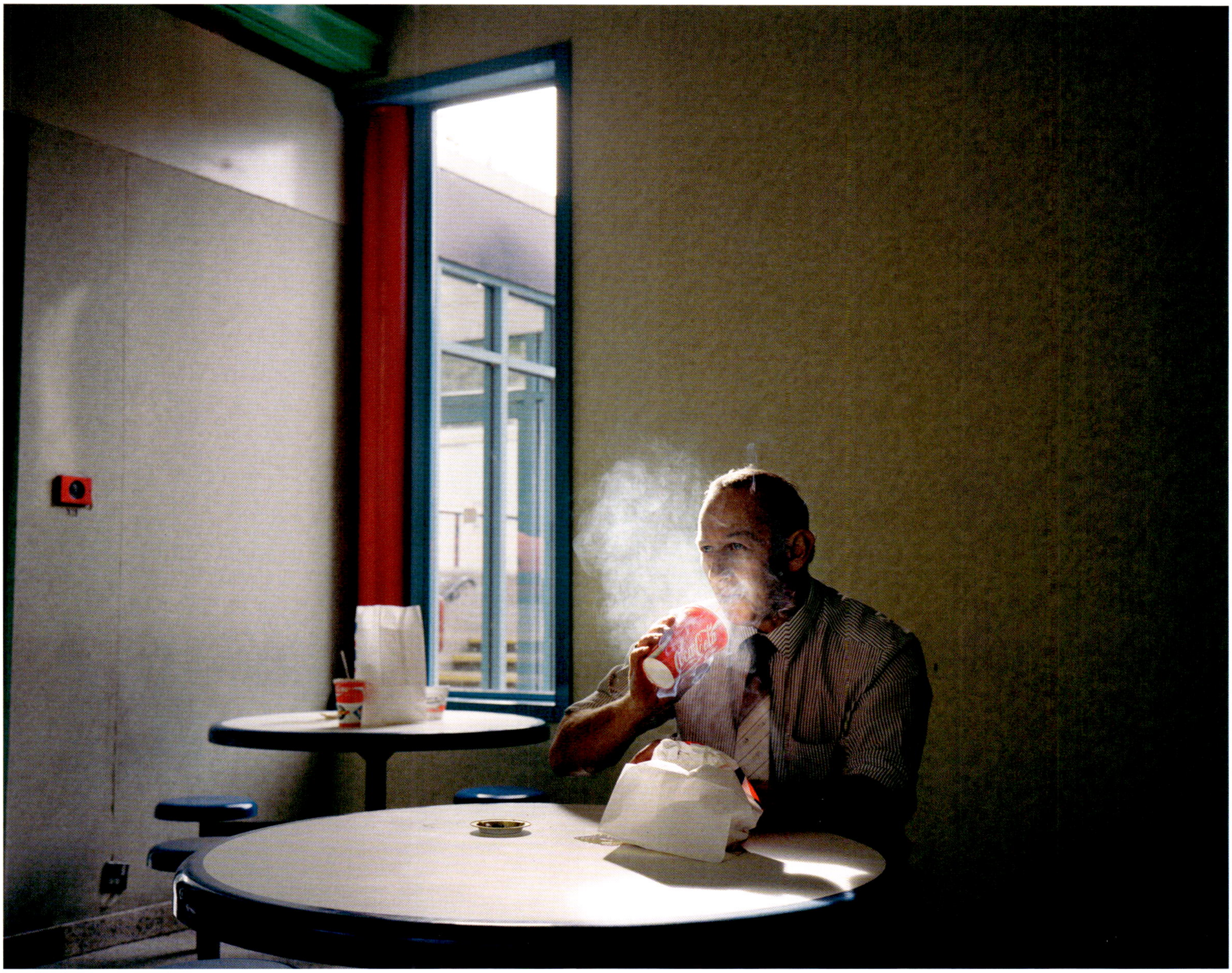
Coca-Cola

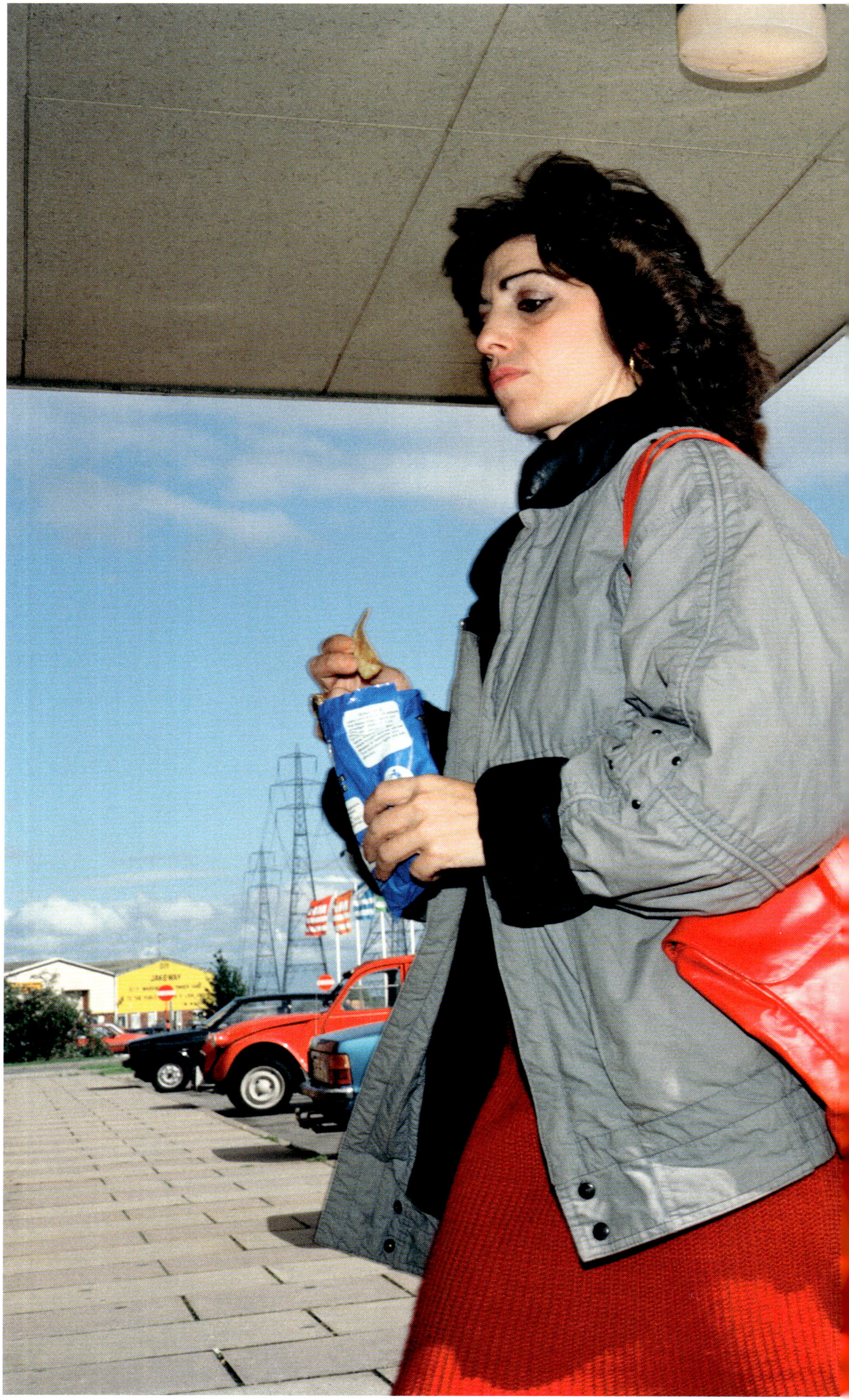

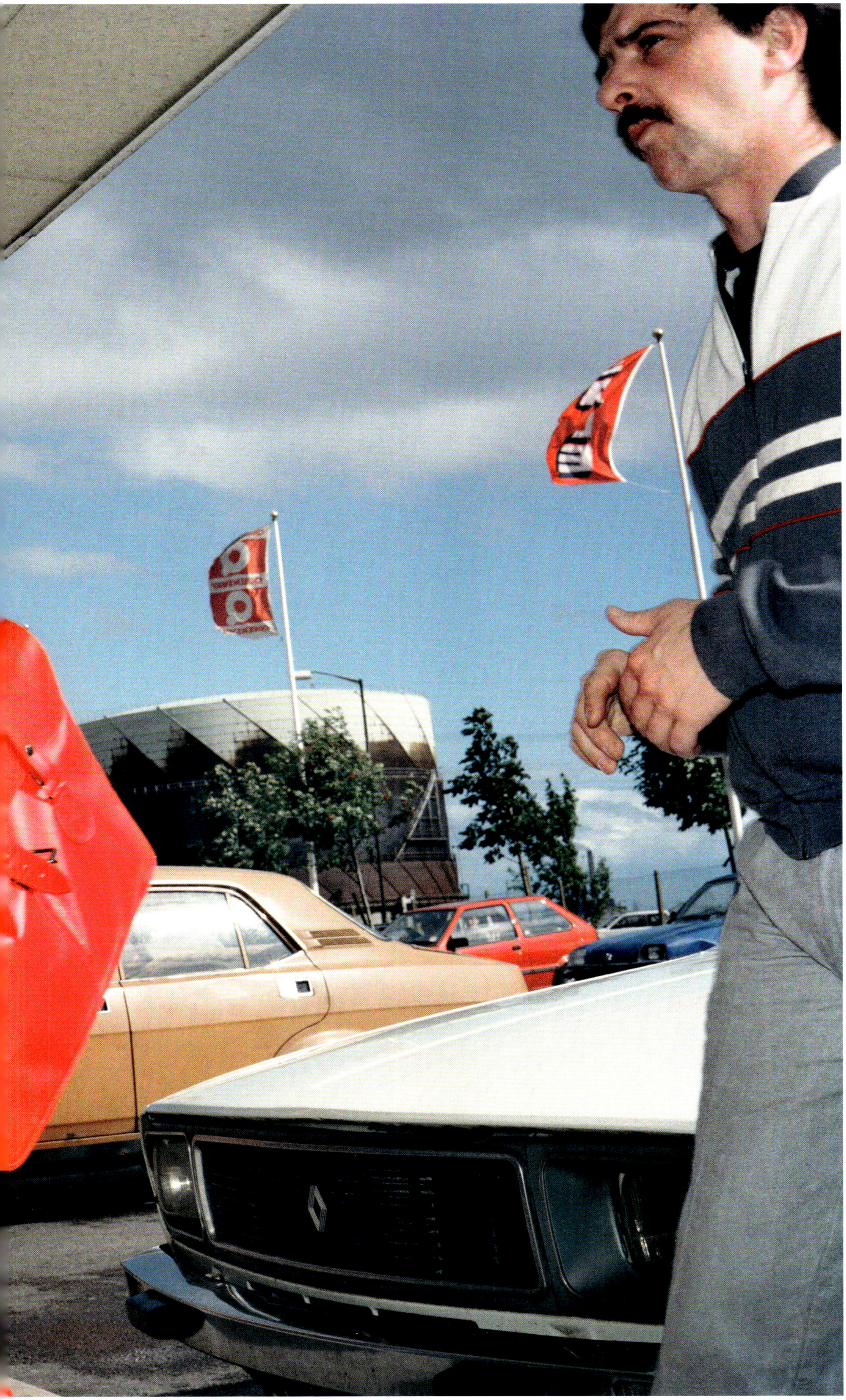

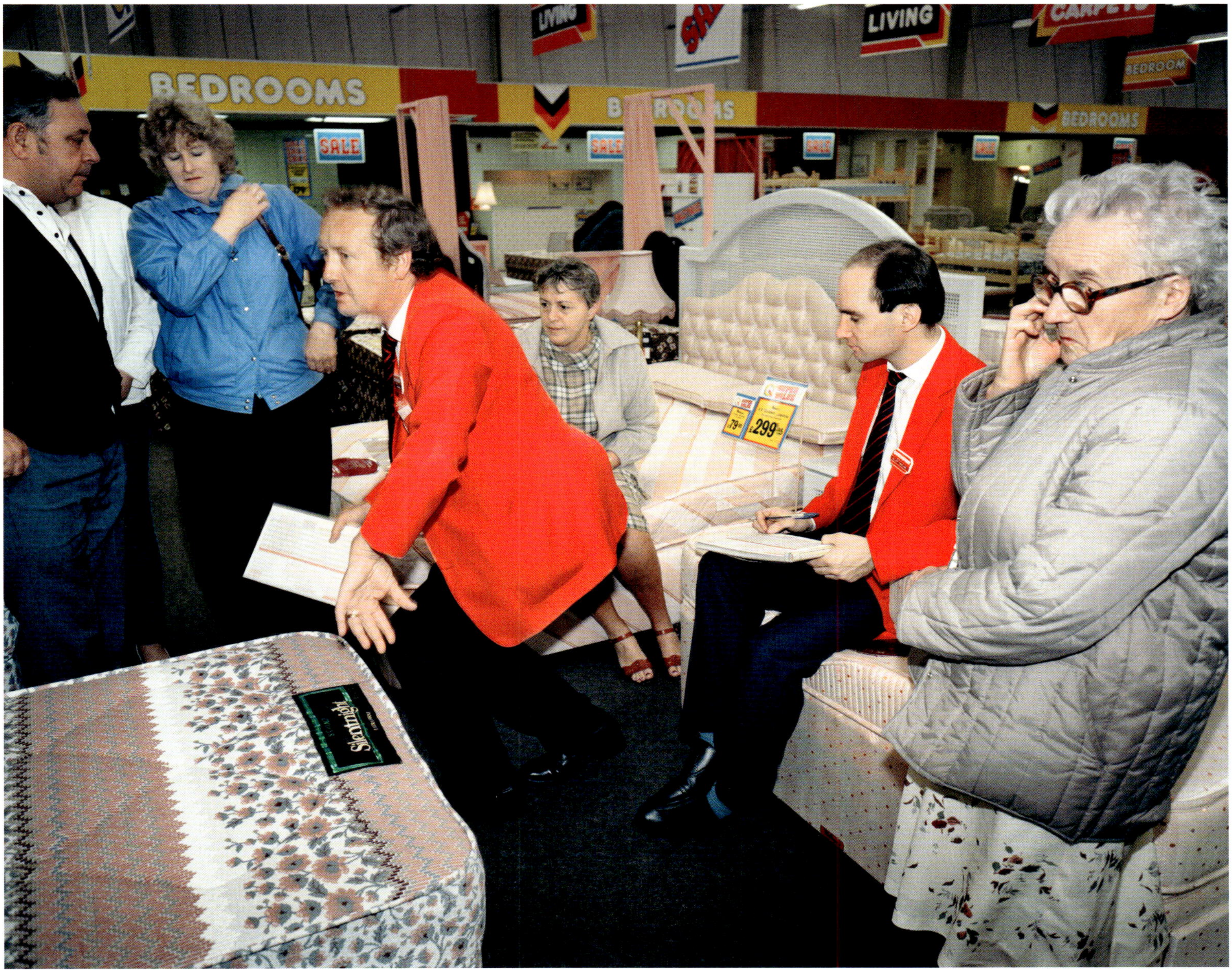
LIVING
LIVING
BEDROOMS
BEDROOMS
SALE
Silentnight

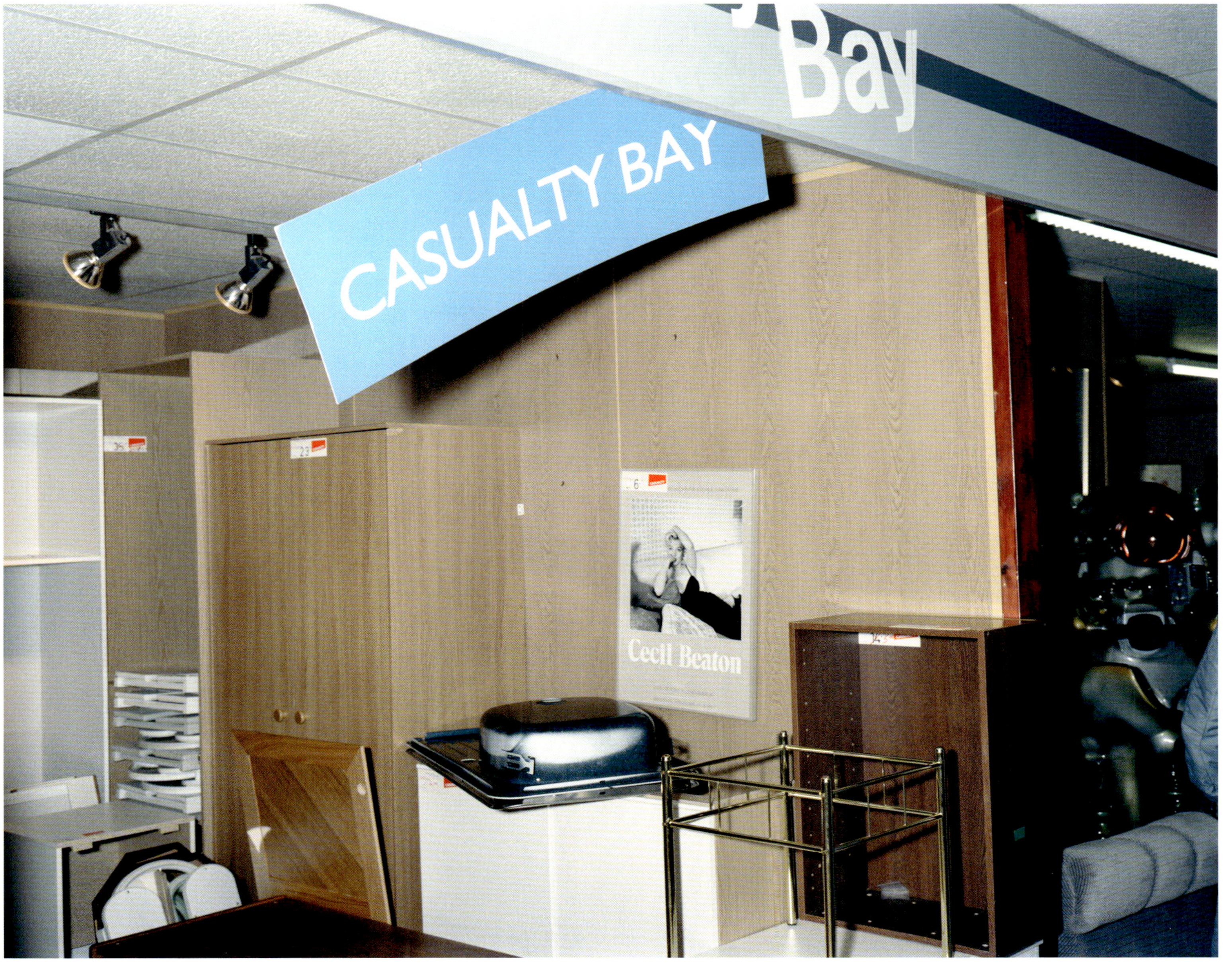
Bay
CASUALTY BAY
Cecil Beaton

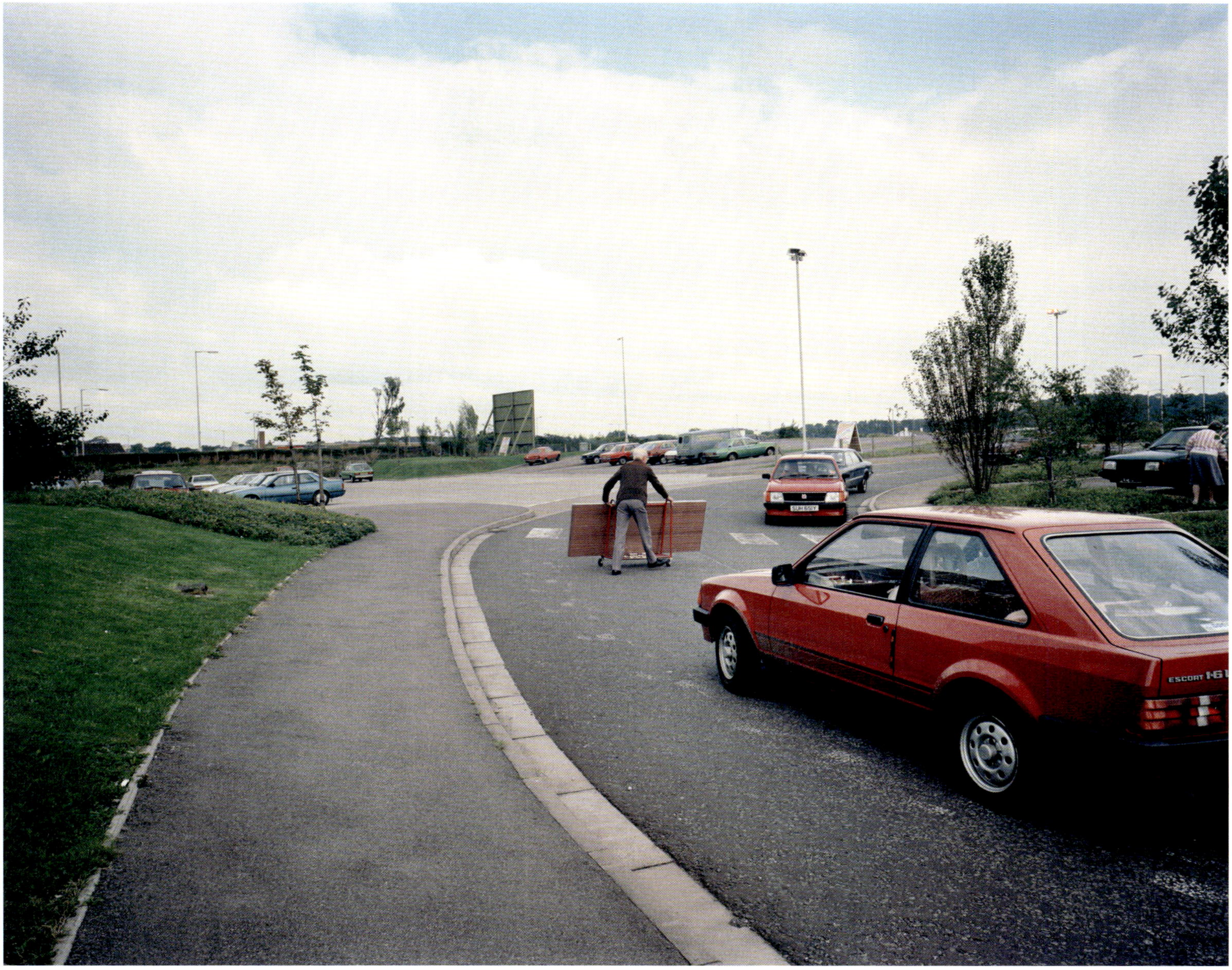
ESCORT 1·6

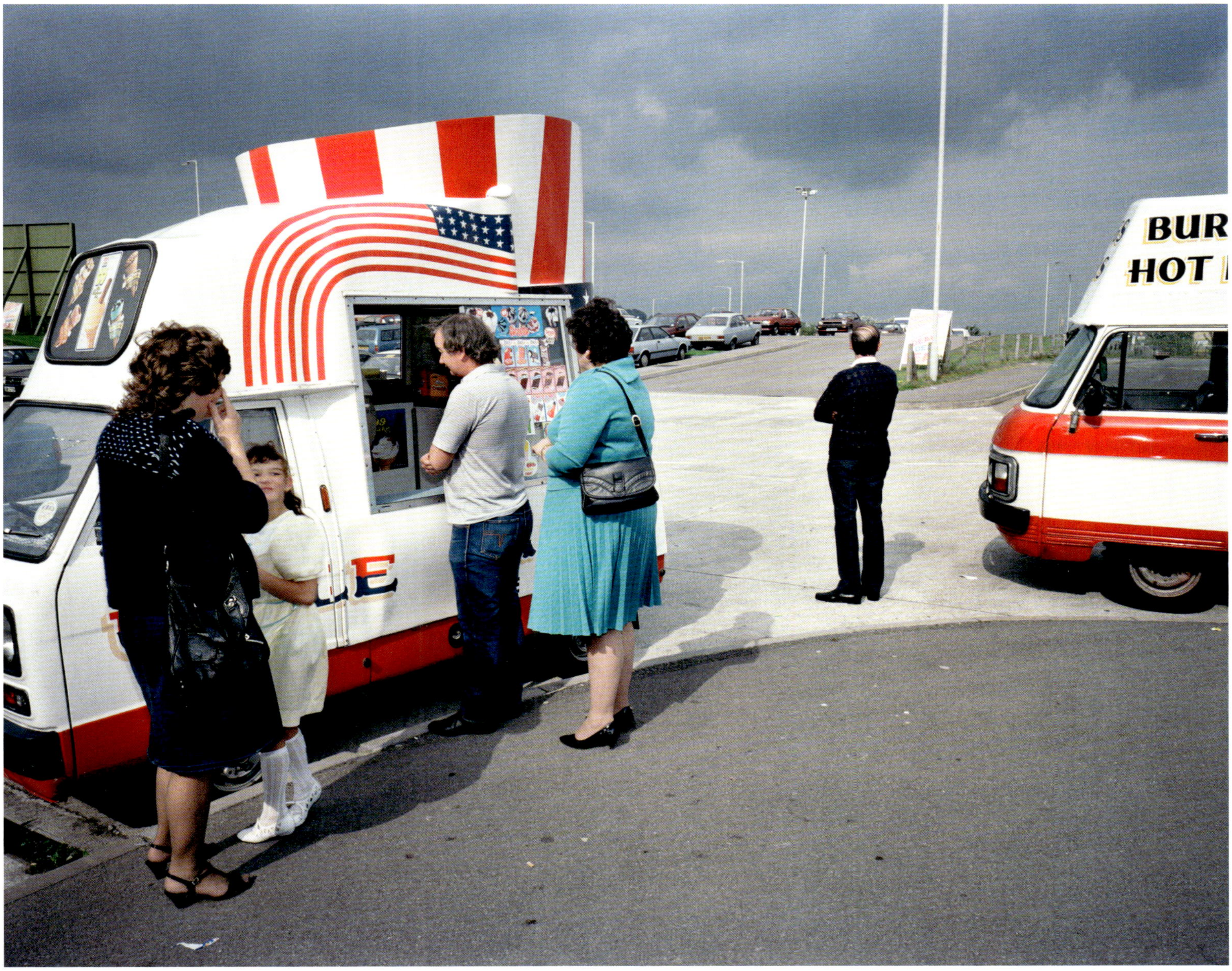
BUR
HOT

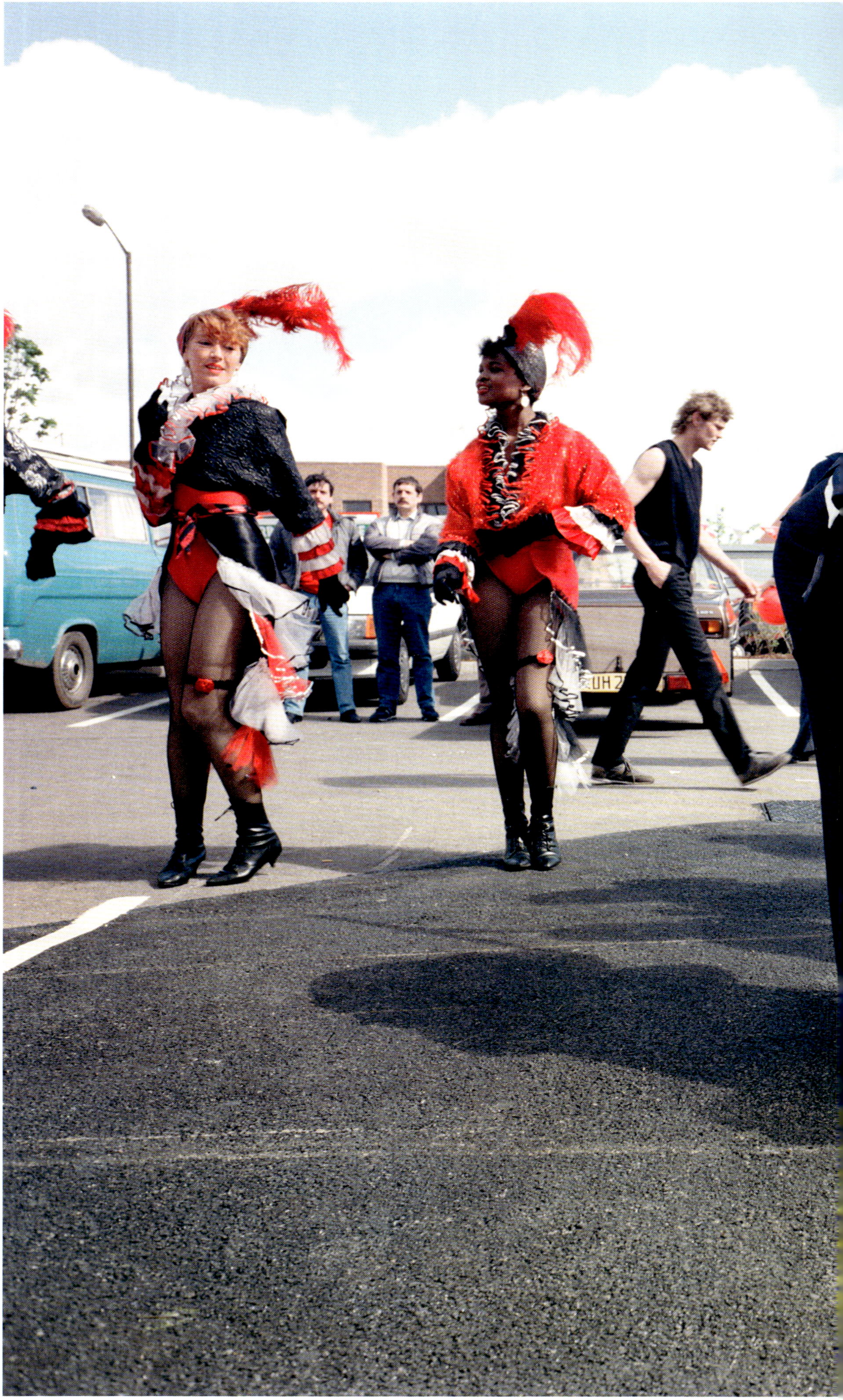

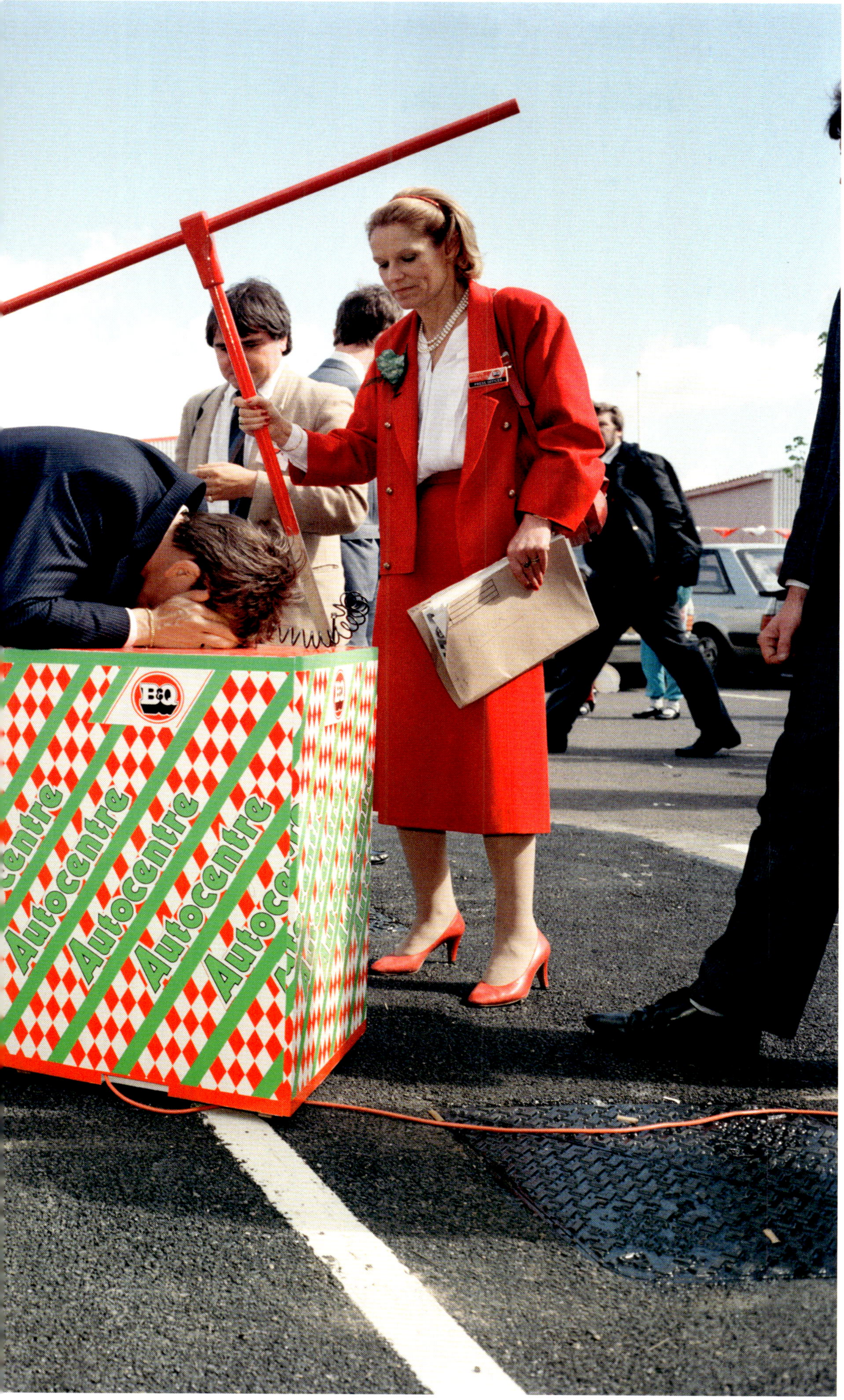
B&Q
Autocentre
Autocentre
Autocentre
Autocentre

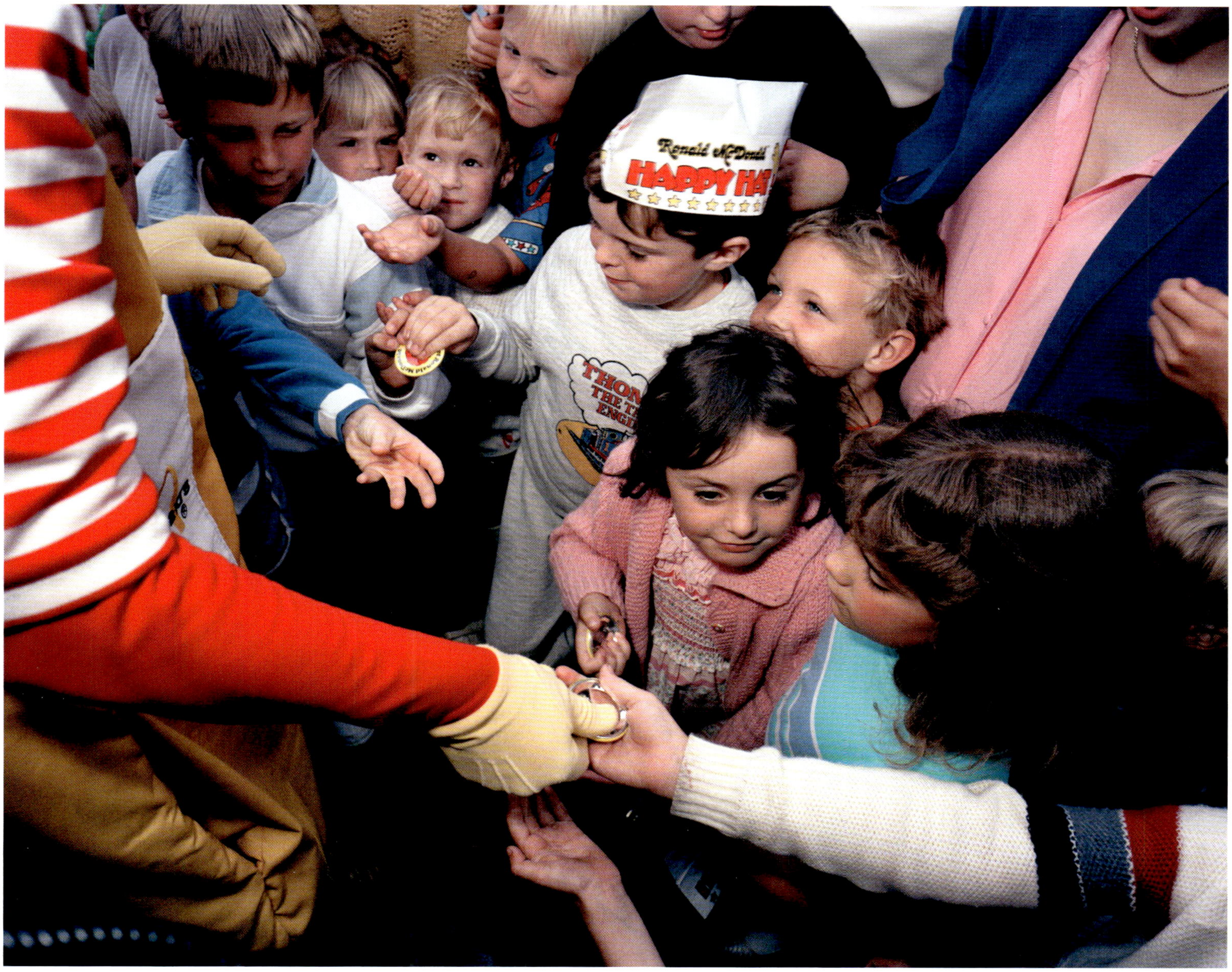
Ronald McDonald
HAPPY HA

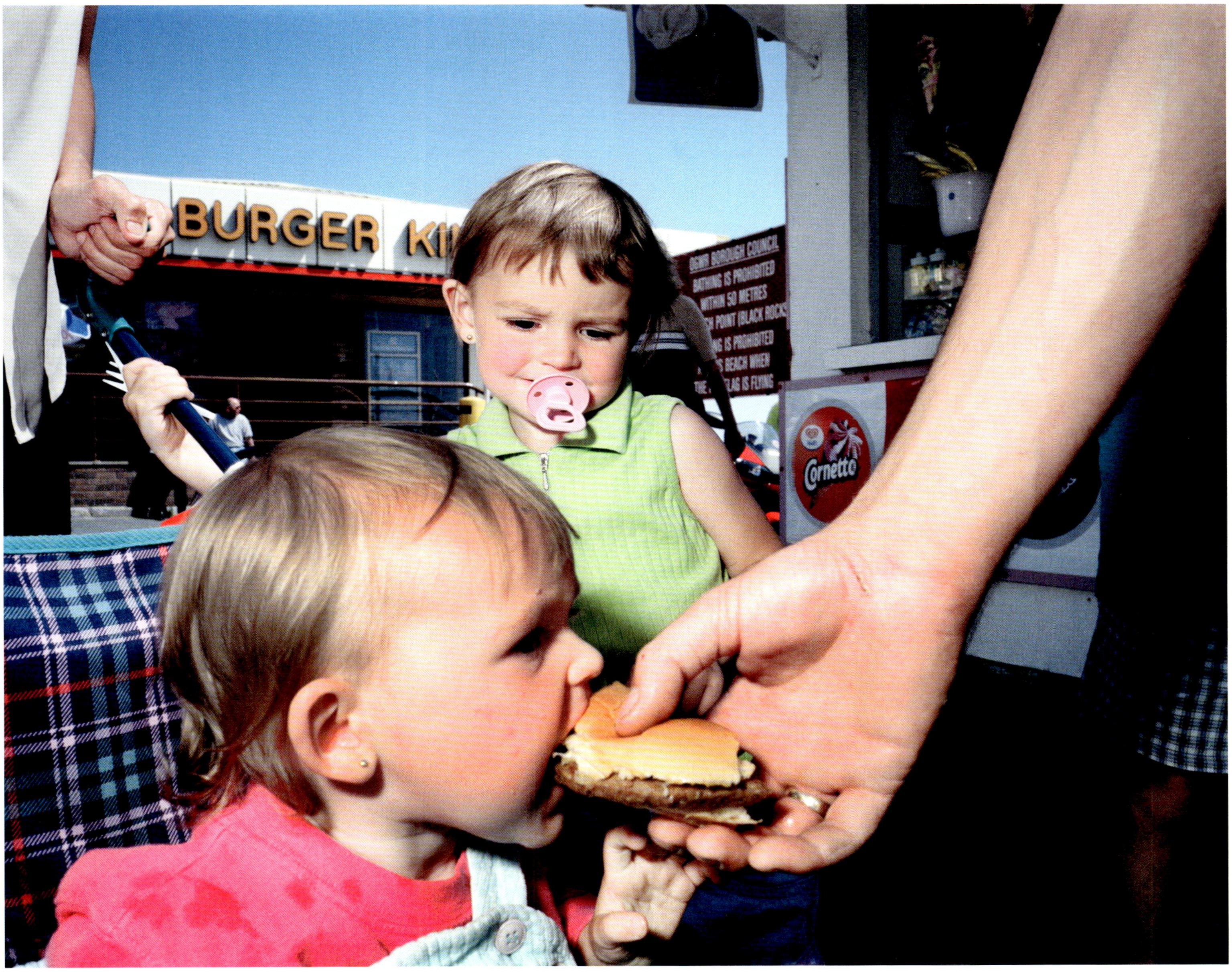
BURGER KI
OGWR BOROUGH COUNCIL
BATHING IS PROHIBITED
WITHIN 50 METRES
Cornetto

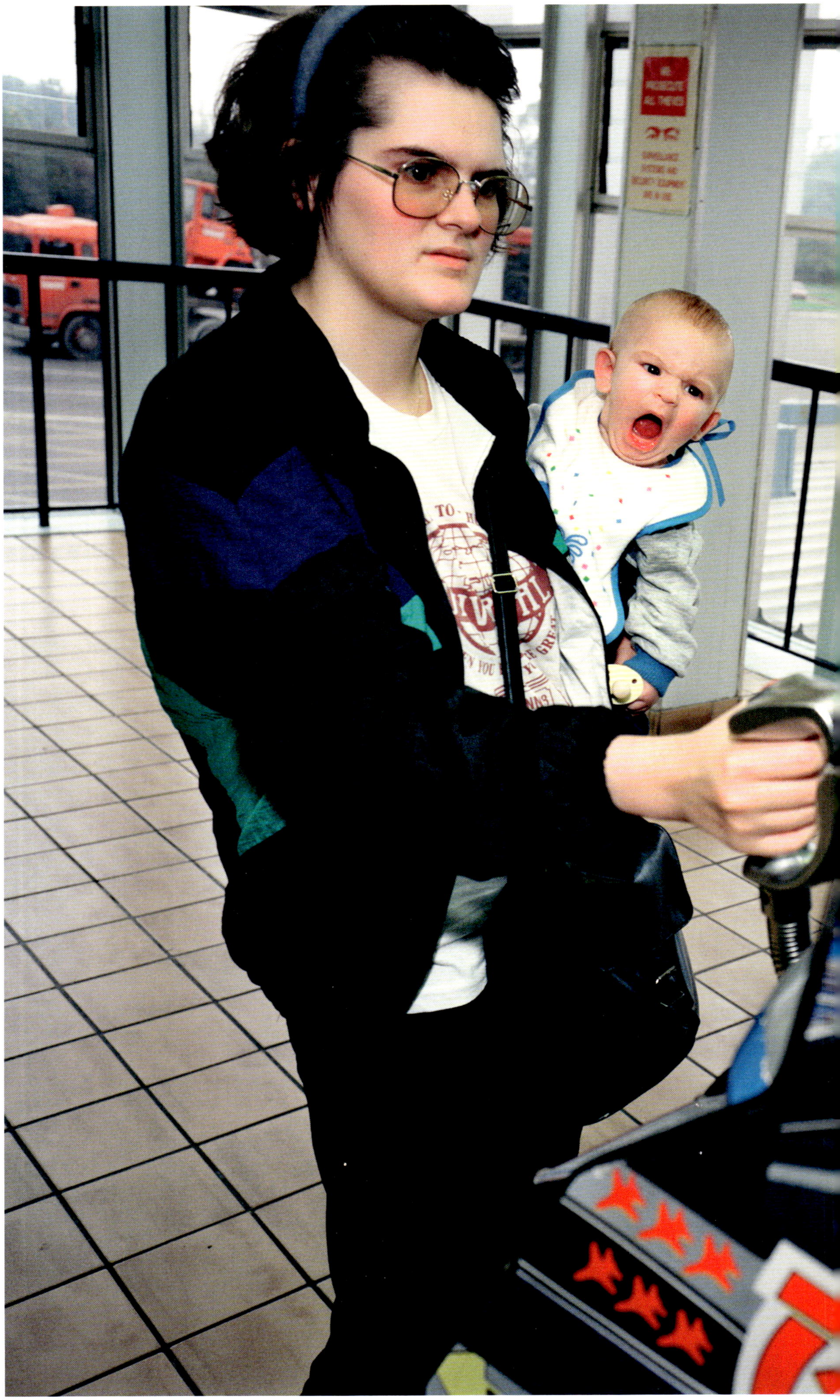

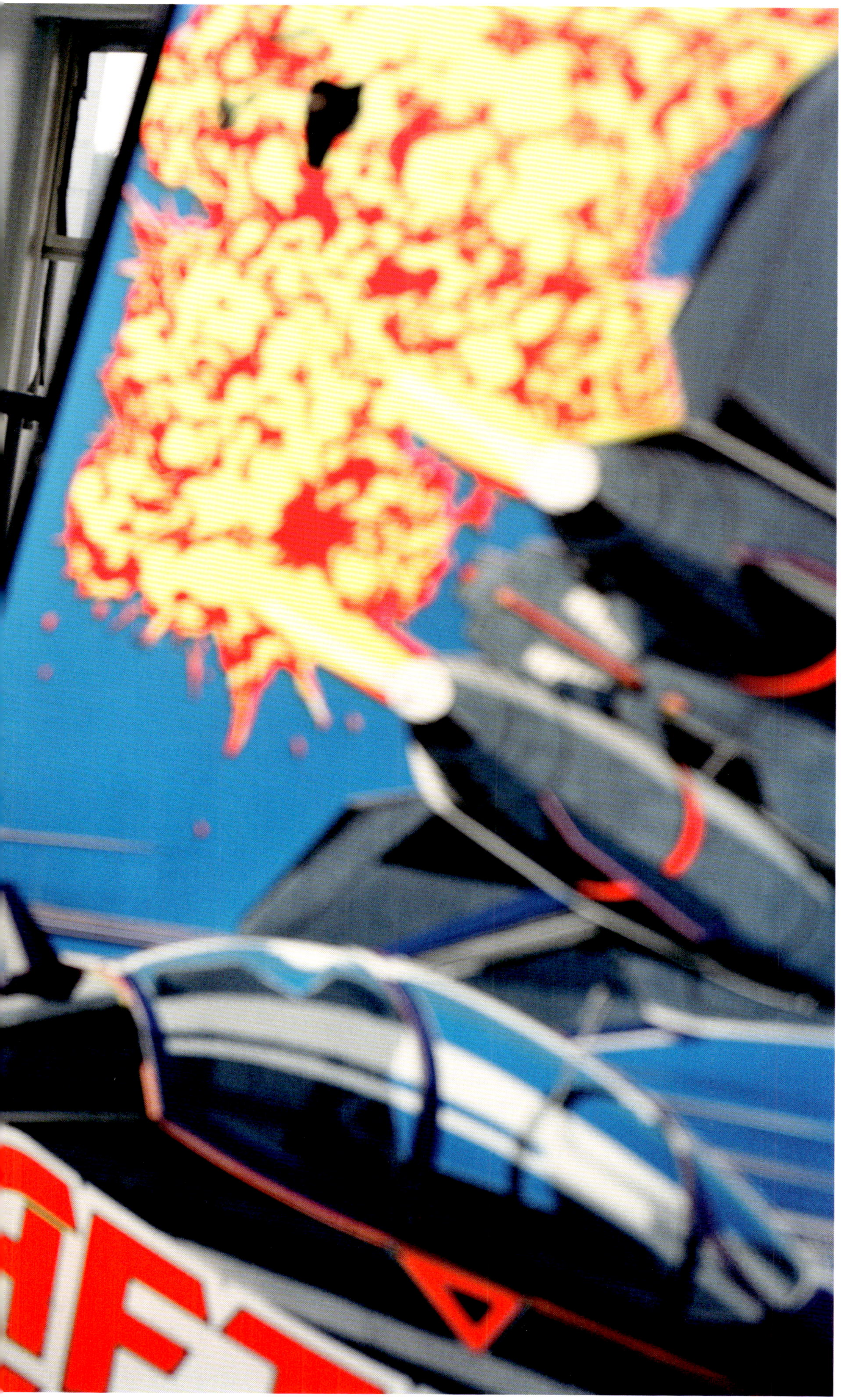

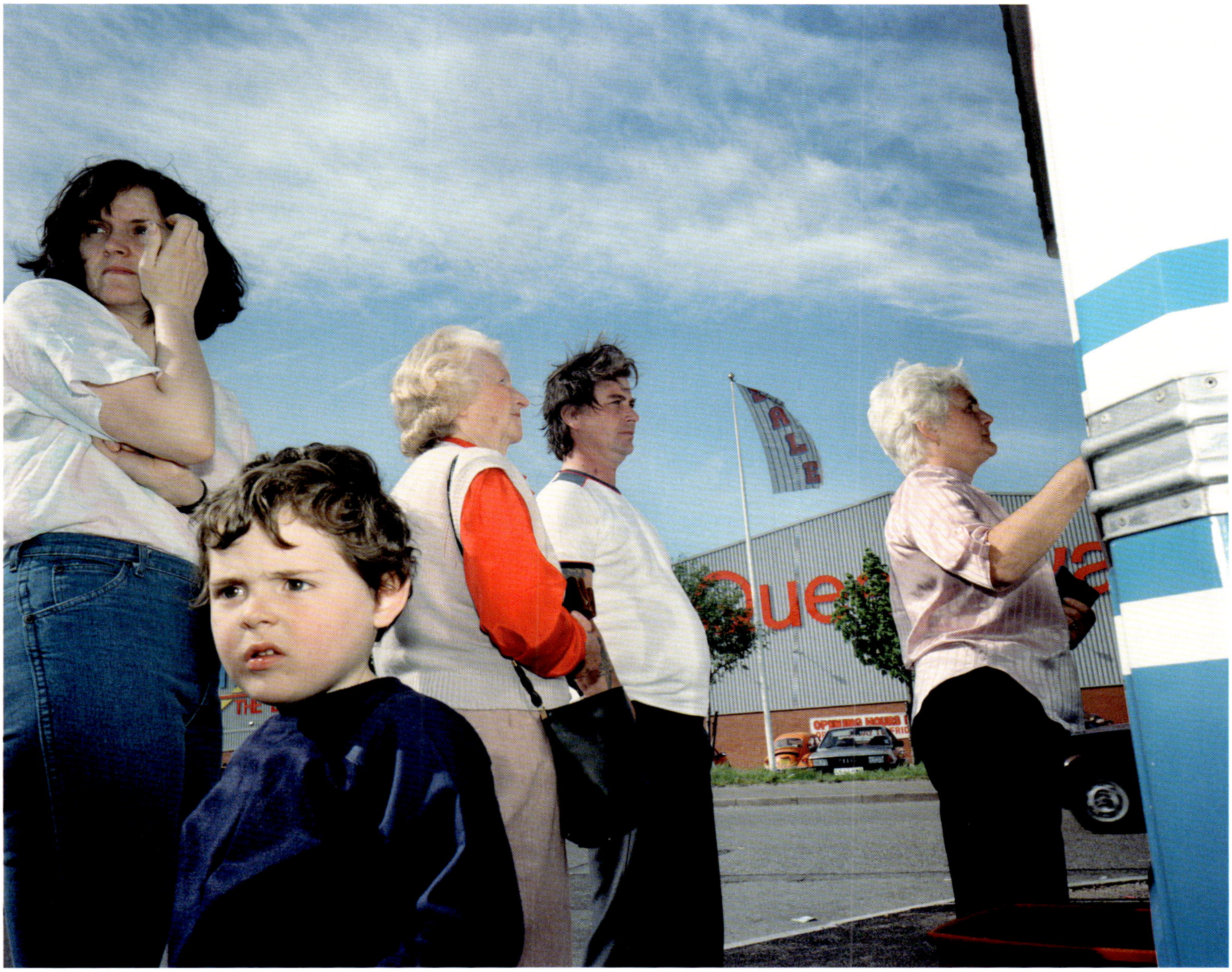

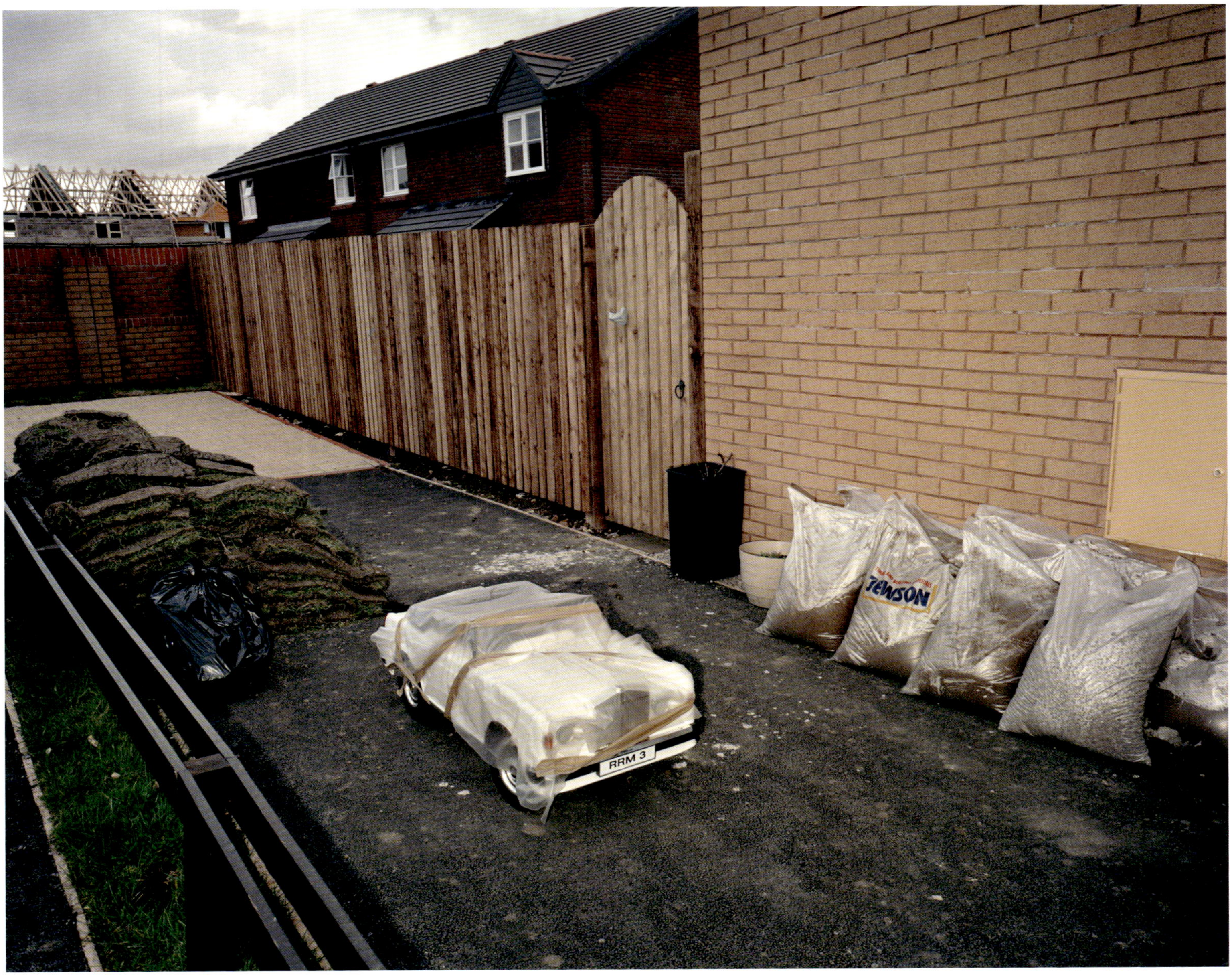
JEWSON
RRM 3

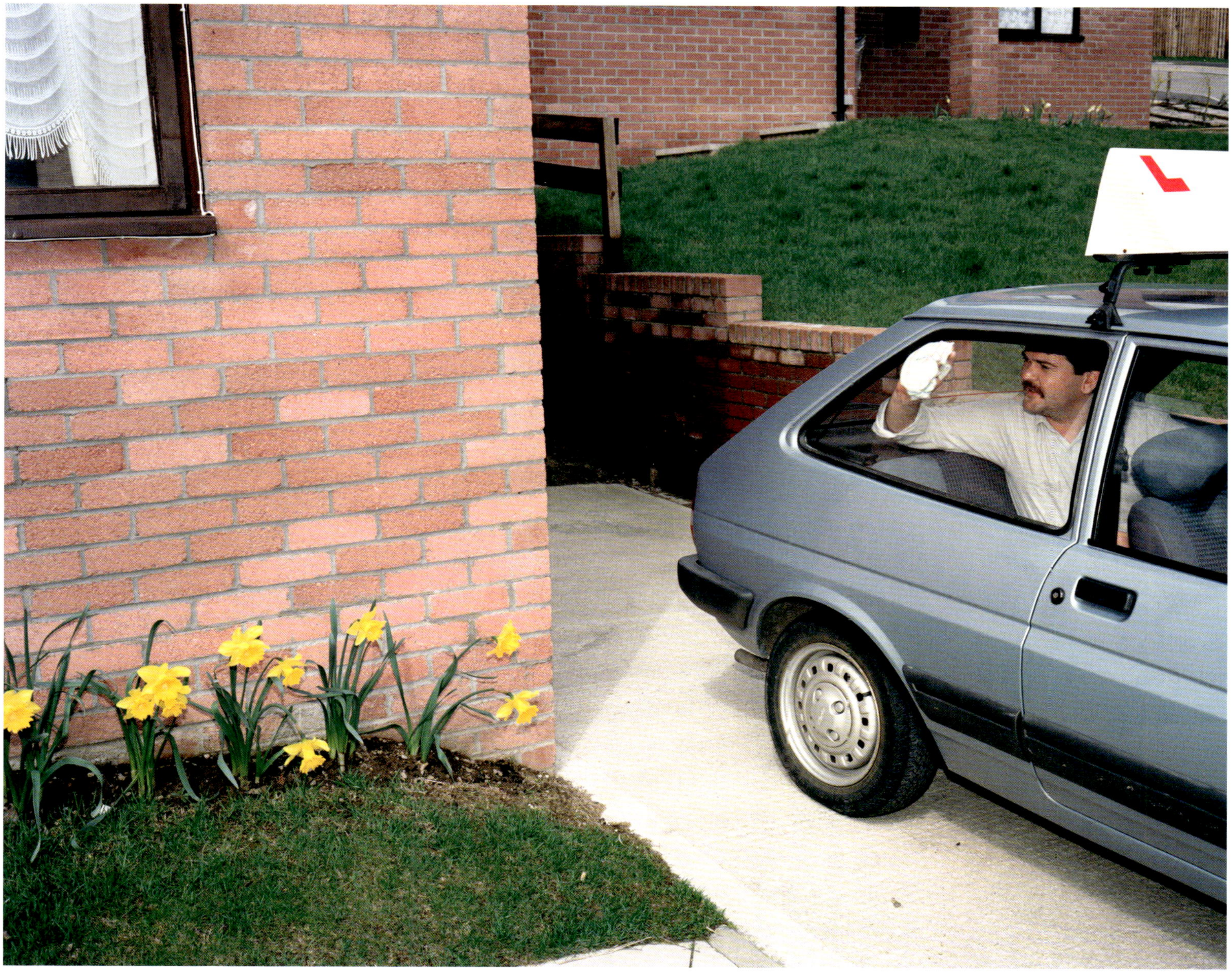

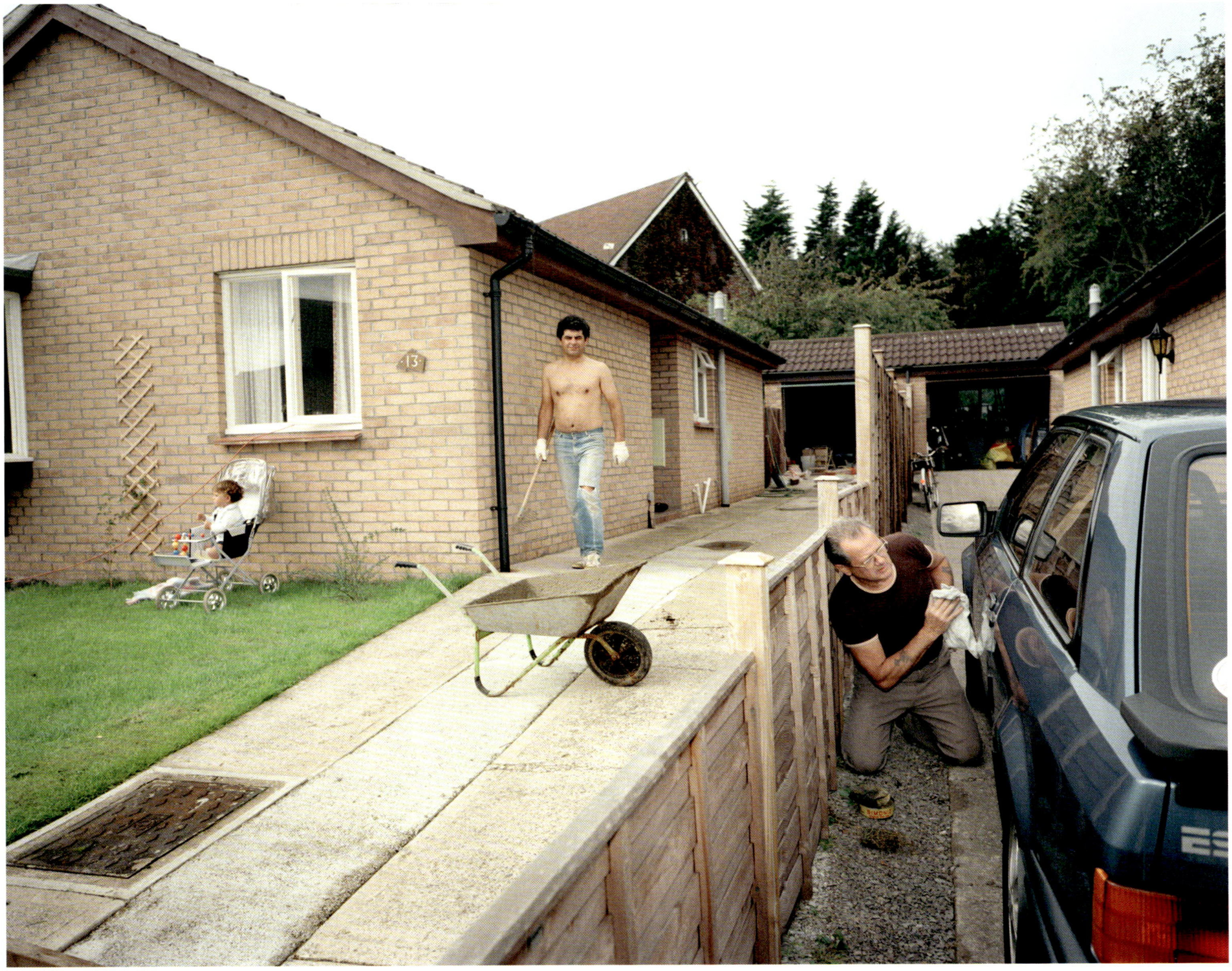

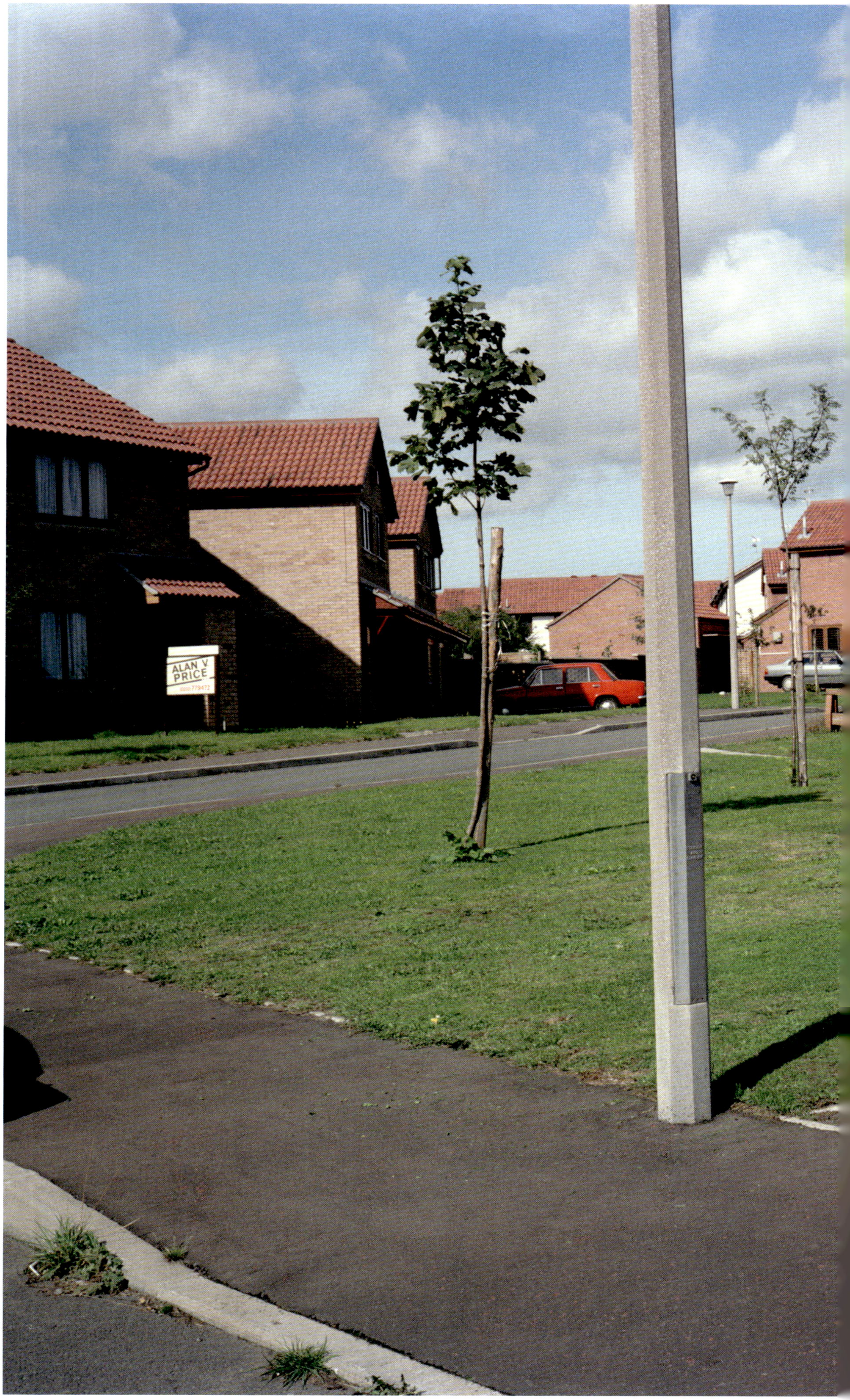
ALAN V
PRICE

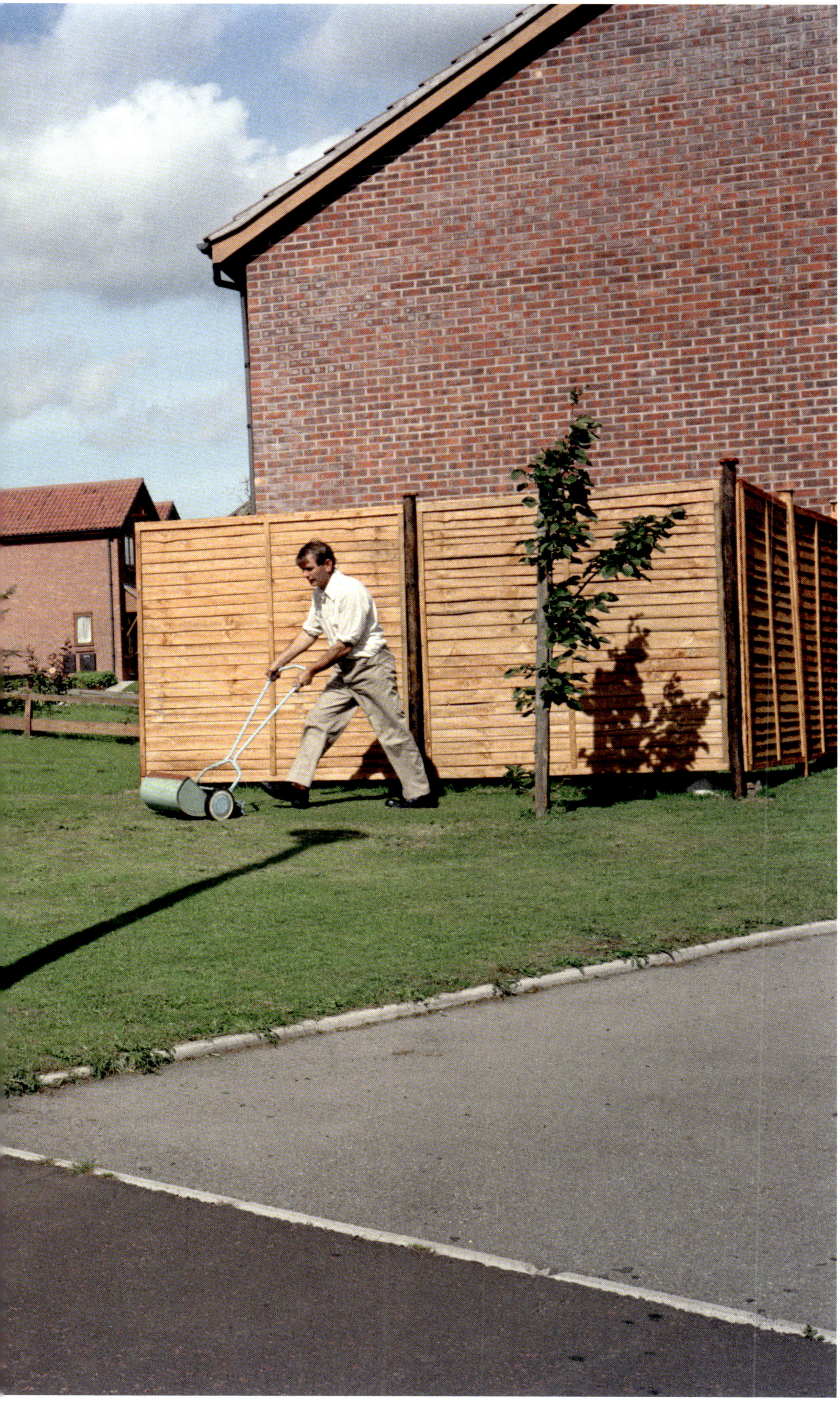

The decline of manufacturing industries in Britain throughout the 1980s forced the collective imagination of Britain to retreat into a time of more certainty. A time of empire, a time of full employment, a time of paternalistic benevolent mill owners and a time of the pastoral and picturesque. This desire for an illusion of stability was serviced by the heritage industry; with its themed industrial museums and country houses, heritage offered a novel (if spurious) sense of place and identity to a country which had lost its old 'eternal truths' of industry and empire, reassuring us that our lives are better in the new service economy than those of our parents in 'the bad old days' of the industrial past. But these heritage centres did not recover the past—they re-created it. The heritage process irons out differences, glosses over contradiction and unifies all the conflicting dynamics of the past into a single romantic and idealised version of it.

This notion of a manufactured history, at a time of economic uncertainty, would be the subject of my second book, *Flogging a Dead Horse*, published in 1993 by Cornerhouse Publications.

1989–93

Flogging a Dead Horse

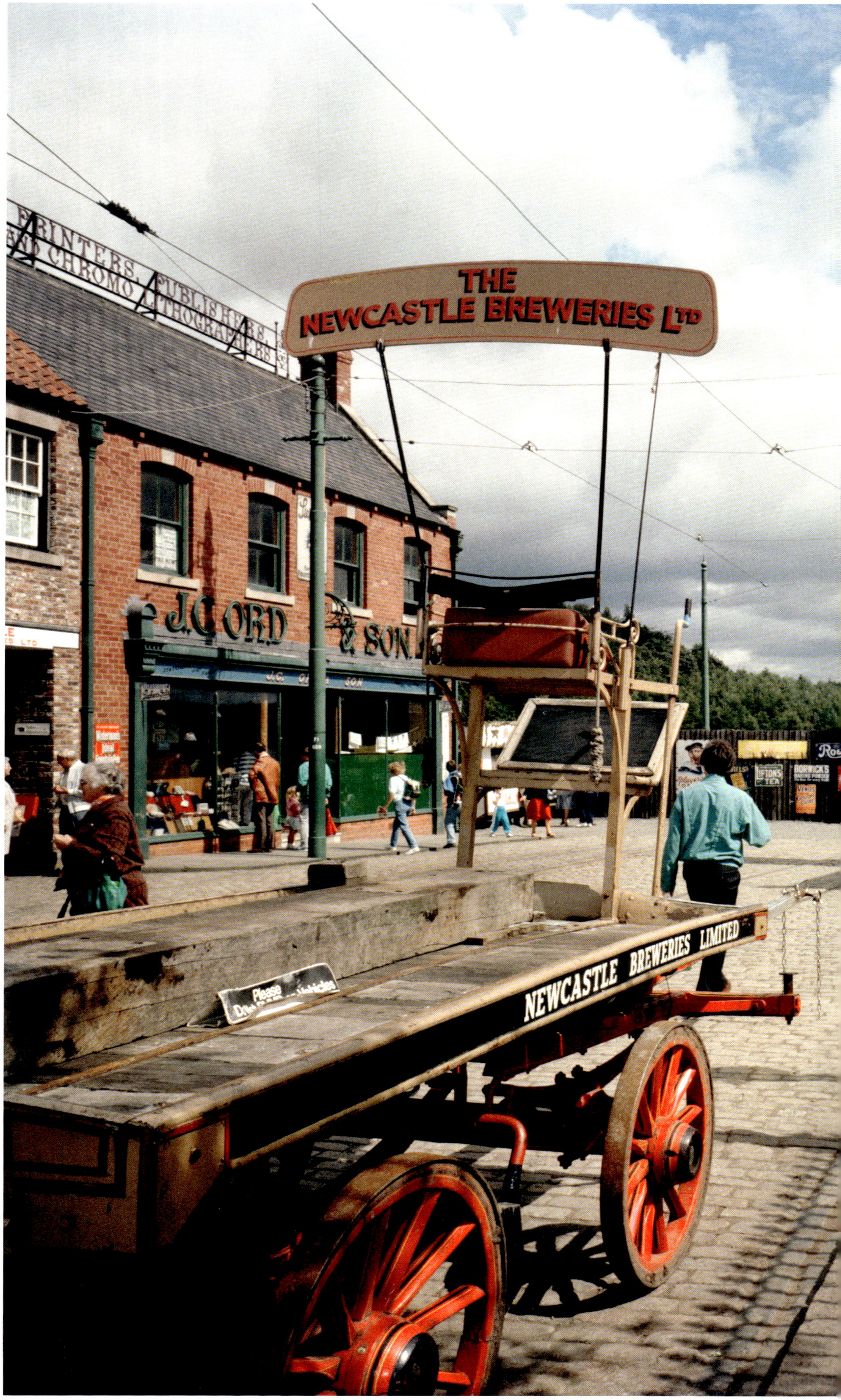
PRINTERS, PUBLISHERS
AND CHROMO LITHOGRAPHERS
THE
NEWCASTLE BREWERIES LTD
J.C. ORD & SON
NEWCASTLE BREWERIES LIMITED

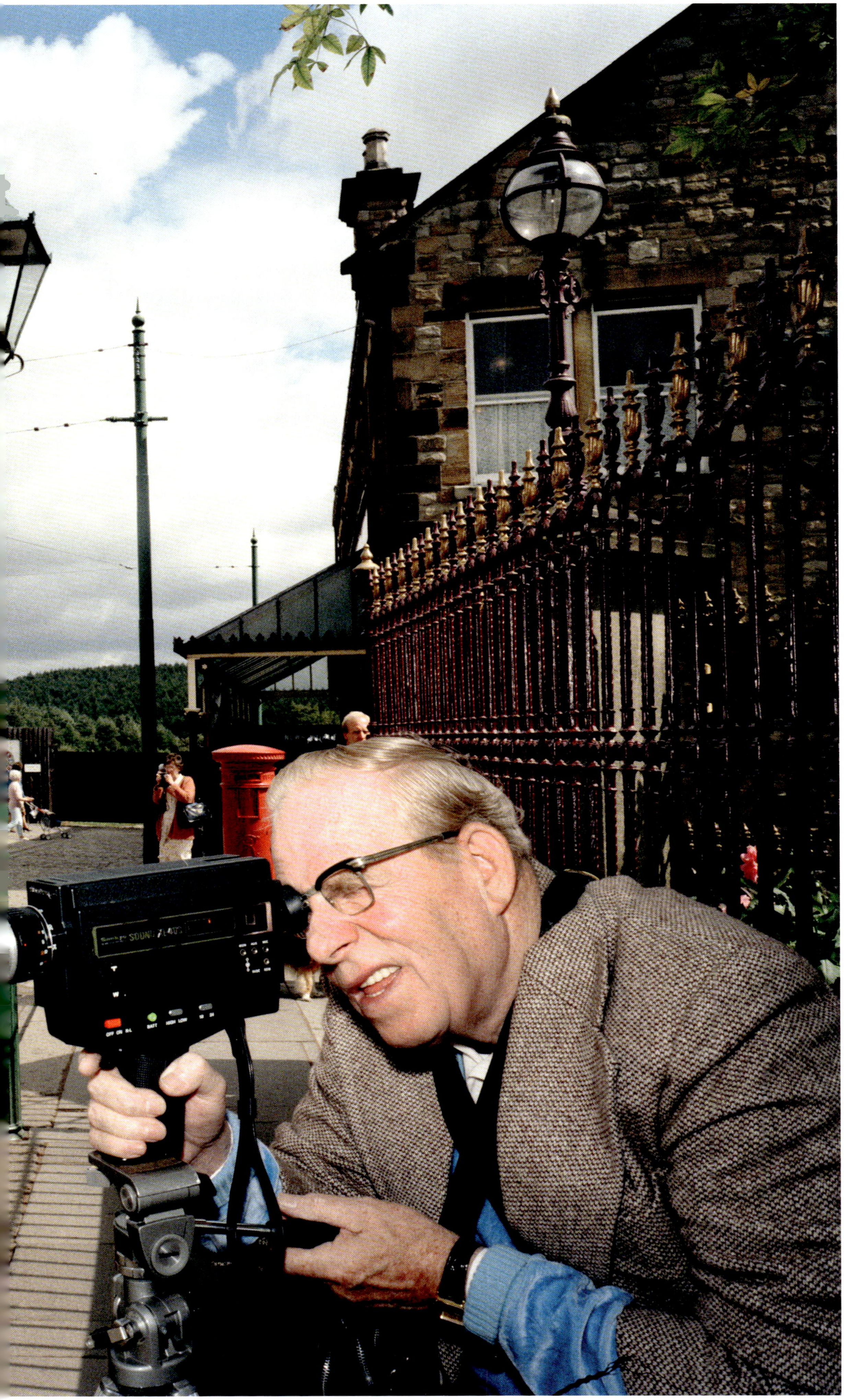

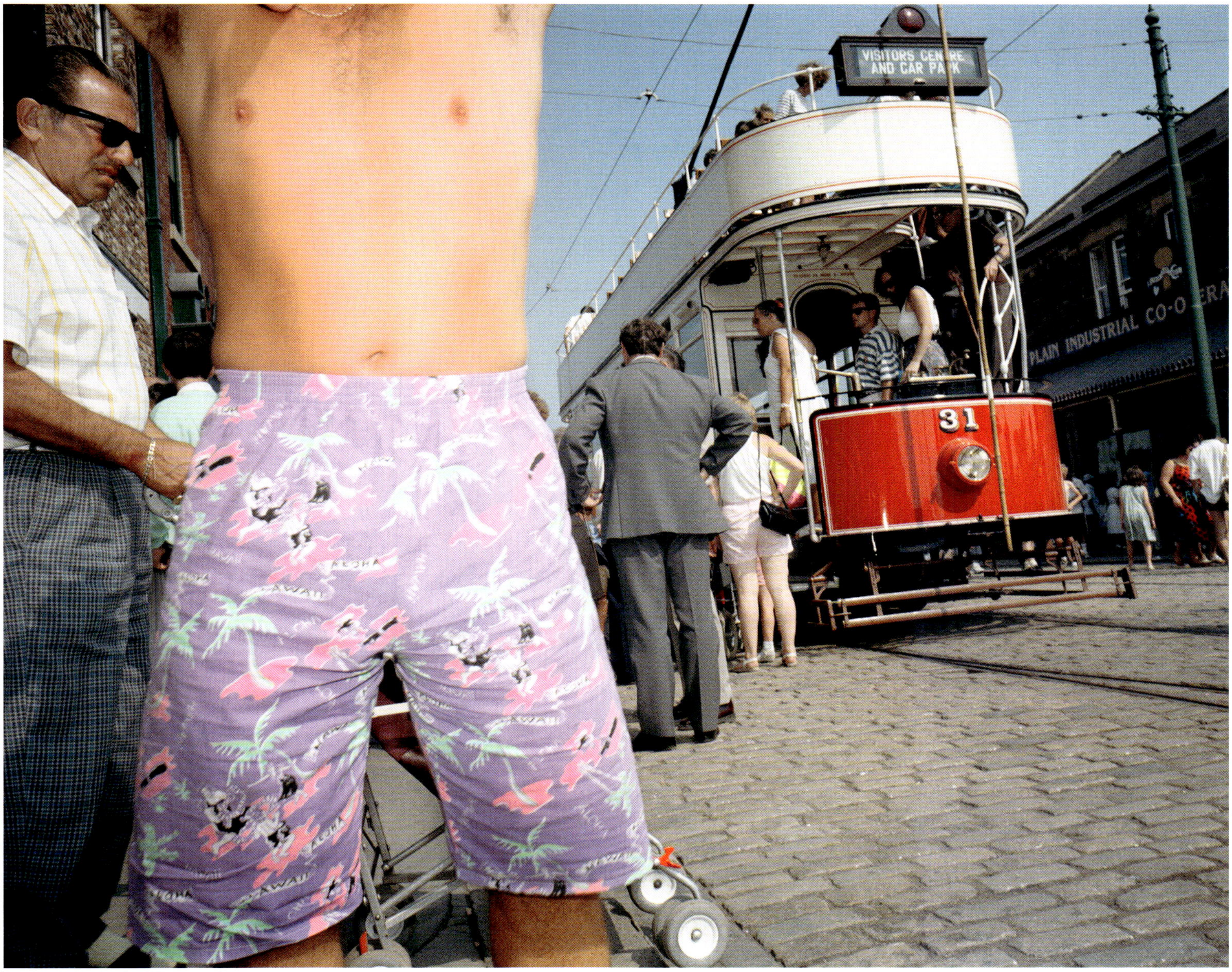
VISITORS CENTRE
AND CAR PARK
31

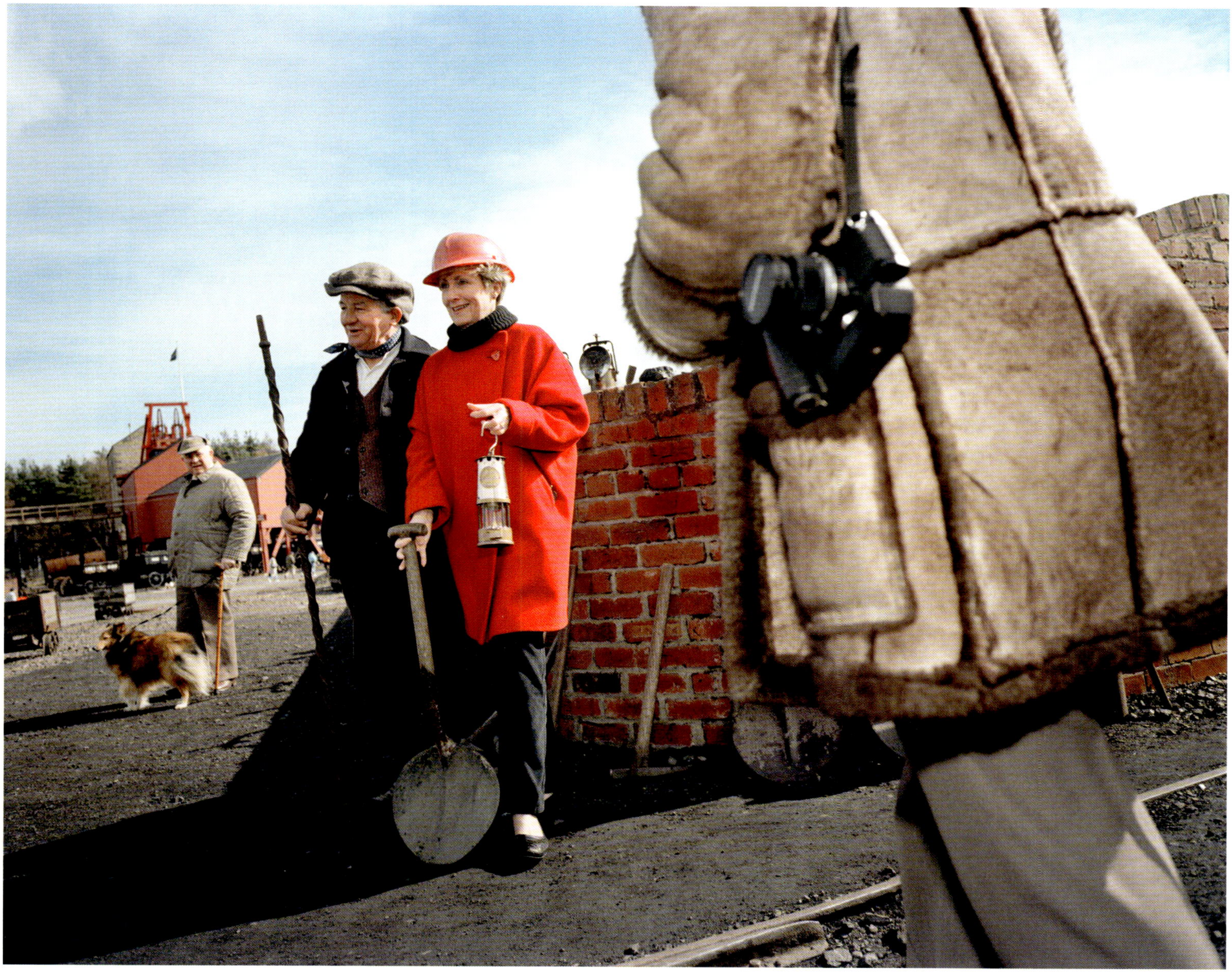

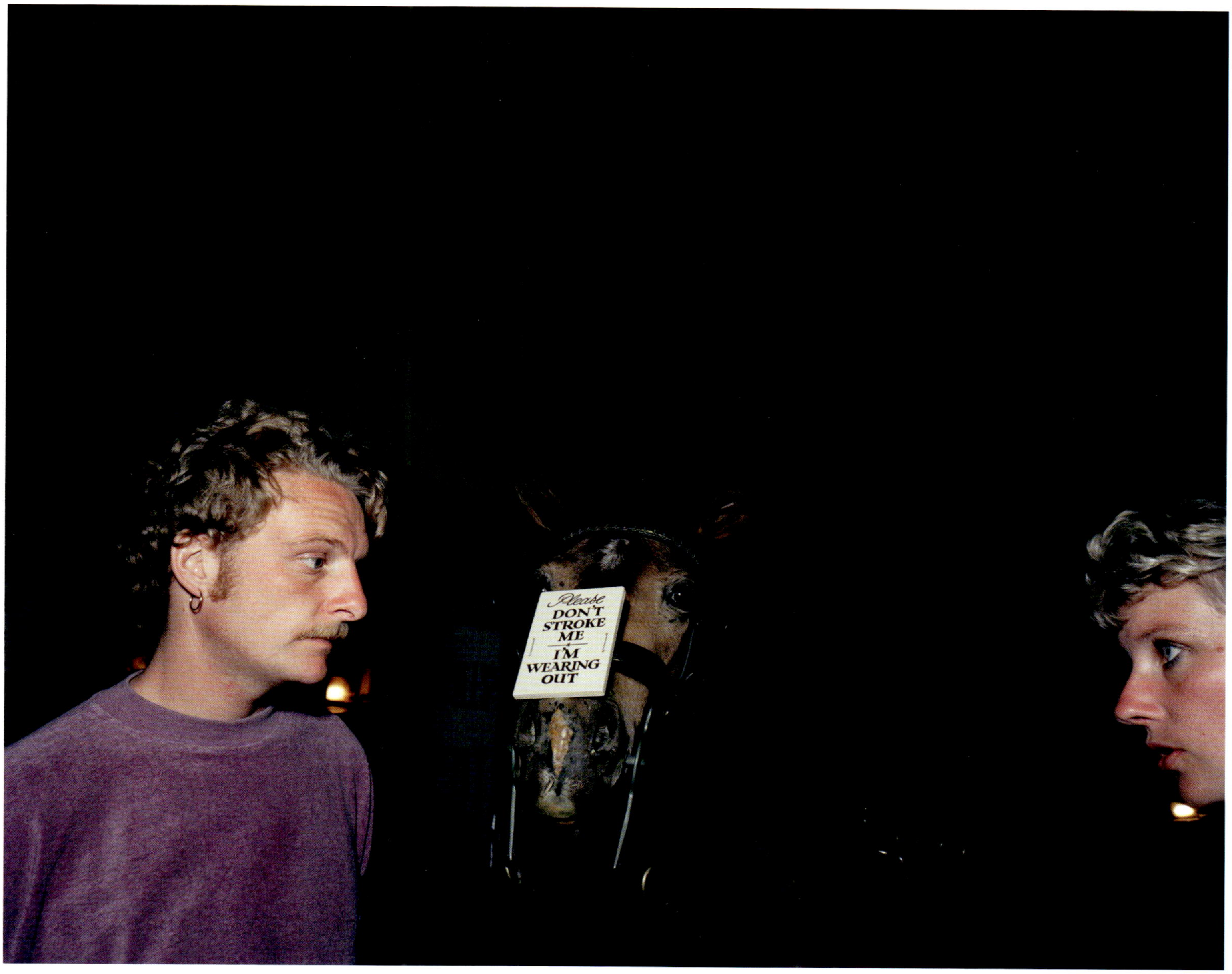
Please
DON'T
STROKE
ME
I'M
WEARING
OUT

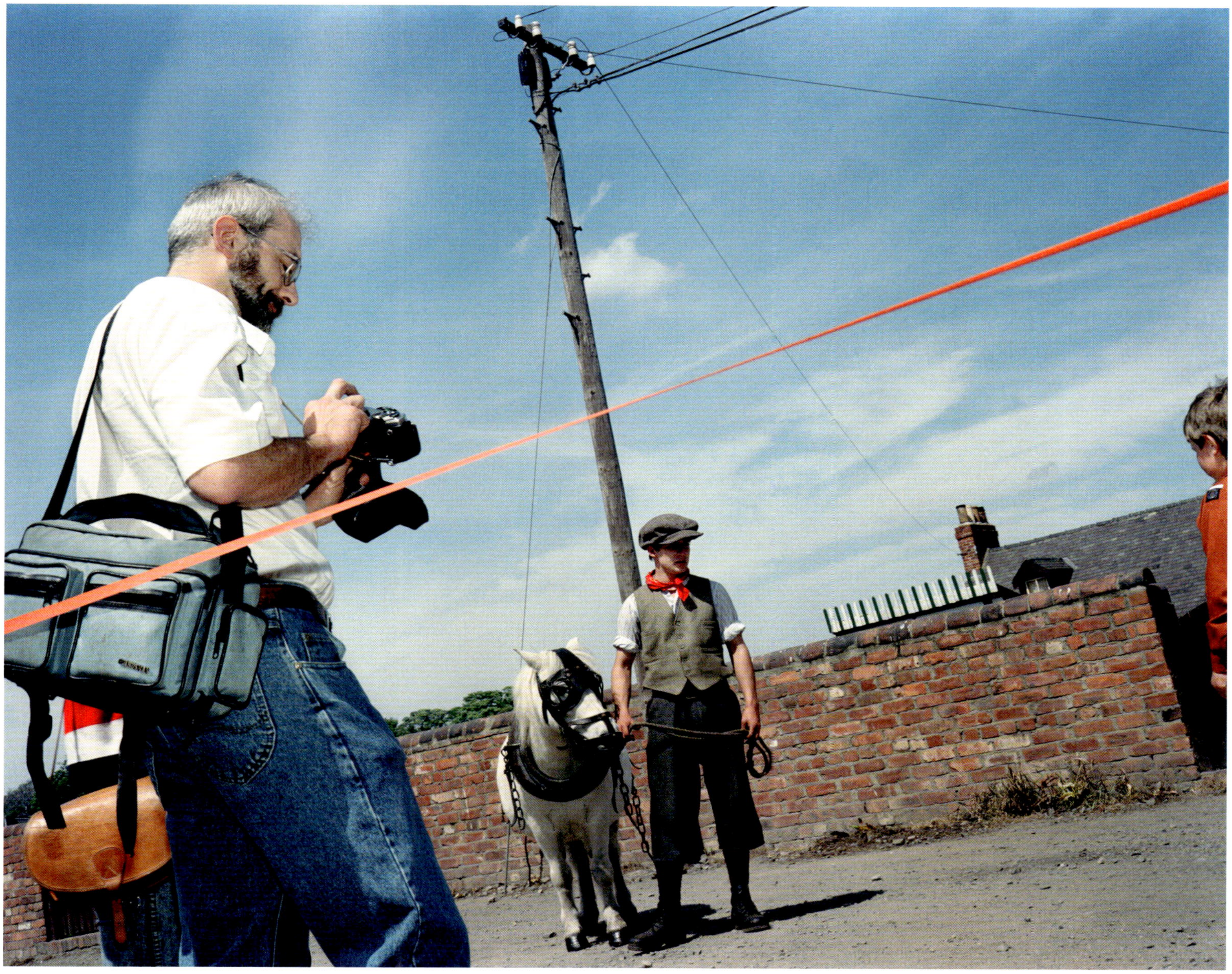

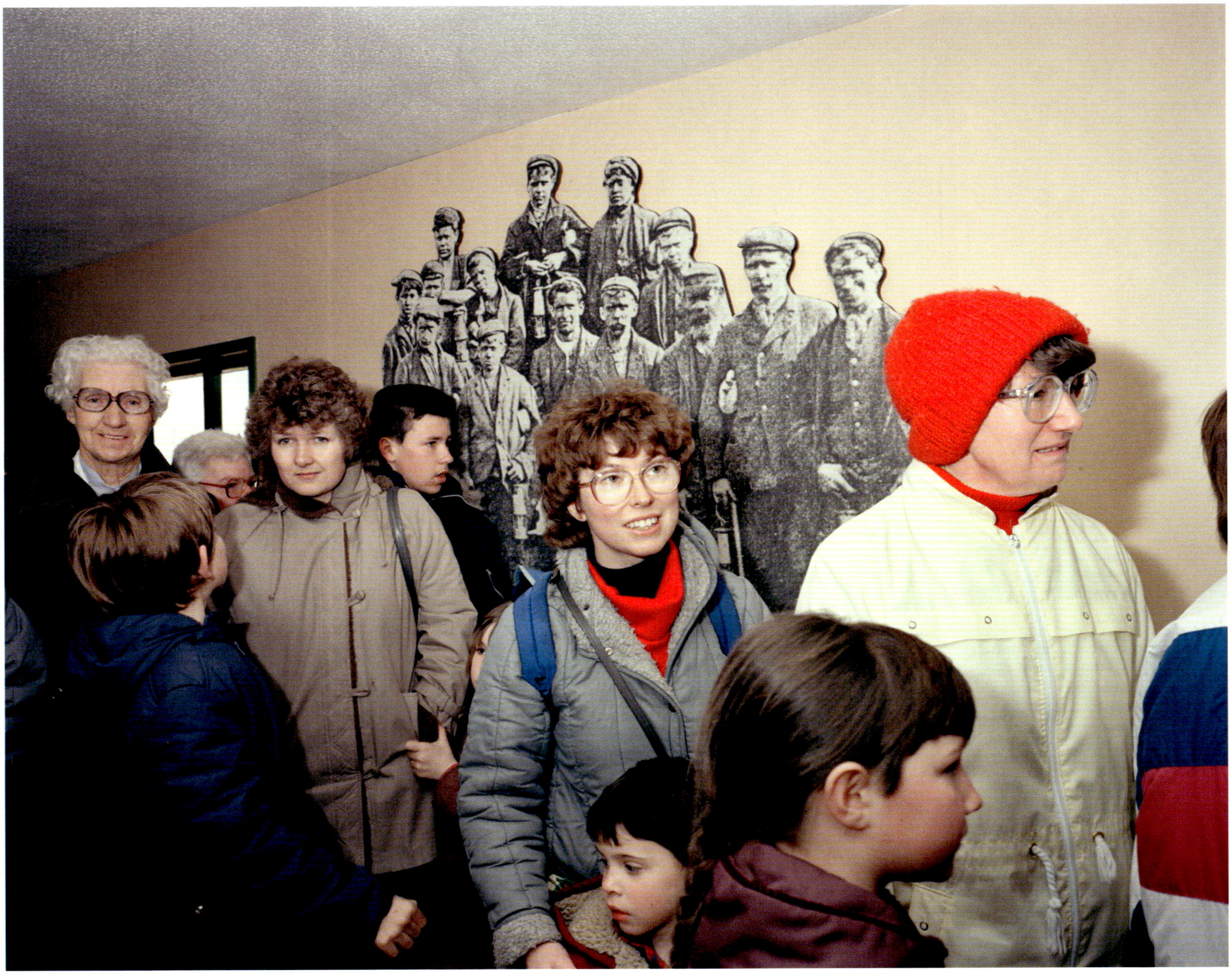

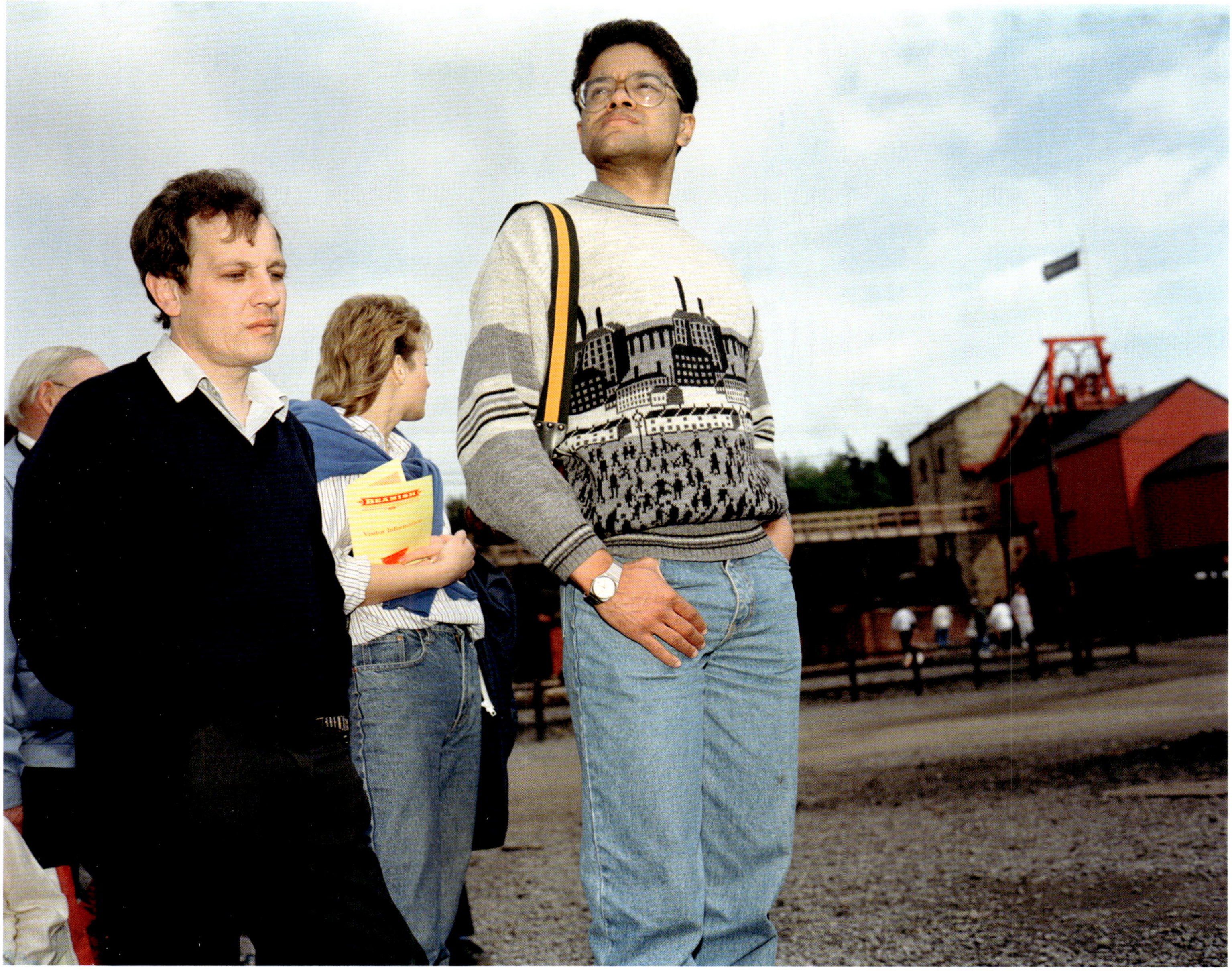
BEAMISH

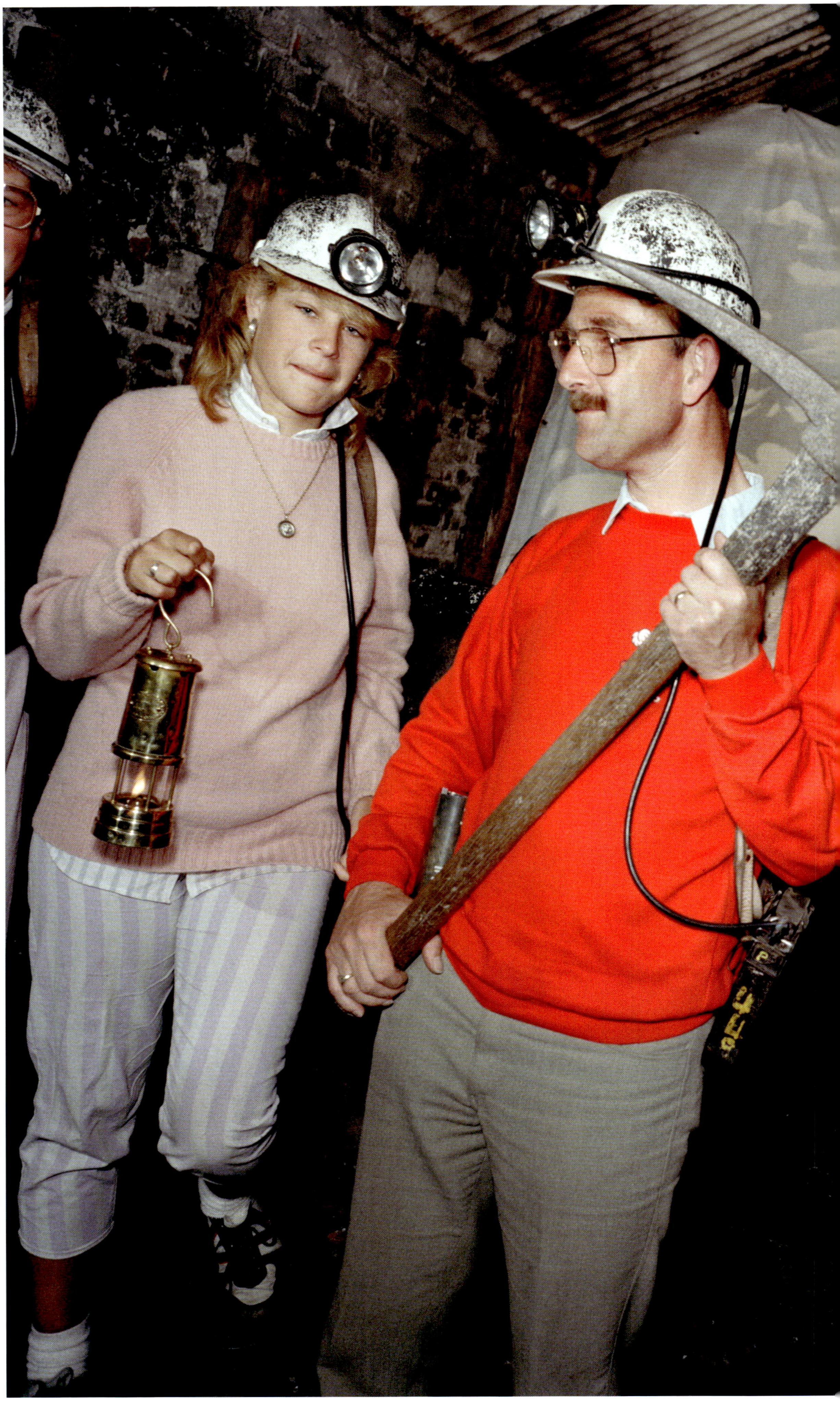

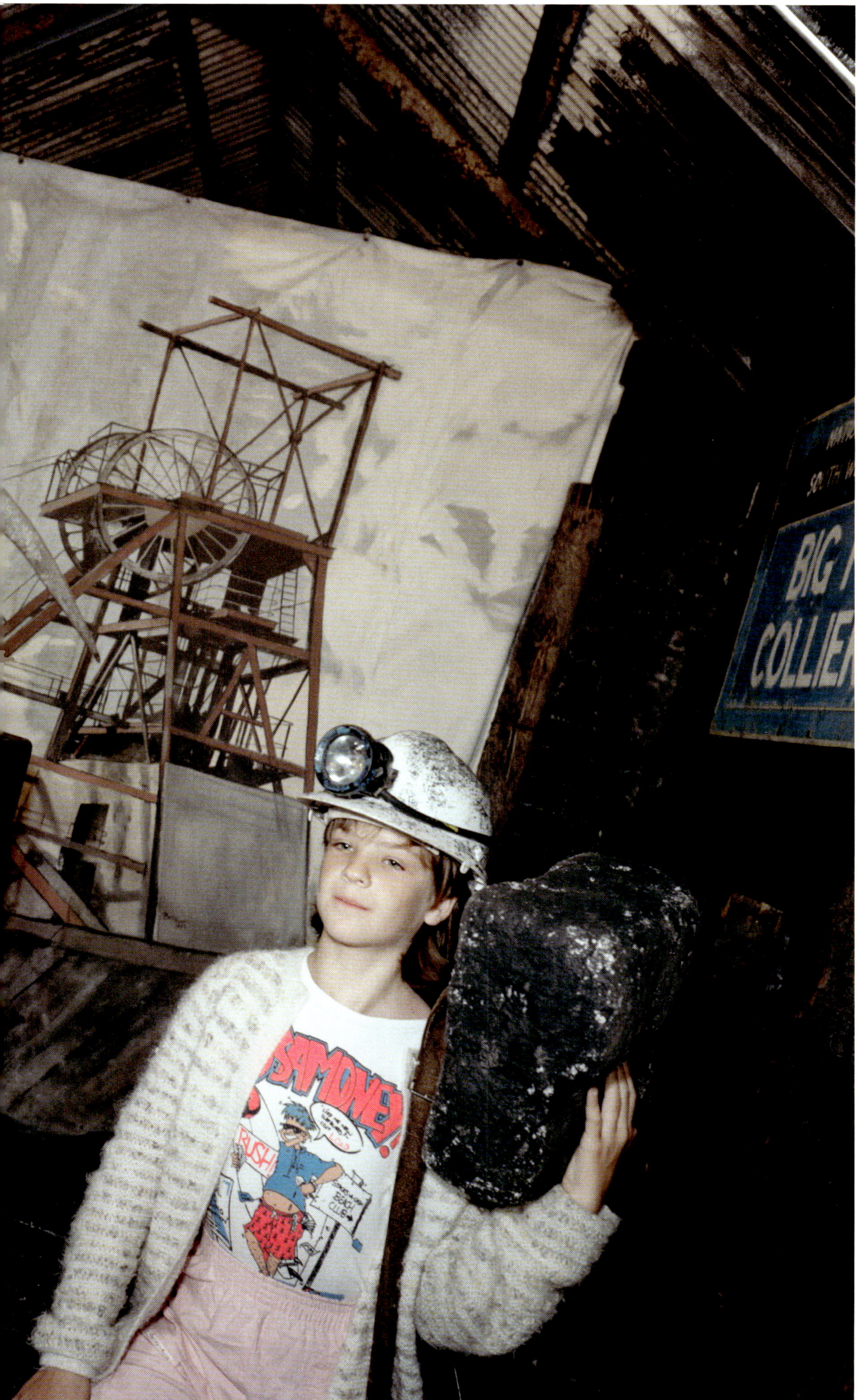

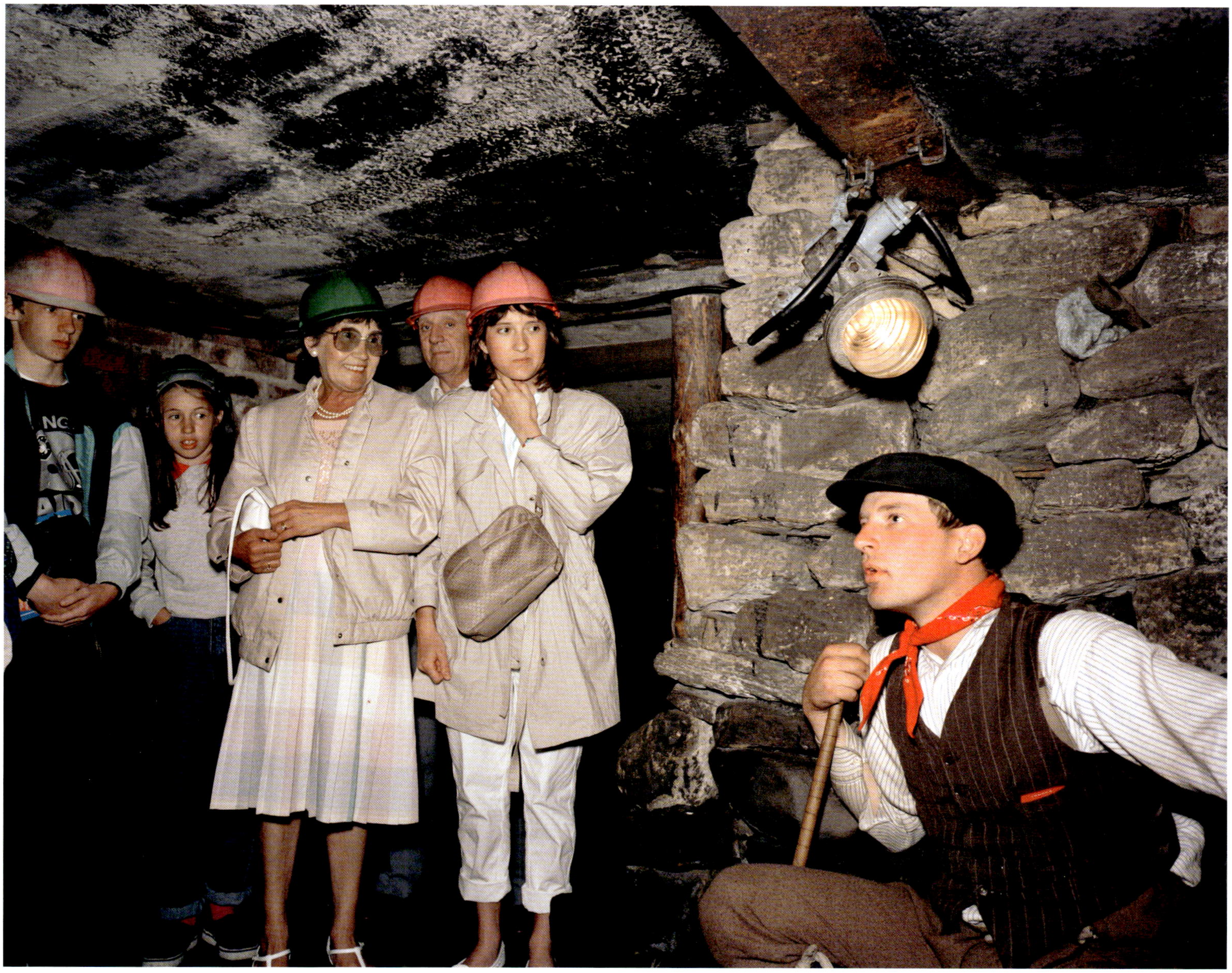

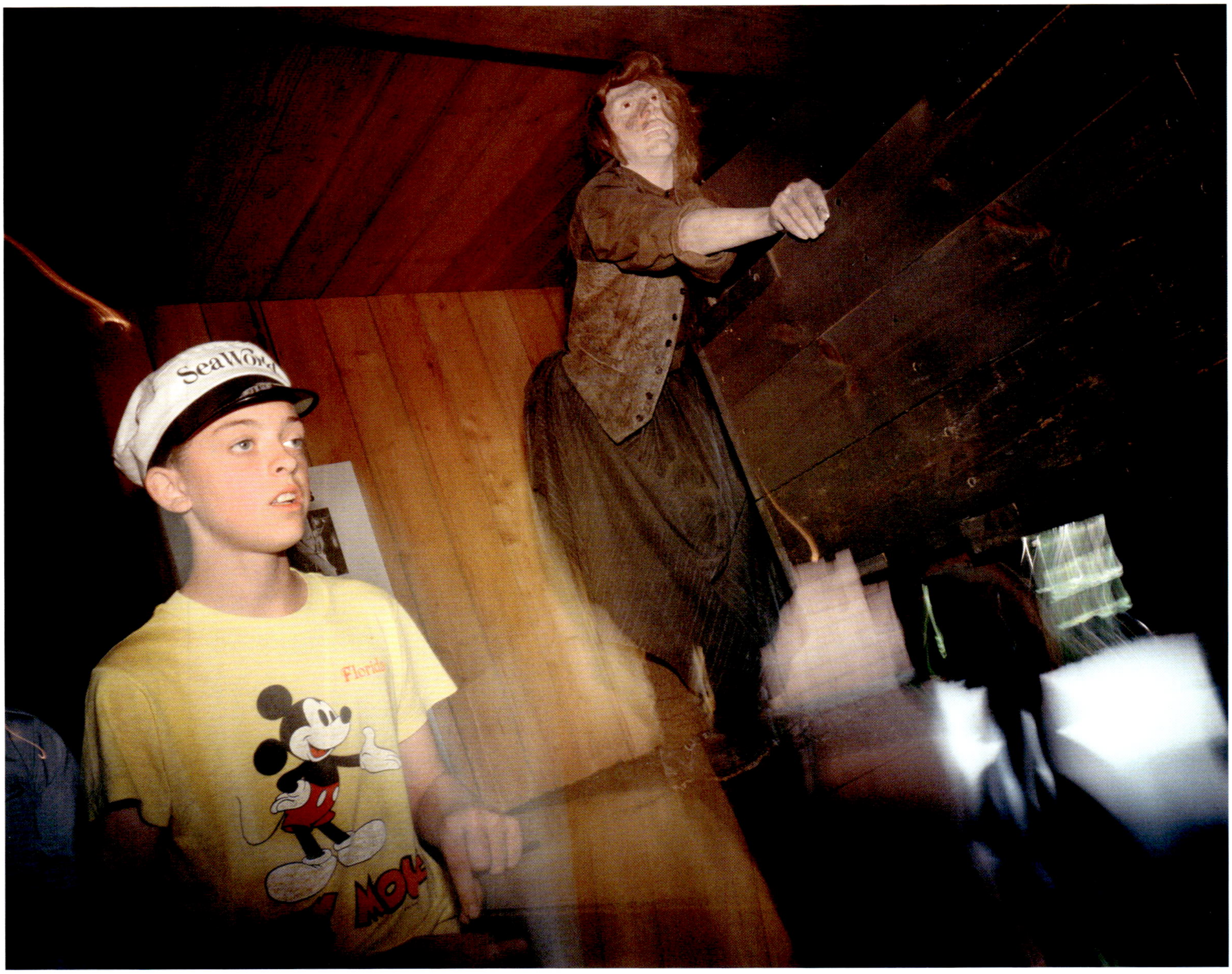

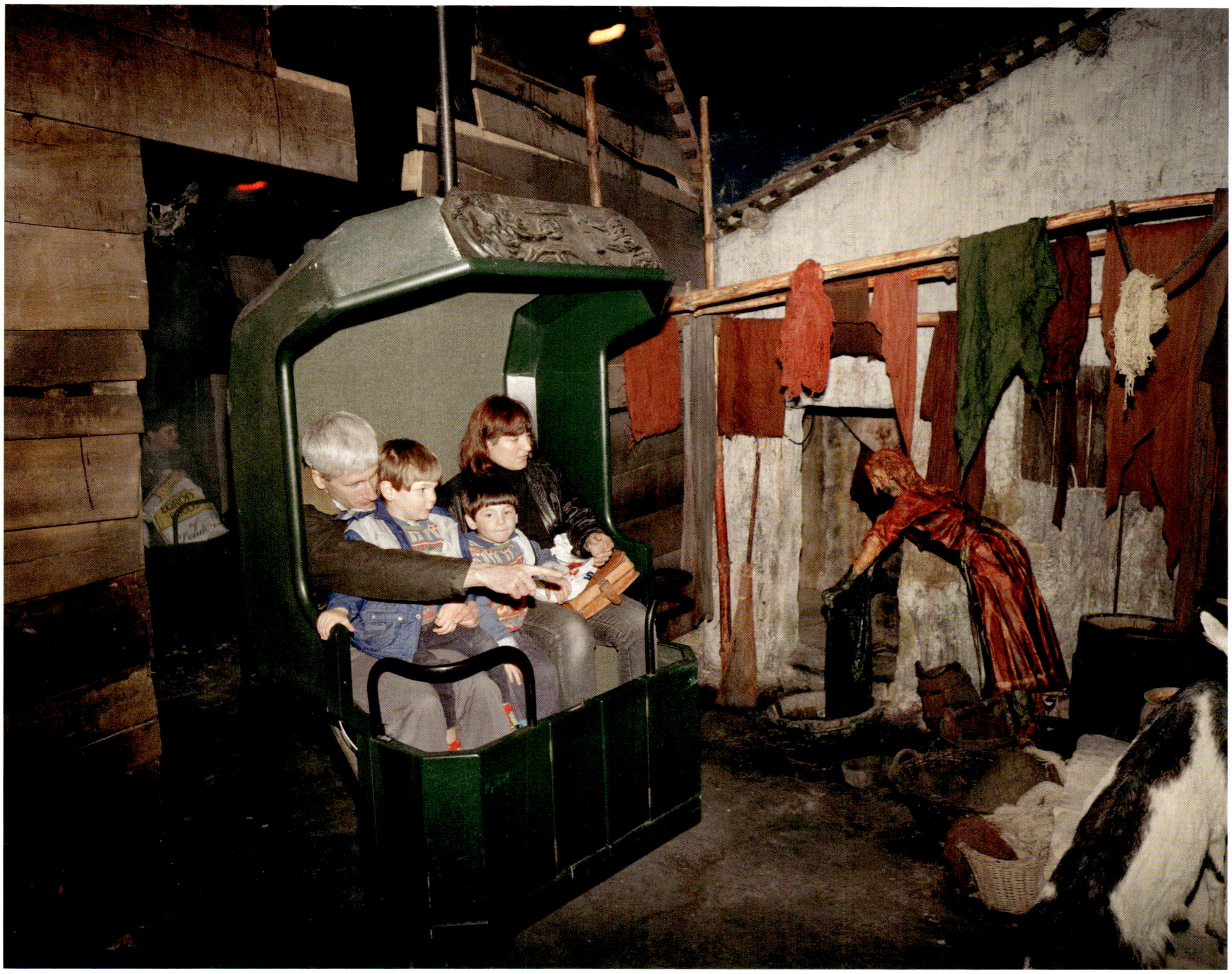

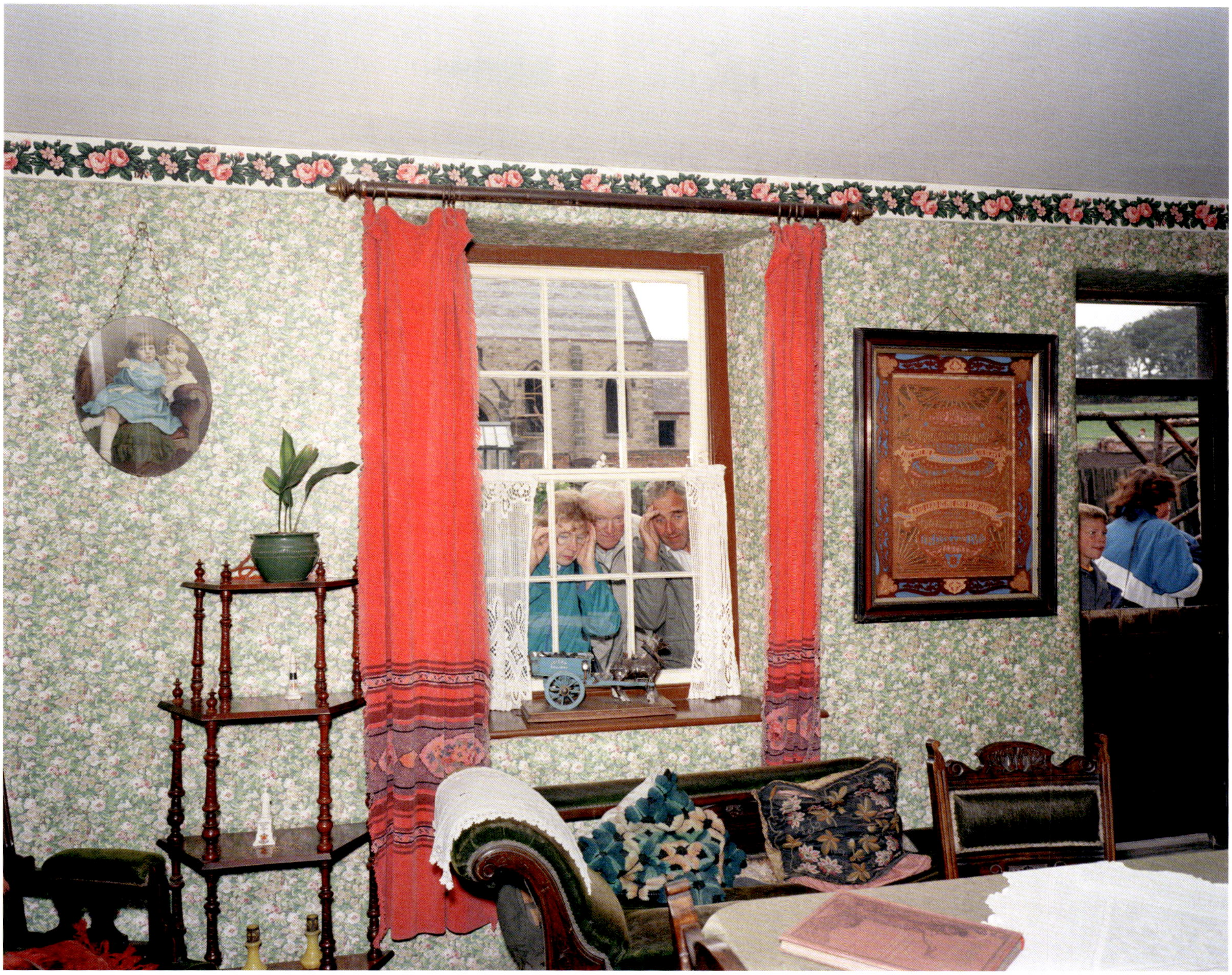

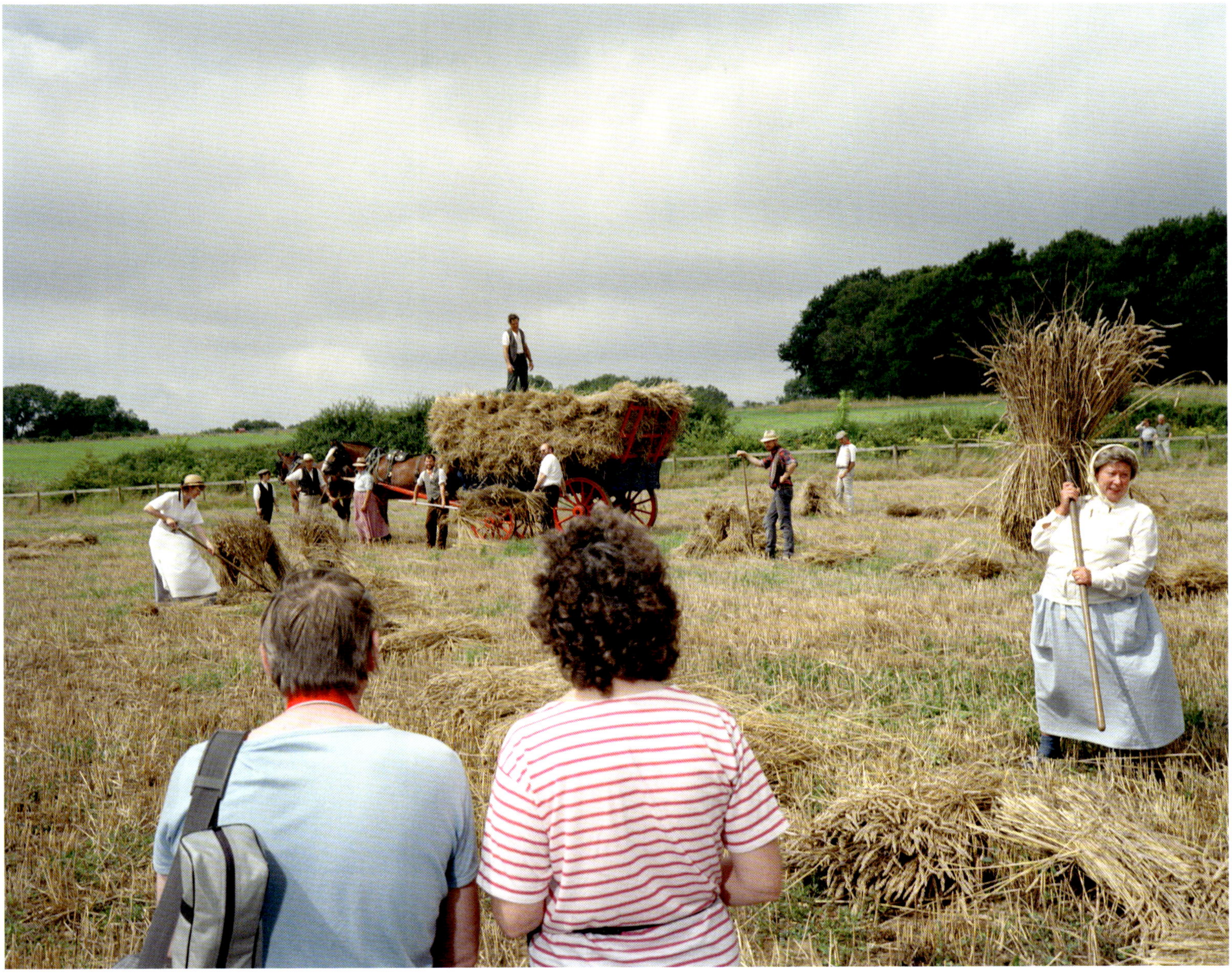

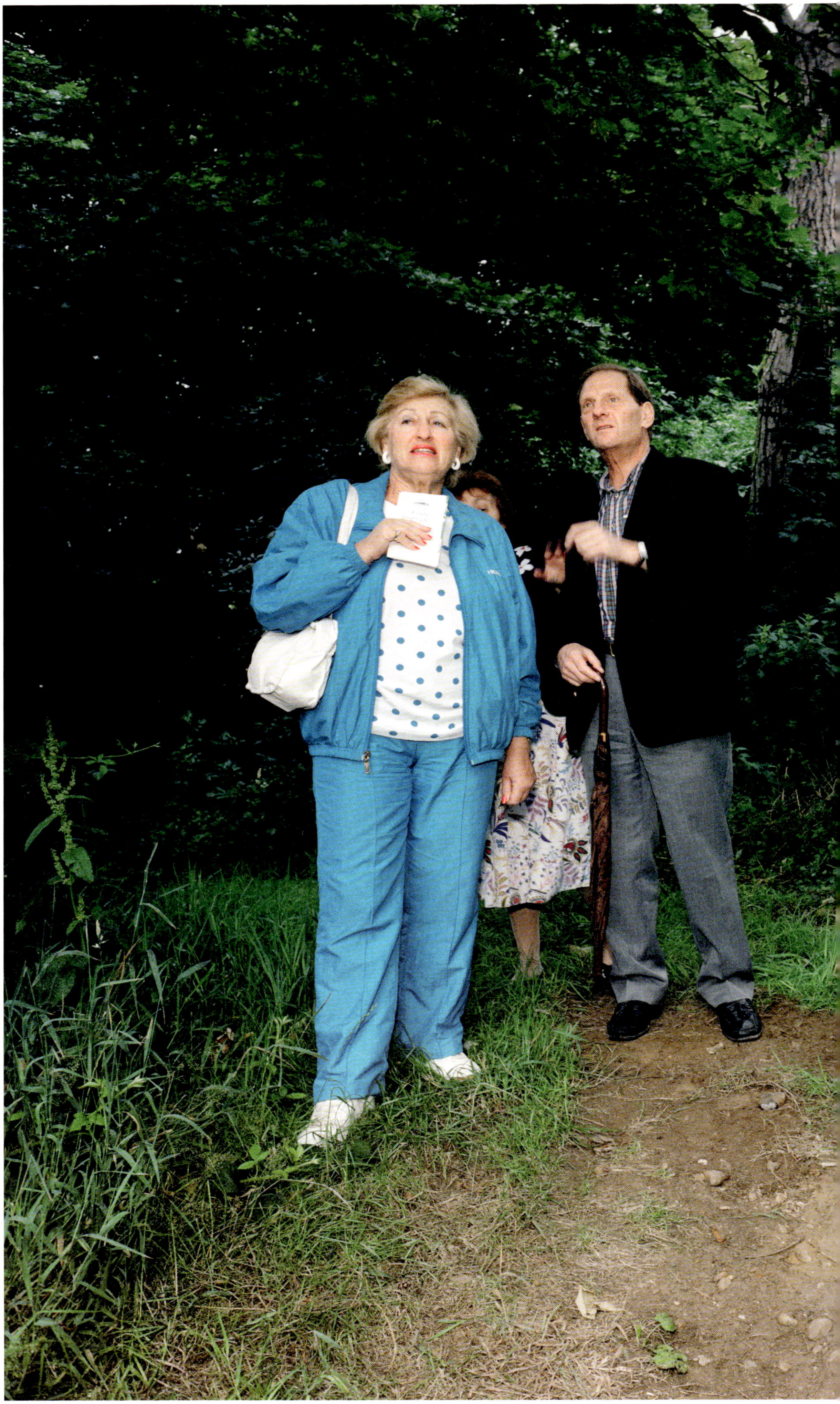

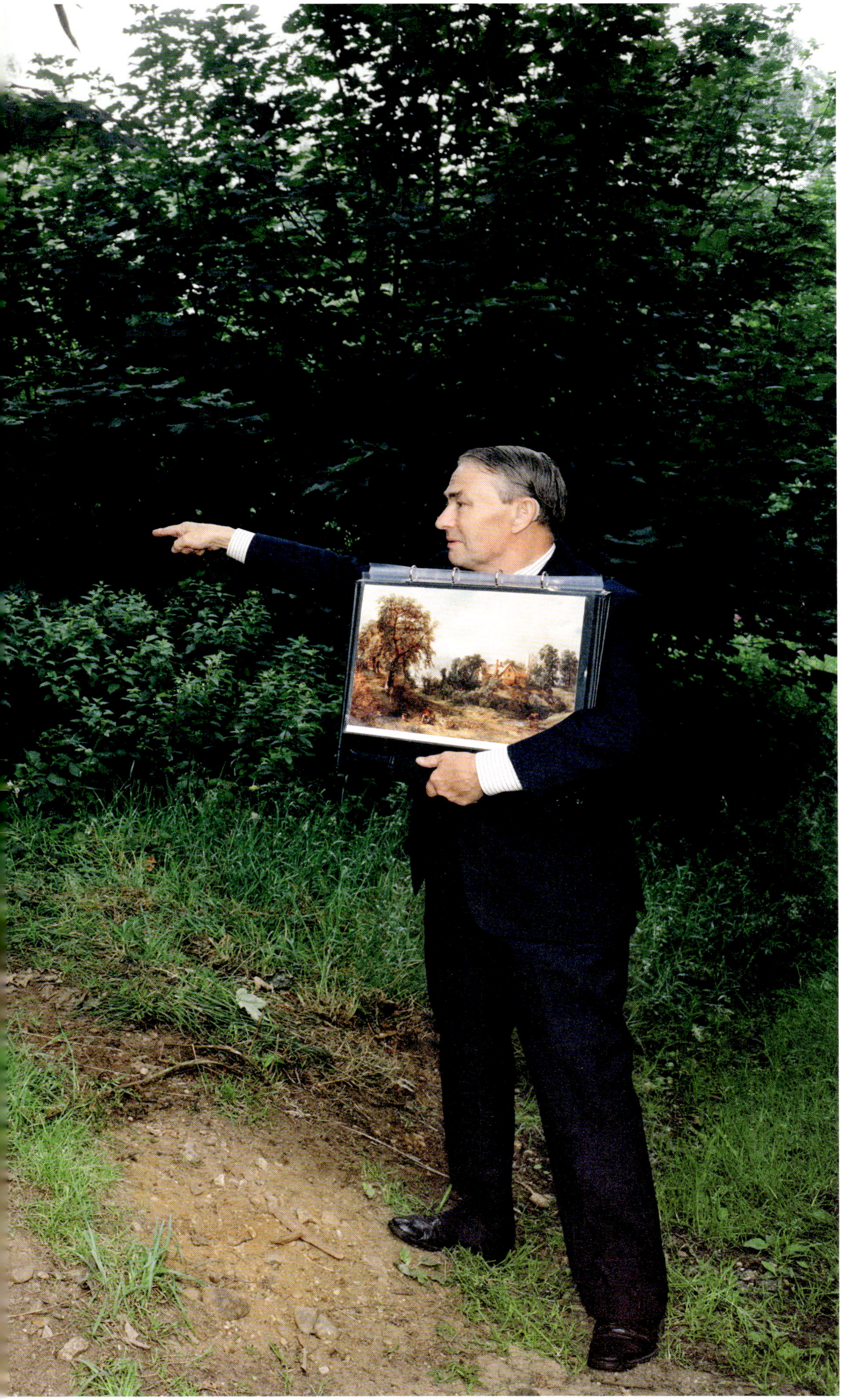

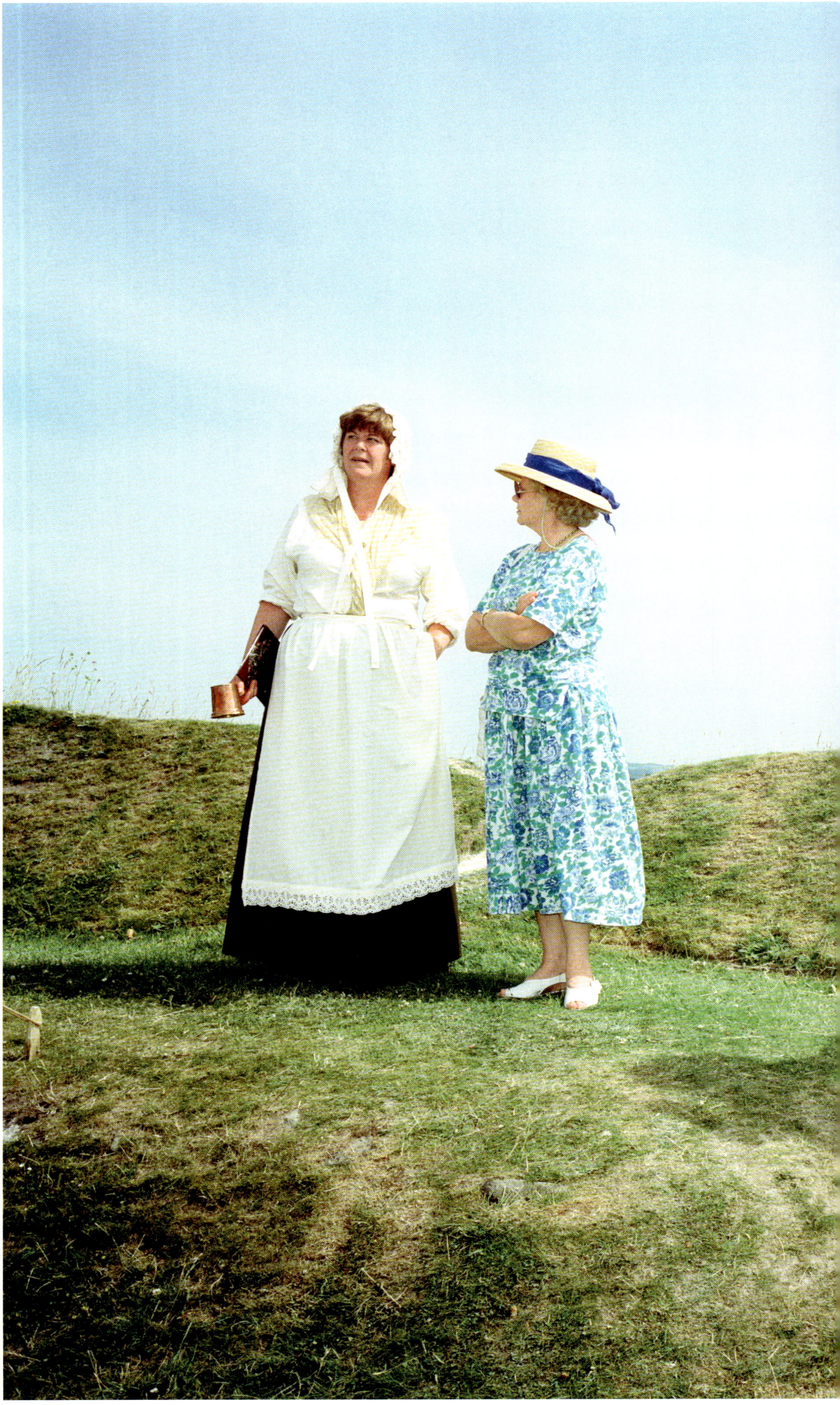

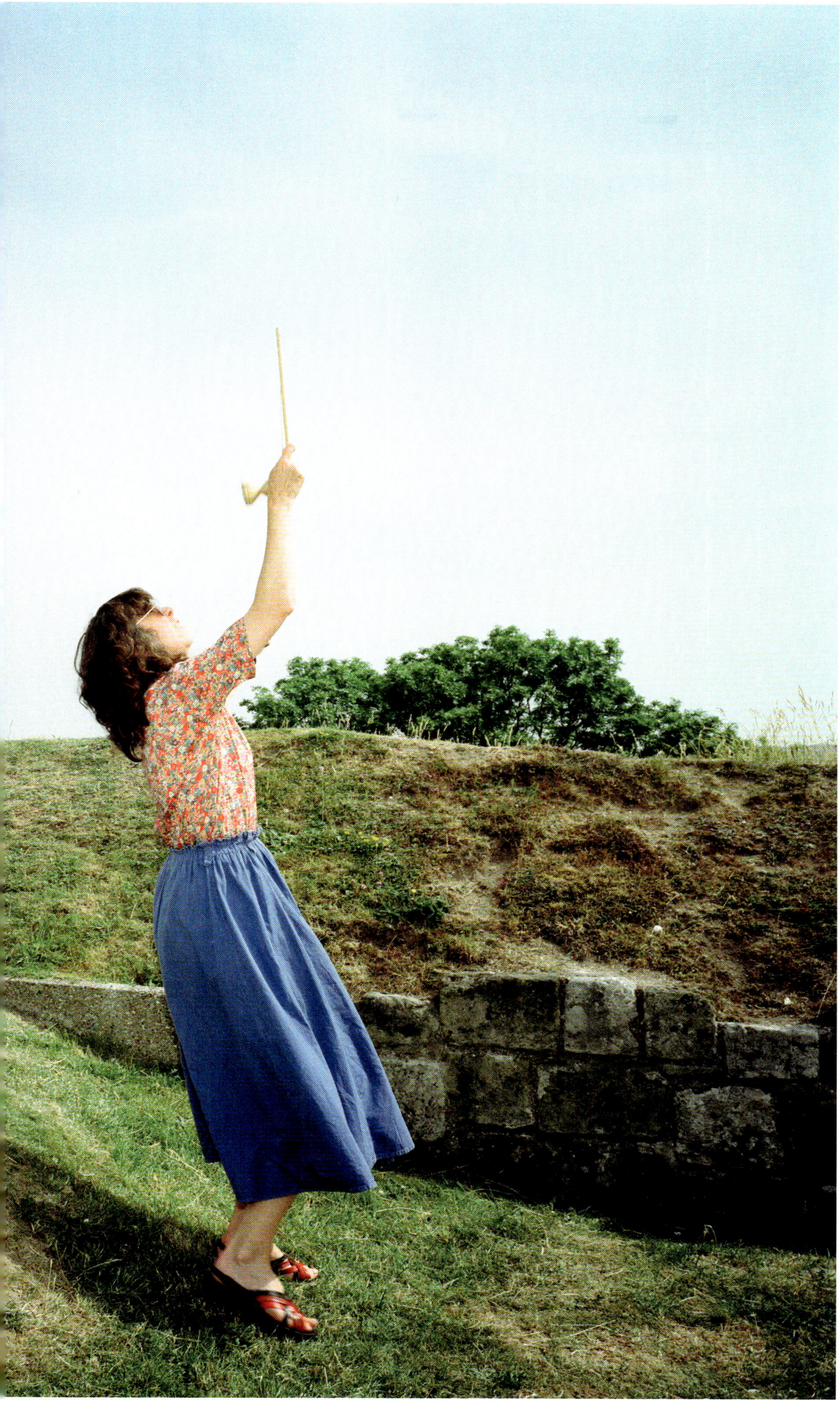

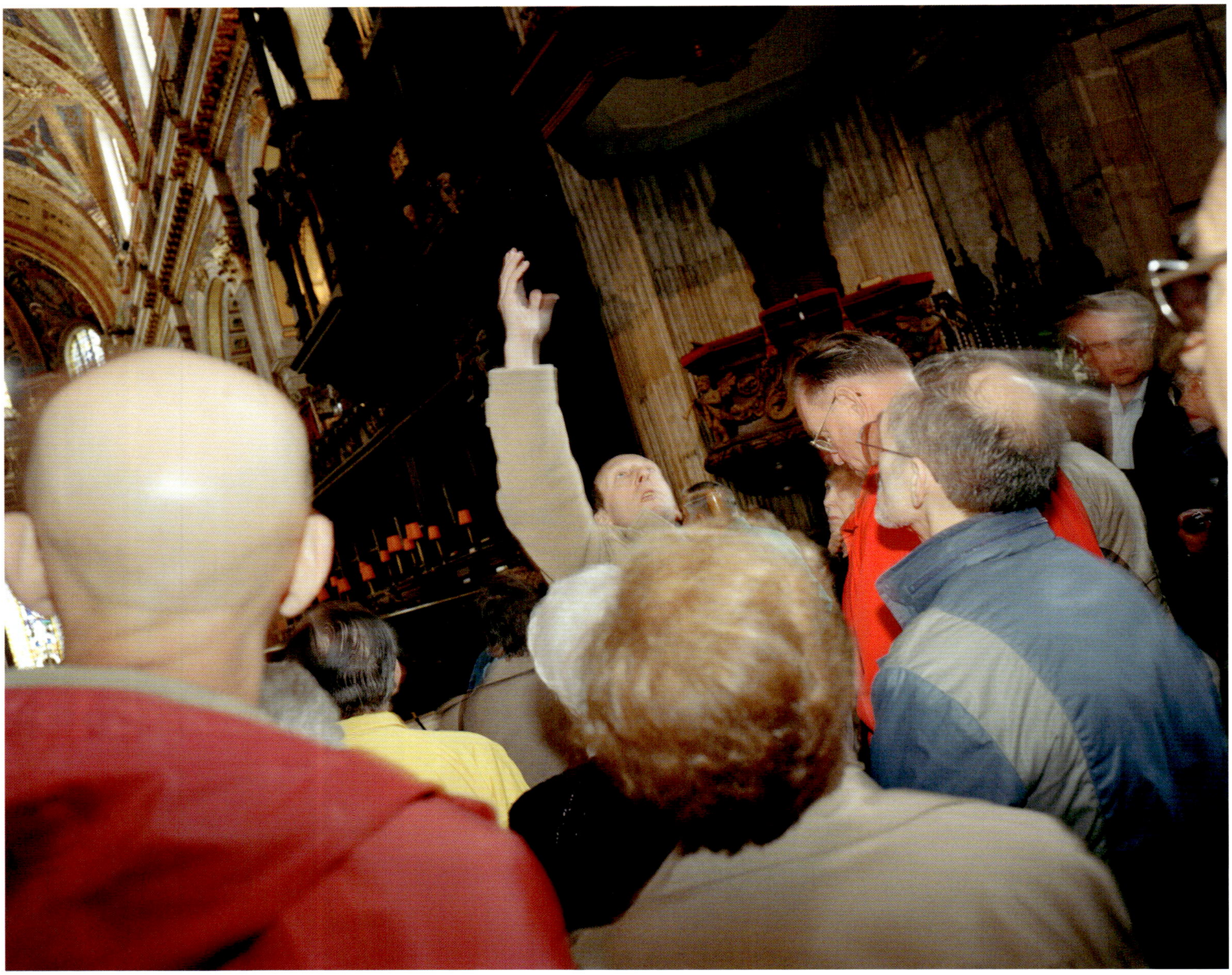

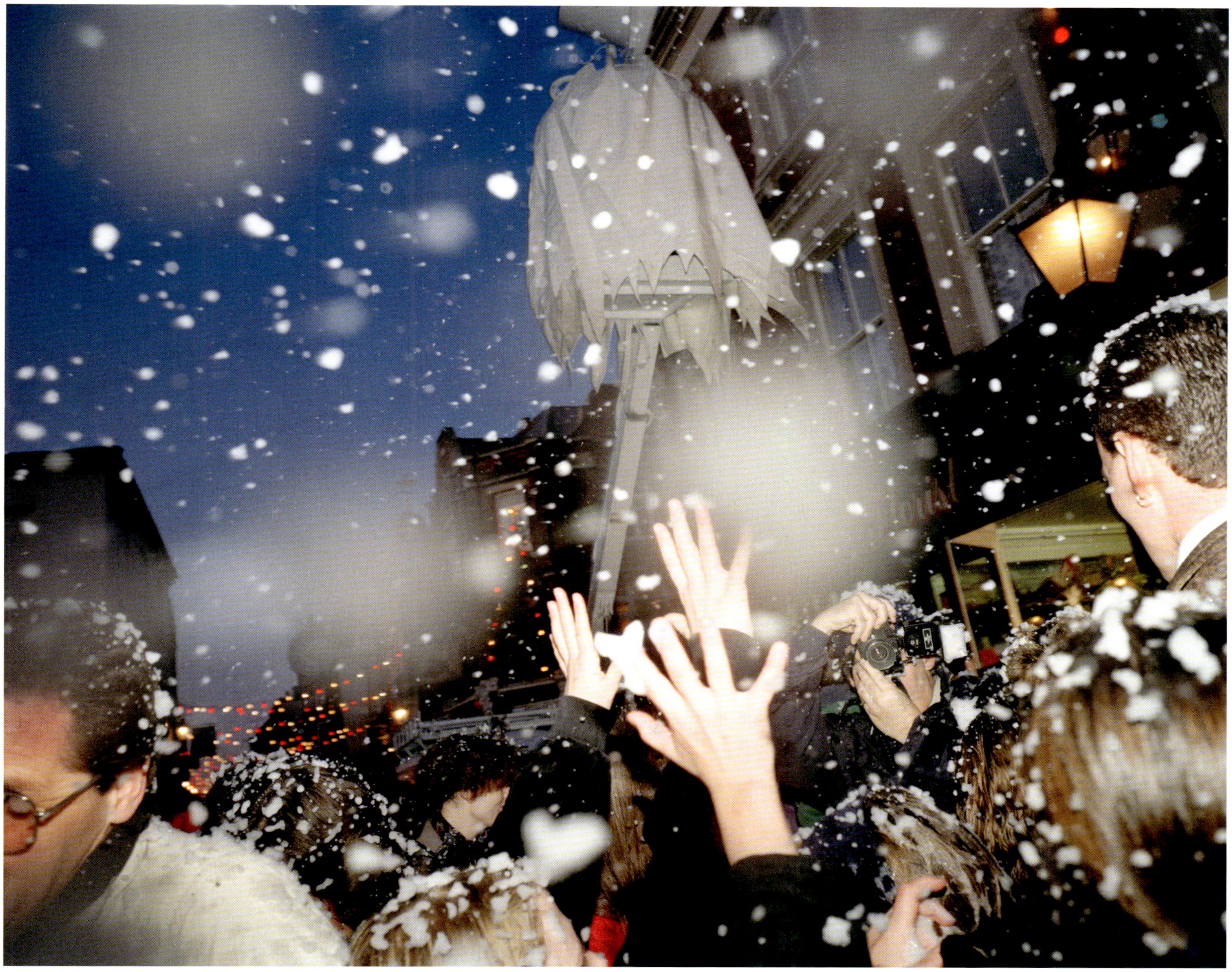

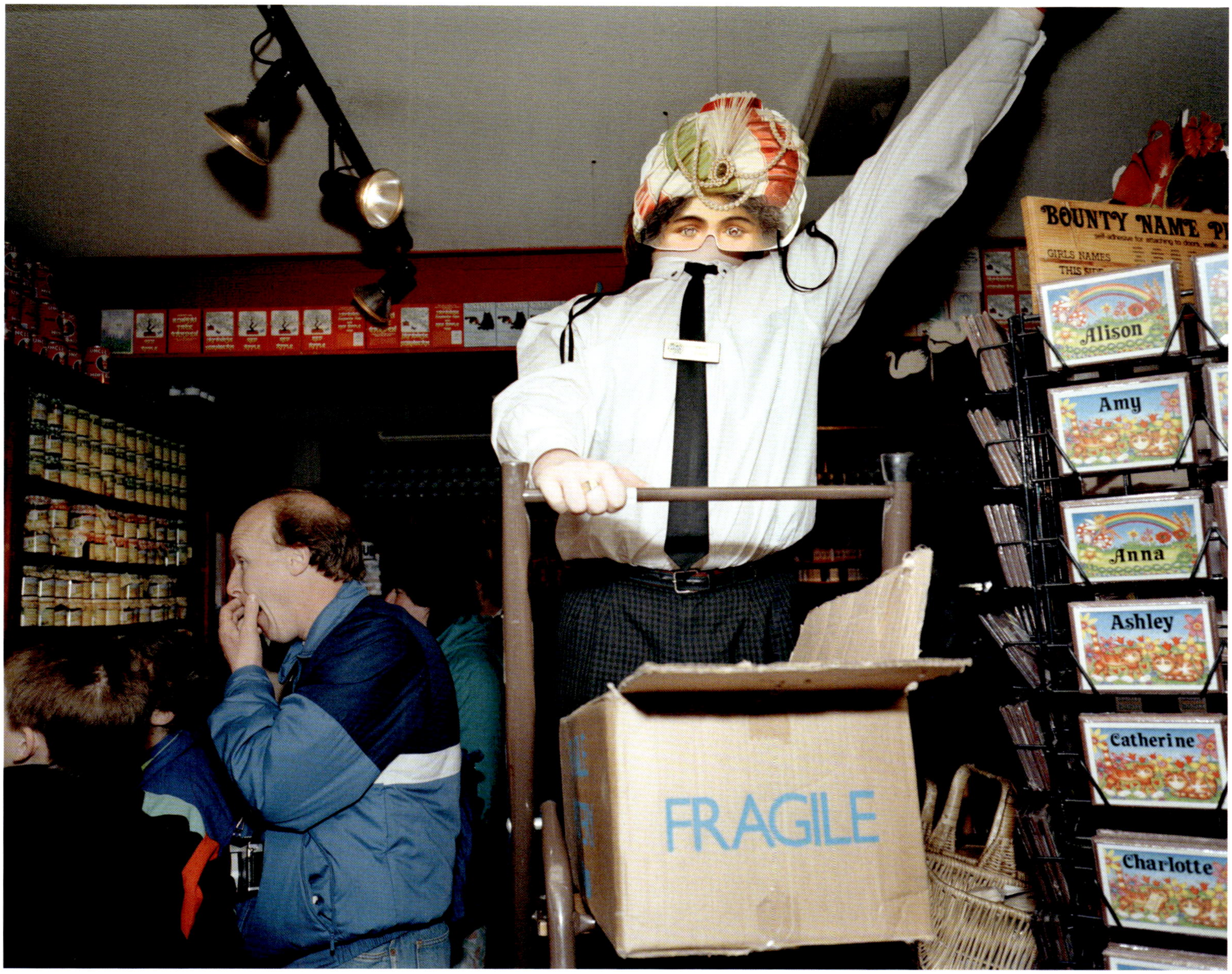
BOUNTY NAME
GIRLS NAMES
Alison
Amy
Anna
Ashley
Catherine
Charlotte
FRAGILE

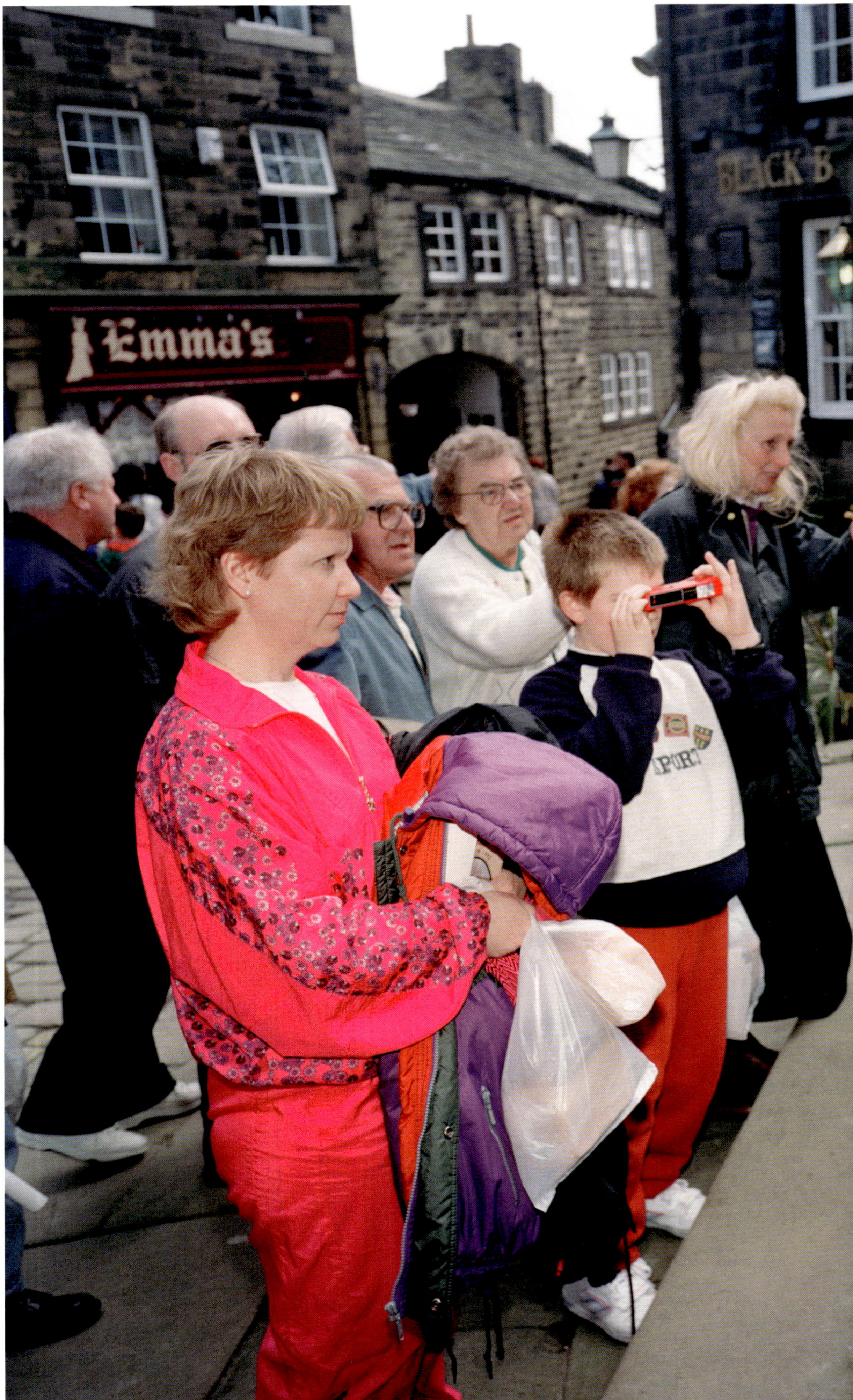
Emma's
BLACK B

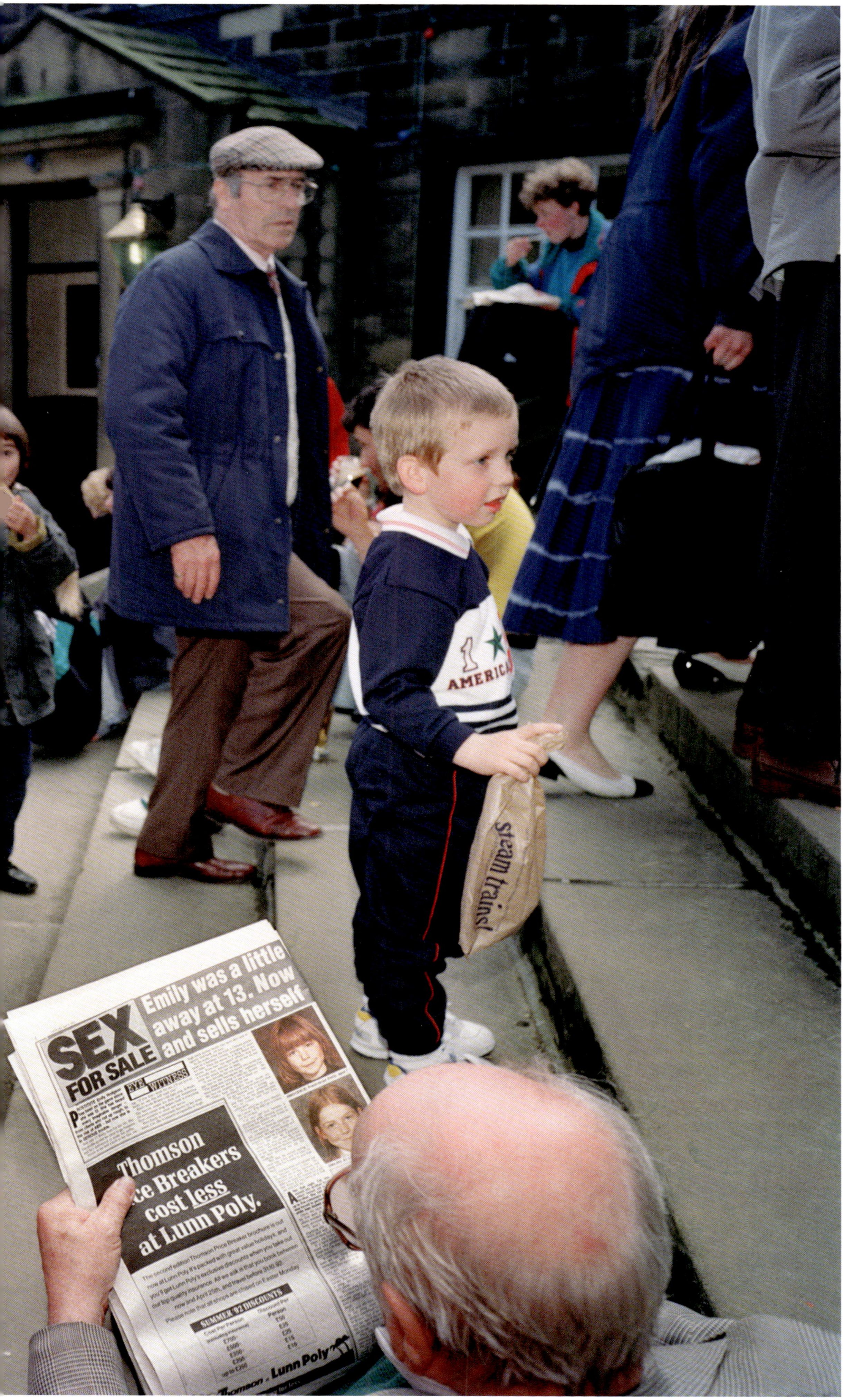
Emily was a little
away at 13. Now
and sells herself
SEX
FOR SALE
Thomson
ce Breakers
cost less
at Lunn Poly.
SUMMER '92 DISCOUNTS
Lunn Poly
AMERICA
steam trains!

Up until the publication of my second book, *Flogging a Dead Horse* (1993), I had worked as a photographic technician on the Documentary Photography course at Newport. At the time of the book and exhibition of *Flogging a Dead Horse*, I started to receive requests from picture editors of magazines to work for them on assignments. In many ways my time studying under Magnum's David Hurn at Newport had prepared me for this experience, and I willingly embraced the opportunity. For the next fifteen to twenty years I would work regularly on assignment for publications like the *Sunday Times Magazine*, and also on commercial advertising campaigns for clients such as Volkswagen, Fujifilm and Nissan.

The advertising world in particular was all-consuming. When I wasn't working on a campaign, I would be in meetings talking about the next one or scouting locations. I became further and further removed from the independent world of photography which had given me so much. I no longer had time to attend festivals or private views, and I slowly lost contact with photographers who were friends and whose work I respected. It was whilst articulating these frustrations to Patrick Sutherland and Paul Lowe, who were themselves ex-Newport students, that they offered me a commission which would result in the work 'From a Distance' (2012). Both Patrick and Paul were teaching at London College of Communication (now part of University of the Arts London), in the Elephant and Castle area of London. They were about to embark on a series of commissions which would document the regeneration of the Elephant and Castle over the ten-year period of its redevelopment. The original idea for the series was to commission a different photographer each year to cover a different aspect of the process of regeneration. Mine was the first, and I was very sure from the outset—having spent most of my professional life trying to negotiate access to subjects—that I simply wanted to photograph the ebb and flow of the streets. In truth I was hoping that the commission would add to a growing set of photographs I had started to make elsewhere on the streets of London (some of which are included here), and that these might reignite my passion for independent picture making.

As with many projects I have undertaken, there was a personal connection. The area of the Elephant and Castle was the home of one of London's longest-established working-class communities, who were being 'decanted', to use the developers' jargon, from their council properties to clear the way for the construction of luxury apartments. At the same time my parents were being forced to leave the house in which I was born, the one which had been the family home for over fifty years, because the council had sold this particular area of the estate in Bradford to a private developer.

2012

From a Distance

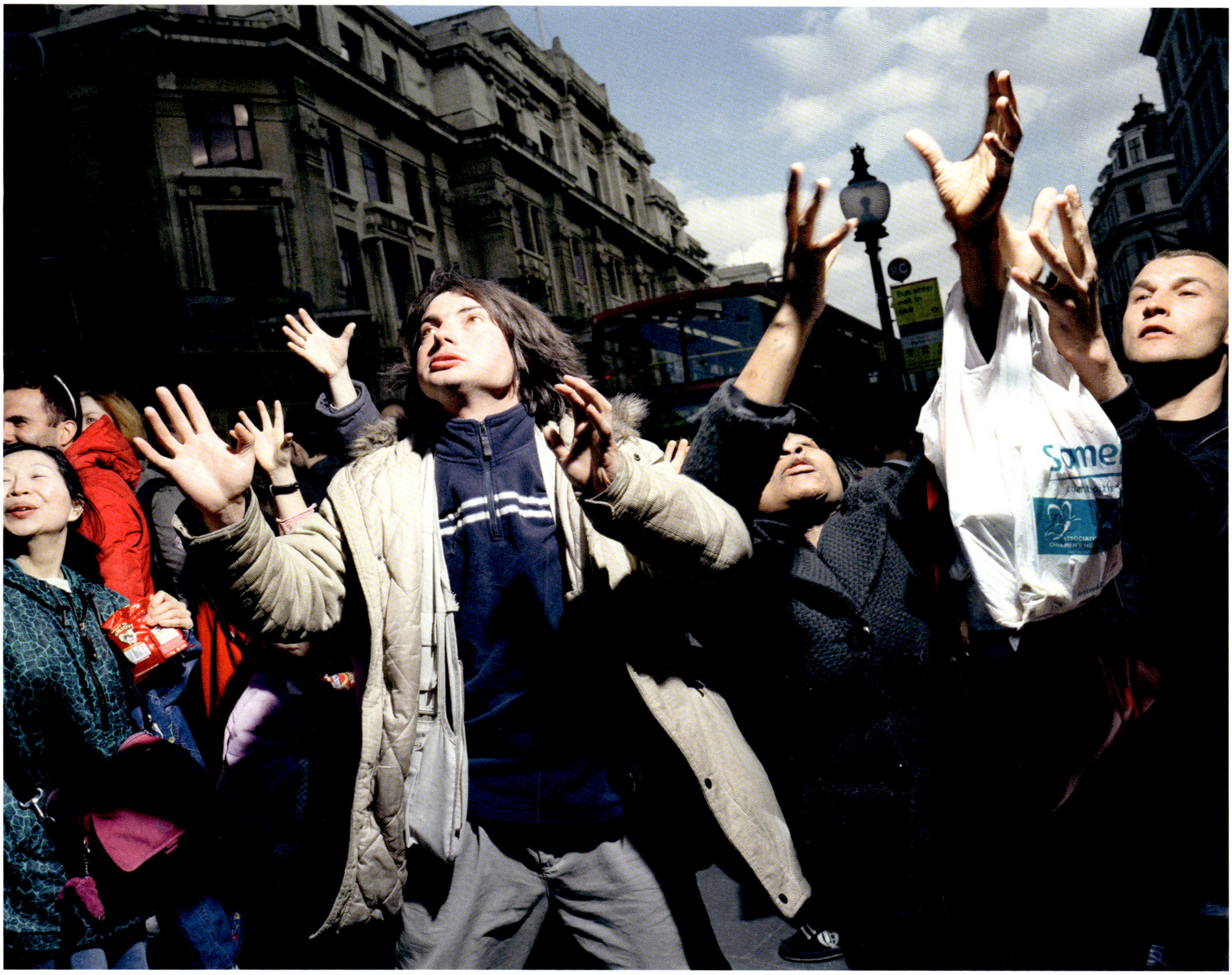

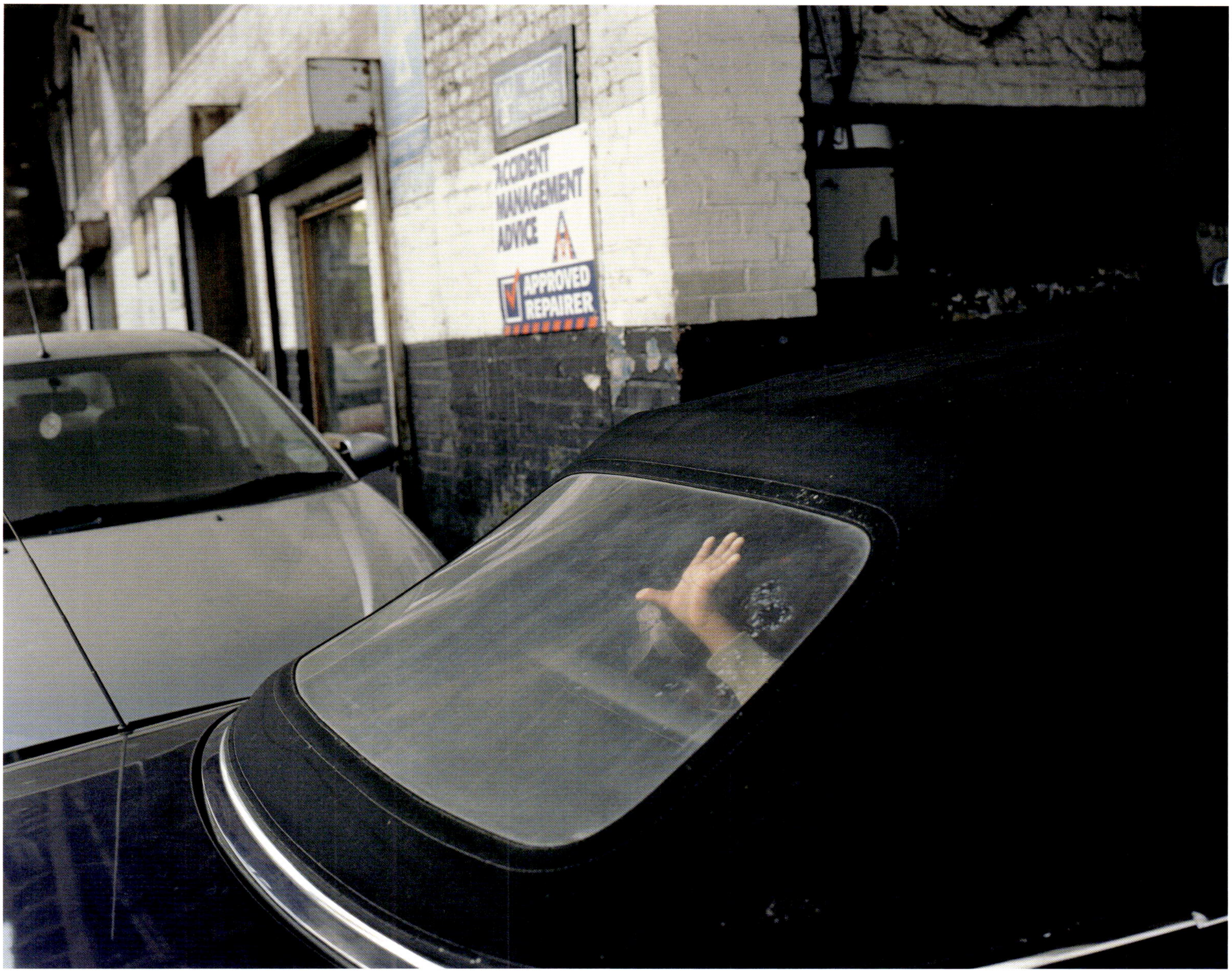
ACCIDENT
MANAGEMENT
ADVICE
APPROVED
REPAIRER

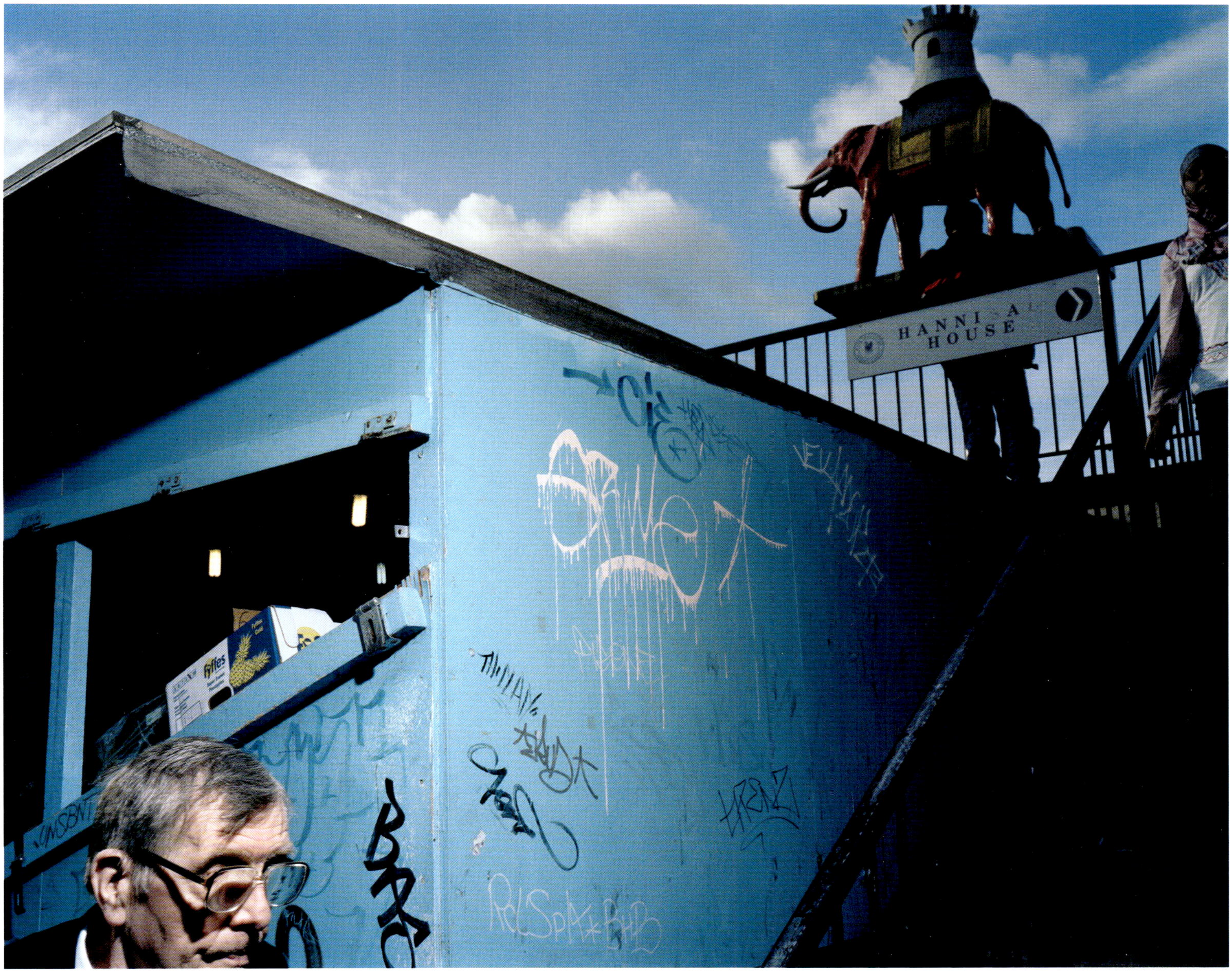
HOUSE

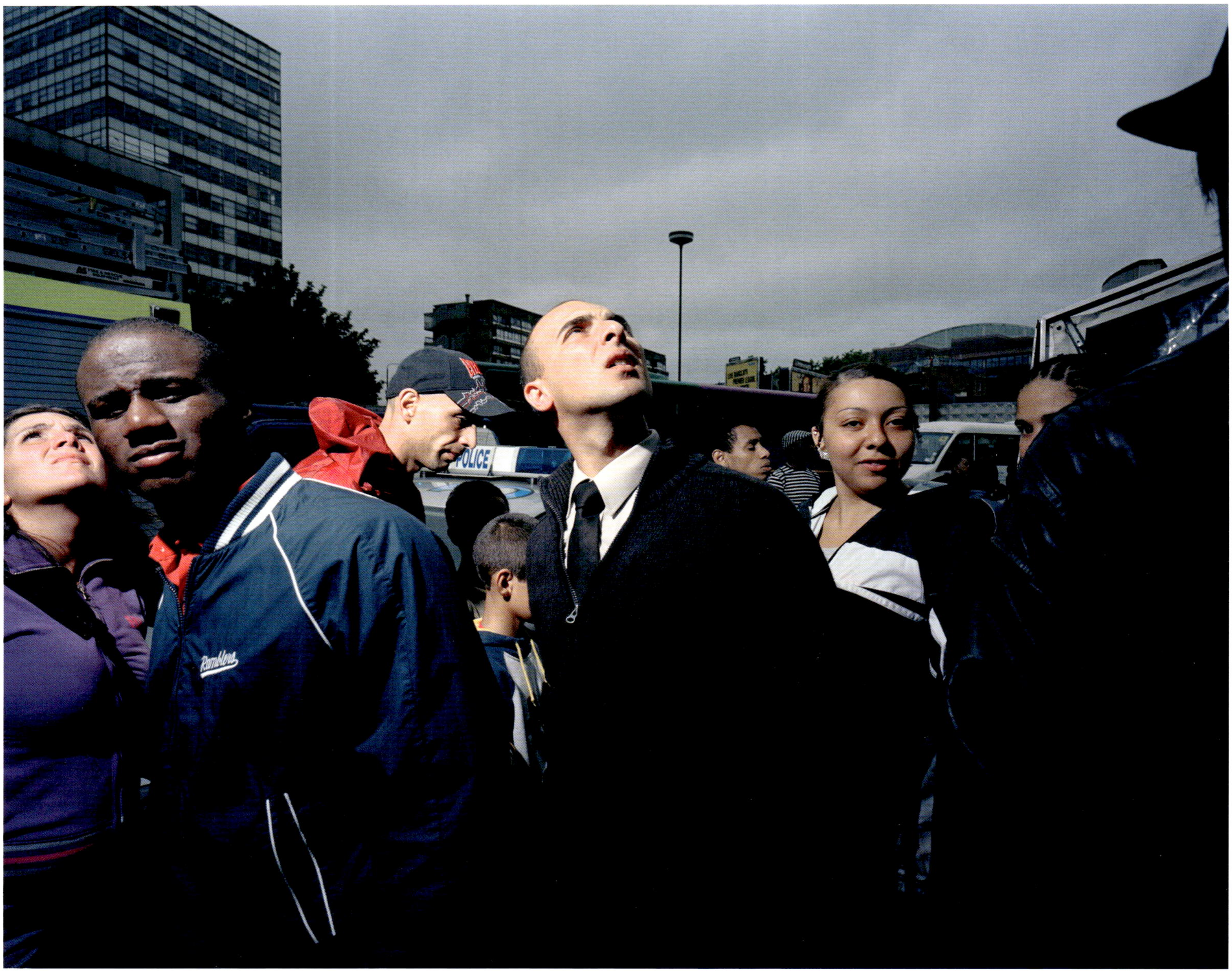
POLICE
Ramblers

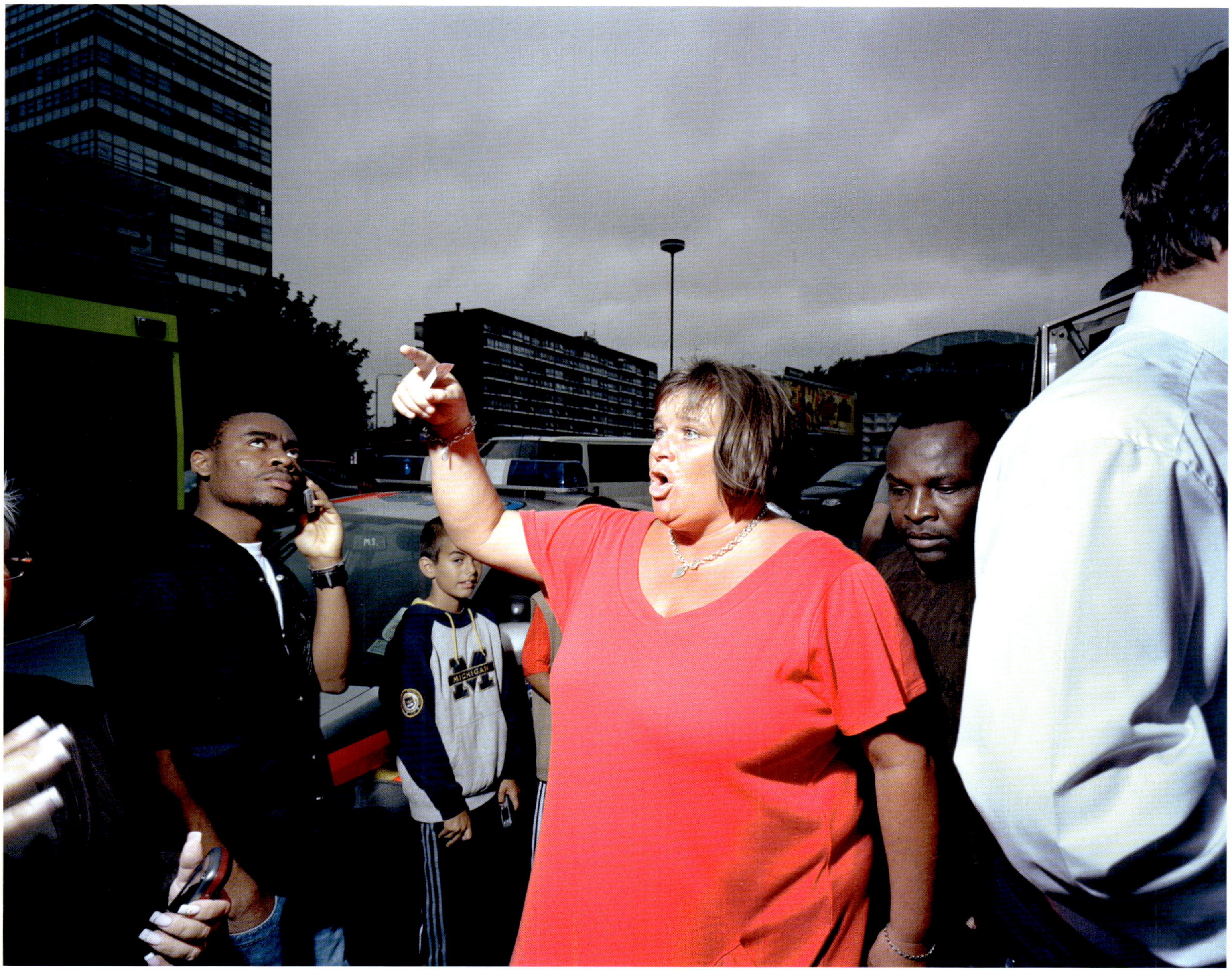
MICHIGAN

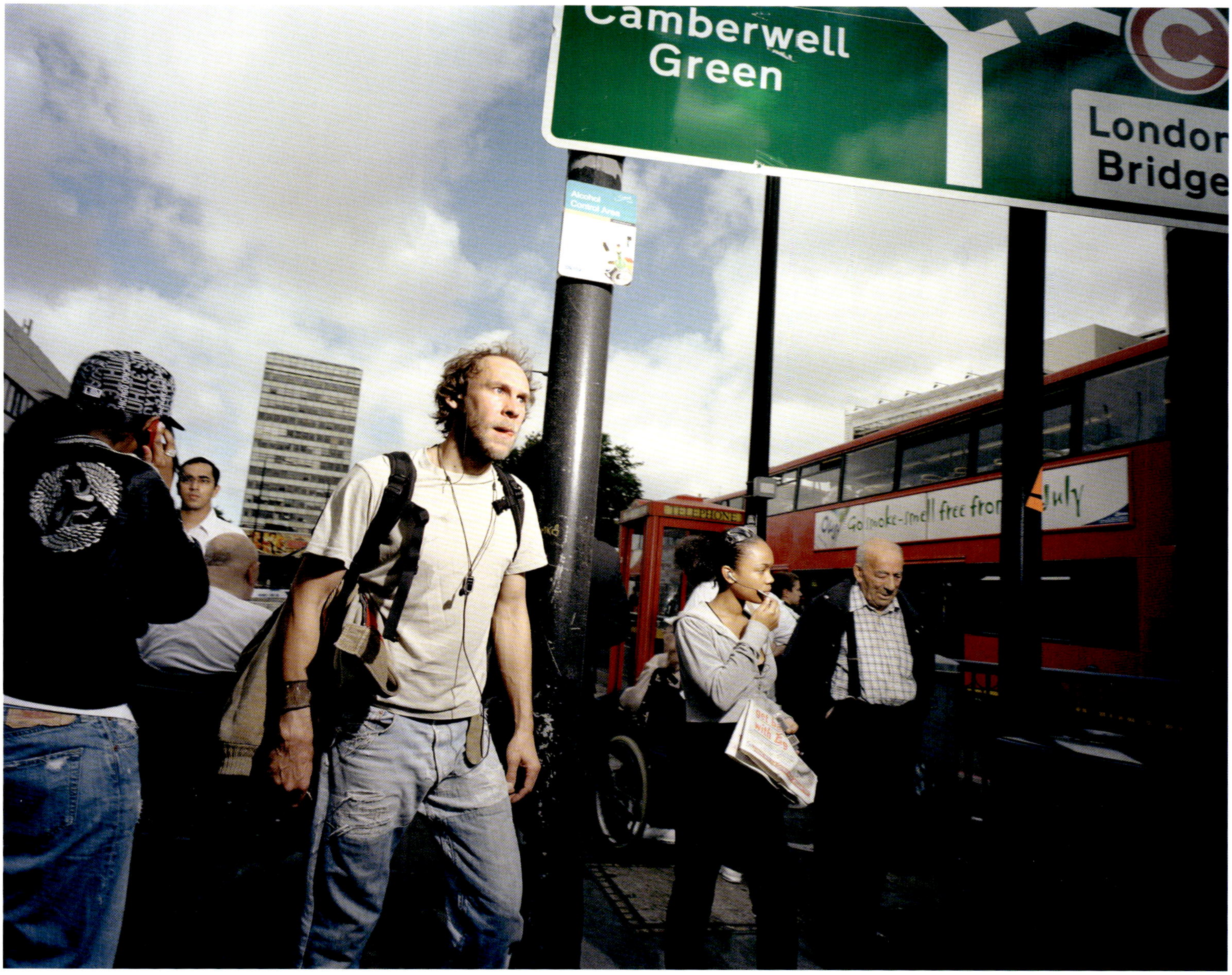
Camberwell
Green
London
Bridge
TELEPHONE

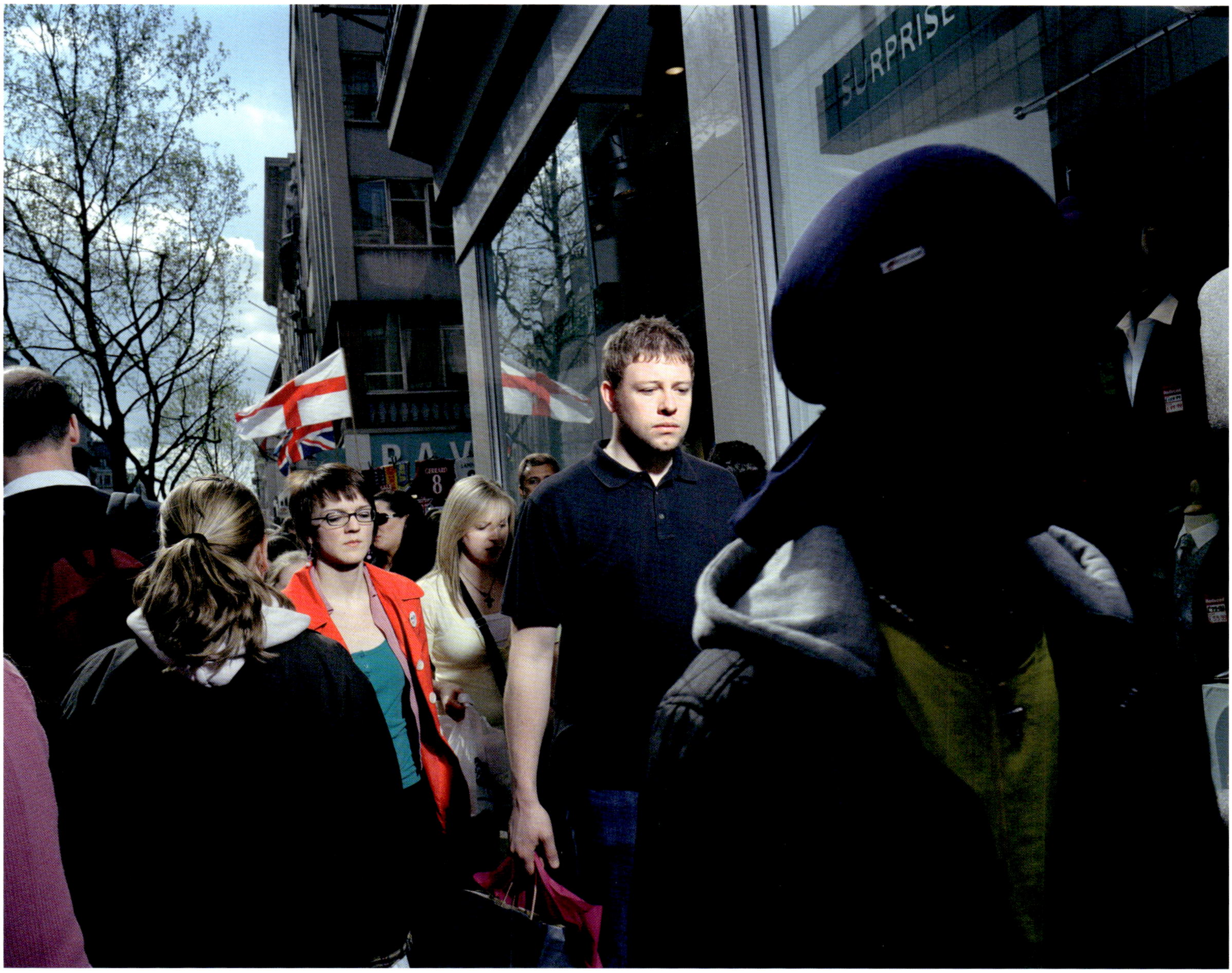
SURPRISE

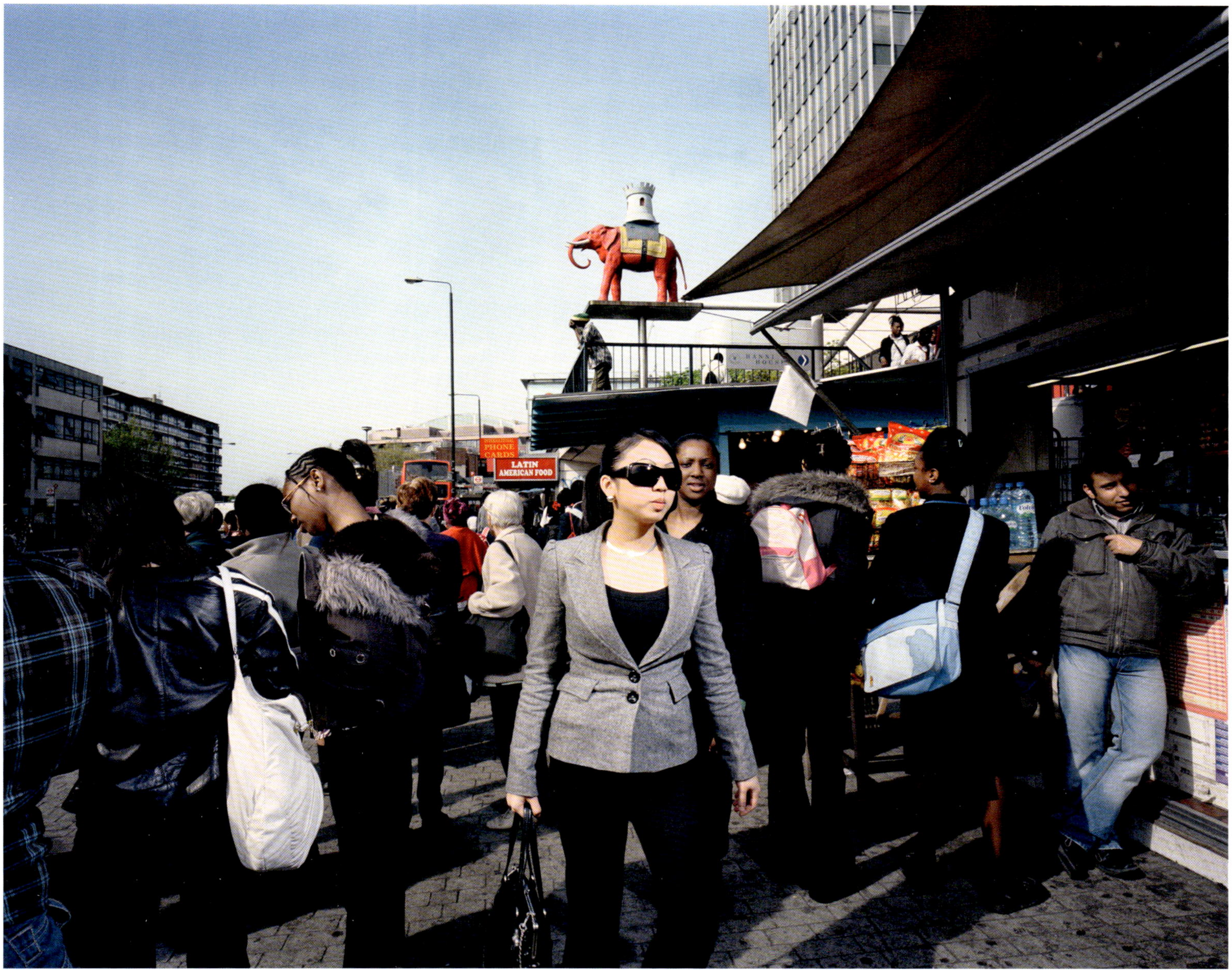
PHONE
CARDS
LATIN
AMERICAN FOOD

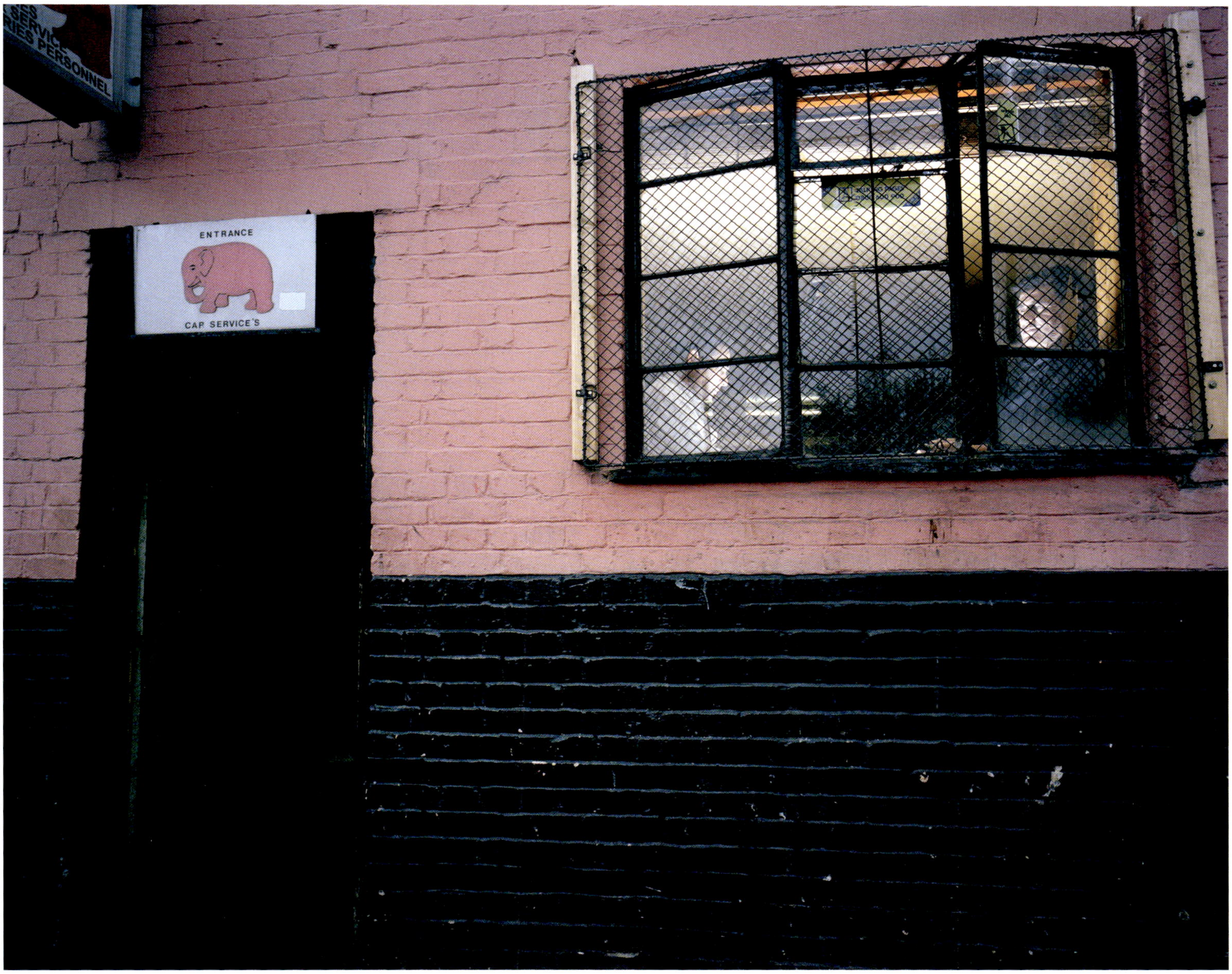
ENTRANCE
CAP SERVICE'S

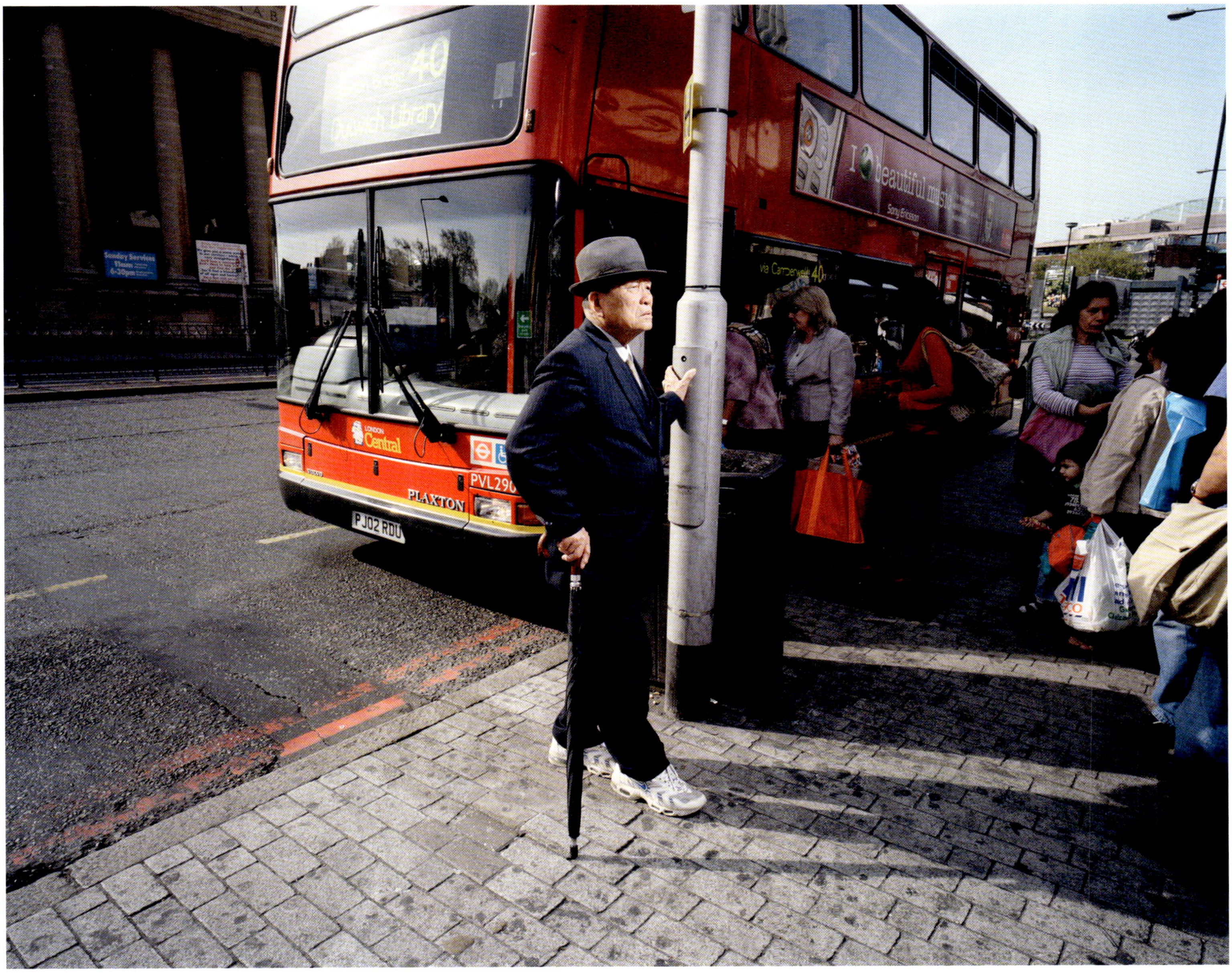
40
Dulwich Library
LONDON
Central
PLAXTON
PJ02 RDU
beautiful music
Sunday Services

David Chandler is a writer, curator and editor. Formerly Assistant Curator of Photography at the National Portrait Gallery, London; Head of Exhibitions at The Photographers' Gallery, London and Director of Photoworks, Brighton, from 1997 to 2010, he is currently Professor of Photography at Plymouth University. David has written widely on photography and the visual arts for many books and journals, including recent monographic essays on the work of Paul Graham, Peter Fraser, Helen Sear, Tom Wood, Rinko Kawauchi, Nigel Shafran, Ori Gersht and Vanessa Winship.

Stuart Cosgrove is from Perth, Scotland and is a writer and broadcaster. He is the author of *Memphis 68: The Tragedy of Southern Soul*, which was awarded the Penderyn Award as Music Book of the Year in 2018. He is widely respected as the UK's most influential writer on the history of soul music, for his epic trilogy of *Detroit 67: The Year that Changed Soul* nominated as Best Music Book of 2016, and the forthcoming *Harlem 69: The Future of Soul*. He has been a staff writer with the black music paper *Echoes* and Media Editor for *NME*.

Stuart has held multiple positions as a television executive with the UK broadcaster Channel 4 and in 2005, he was named Broadcaster of the Year in the Glenfiddich Spirit of Scotland Awards. He has been the recipient of numerous awards including a BAFTA in 2012. Stuart currently presents BBC Scotland's popular radio show 'Off the Ball' and is a regular guest commentator on BBC Scotland's Media Show.

Ken Grant was born in Liverpool in 1967. Since the 1980s he has photographed his contemporaries in the city and engaged in sustained projects both in the UK and wider Europe. A book of his Liverpool pictures, *The Close Season*, was published by Dewi Lewis in 2002 and another, *No Pain Whatsoever* was published by Gösta Flemming, Journal in 2014. Recent books include *Flock*, 2014 and a fourth monograph, *A Topical Times for These Times. Book of Liverpool Football* in 2016, with RRB Publishing.

Ken Grant's photographs are held in important collections of photography, including those of the Museum of Modern Art, New York and the Folkwang Museum, Essen. He is currently working on new initiatives with the partnership Northern Narratives and continues to photograph in Northwest England. He teaches Photography at Belfast School of Art.

Paul Reas is one of the most significant photographers to emerge from the new wave of British colour documentary of the mid-1980s. He is part of a pioneering generation of photographers, that included Paul Graham, Martin Parr and Anna Fox, who revealed and critiqued British class and culture. His work is held in many private and public collections and his photographs have been widely exhibited including Impressions Gallery, Bradford; The Photographers' Gallery, London; Rencontres d'Arles, France; Foto International, Rotterdam; and Jeu de Paume, Paris. Through his significant commercial practice, Reas has worked for such editorial clients as the *Sunday Times Magazine*, *Telegraph Magazine* and *Observer Magazine* among many others. He has also created a number of award winning advertising campaigns for clients such as Volkswagen, Sony PlayStation, Honda Motor Company, Ltd. and Transport for London.

He is currently the Course Leader of the Documentary Photography course at the University of South Wales.

Val Williams is a curator, writer and editor, based in London and the South Coast. She is Professor of the History and Culture of Photography at the University of the Arts London and is the founder and director of the UAL Photography and the Archive Research Centre (2003–2018) of Impressions Gallery. She is co-founder of the Shoreditch Foto Biennale and Moose on the Loose Biennale of Research. Williams is also an editor of the *Journal of Photography & Culture* and a Board member of Fast Forward: Women in Photography, a platform designed to promote and engage with women in photography across the globe.

Her recent curated projects include *Tish Murtha* (The Photographers' Gallery, London 2018); *How We Are* (Tate Britain, London 2007); *Daniel Meadows: Early Photographs* (Library of Birmingham 2014 and touring); *Martin Parr Retrospective* (Barbican Art Gallery, London 2002 and touring).

For Magali
and for Tom and Rosie

Acknowledgments
Over the years many people have contributed so much to my work. Whilst it is impossible to acknowledge everyone I would like to thank the following:

David Chandler, Stuart Cosgrove, Ken Grant and Val Williams for their kind and insightful essays in this book; Stuart Smith and Claudia Paladini at GOST books for guiding me through the process of publishing; to David Hurn, Clive Landen, Daniel Meadows, Ron McCormick, Keith Arnatt, Ian Walker, Paul Hill, Paul Trevor, Martin Parr and Sue Packer, under whom I had the privilege of studying at Newport; to Mark Power, Jim Cooke, Xavier Ribas, Judith Katz, Karen Norquay and Denis Doran with whom I spent many enjoyable years teaching at the University of Brighton; to all the staff and photographers at Network Photographers; to James and Claire Hyman for their continued support; to David Barnes and Lisa Barnard, who are my current teaching colleagues on the Documentary Photography course at the University of South Wales Cardiff; to Jane Reas and Carl Potter for their friendship and support; to John and Kendall Wyatt-Clarke and all the staff at Wyatt-Clarke and Jones; and finally to all the people who have willingly let me, as a photographer, into their lives.

Fables of Faubus
First published in 2018 by
GOST Books
8a West Smithfield
London
EC1A 9JR
info@gostbooks.com
gostbooks.com

© GOST Books
Photographs © Paul Reas
Text © Stuart Cosgrove, David Chandler
Ken Grant, Val Williams

Designed by GOST:
Katie Clifford, Gemma Gerhard, Allon Kaye,
Eleanor Macnair, Eleonora Paciullo, Claudia Paladini

Printed in Italy by EBS

British Library cataloguing-in-publication data.
A catalogue record of this book is available from
the British Library.

isbn 978-1-910401-10-1

All rights reserved. No part of this publication
may be reproduced, stored in a retrieval device or
transmitted in any other form or by any other means,
electrical, mechanical or otherwise, without first
seeking the permission of the copyright owners
and the publishers.